THE
Restaurant
Companion™

A guide to healthier eating out

HOPE S. WARSHAW

M.M.Sc., R.D., C.D.E.

SurreyBooks

CHICAGO

THE RESTAURANT COMPANION™: A GUIDE TO HEALTHIER EATING OUT is published by Surrey Books, Inc., 230 E. Ohio St., Suite 120, Chicago, IL 60611. ''The Restaurant Companion'' is a registered trade mark of Surrey Books, Inc.

This book is manufactured in the United States of America.

Second edition. 1 2 3 4 5

Library of Congress Cataloging in Publication Data:
  Warshaw, Hope S., 1954–
    The restaurant companion: a guide to healthier eating out / Hope S. Warshaw.—2nd ed.
      p. 384   cm.
  ISBN 0–940625–93–8 (paper)
  1. Nutrition—Handbooks, manuals, etc.
  2. Restaurants—United States—Handbooks, manuals, etc.   I. Title.
  RA784.W365   1995
  613.2—dc20   95–9953
                                               CIP

For free book catalog and prices on quantity purchases, contact Surrey Books at the above address.

This title is distributed to the trade by Publishers Group West.

Editorial and production: Bookcrafters, Inc., Chicago.
Cover: Joan Sommers Design, Chicago; illustration by Susan Gross.
Interior illustrations: Elizabeth Allen and Laurel DiGangi.

Contents

Acknowledgments . . .

A big thanks to everyone at Surrey Books for their great enthusiasm for *The Restaurant Companion*. To publisher Susan Schwartz for recognizing the need for a how-to guide for healthier restaurant eating years ago and for her support of this second edition. To Gene DeRoin, my editor, who again patiently edited the myriad facts and figures in this compendium. To Julie Mulzoff, Surrey Publicist, who always remembers *The Restaurant Companion* in her marketing and publicity efforts. Many thanks also to Dr. George L. Blackburn for willingly writing the ''Foreword'' to the book.

Thanks also go to the registered dietitians and public relations and marketing representatives who took time to provide the nutrition information for their restaurants. Where exact nutrition information from the restaurant is used, it is indicated. Some nutrition information was estimated based on data from N-Squared Computing, Nutritionist IV for Windows, Diet Analysis Module, Version 3.5, First Data Division, The Hearst Company, 1111 Bayhill Drive, San Bruno, CA 94066. Exchange information is based on the *1986 Exchange Lists for Meal Planning*, The American Dietetic Association, Illinois; and American Diabetes Association, Inc., Virginia.

To . . .

my wonderful expanded family, fabulously supportive friends and professional peers, and clients from whom I continue to learn more than textbooks could ever teach.

Preface

I t has been more than six years since the first edition of *The Restaurant Companion: A Guide to Healthier Eating Out* was published. The response to this book from consumers and professional colleagues has been gratifying.

So why the second edition? Several reasons. I've been writing and talking about healthier restaurant eating over the last 8 years and have collected many more creative tips and tactics, all of which are woven into the pages ahead. The restaurant industry is continually changing—more food is being served faster, continental food has turned into fusion cuisine, rotisserie chicken is giving fried a challenge, and bagels are edging out muffins—to name a few changes. Also, some nutritious changes have occurred in restaurants:

more vegetarian entrees, availability of smaller servings, more nutrition information available, less frowns when you ask to split or share, lighter salad dressings, and more. These changes are all integrated into this second edition.

Though a bit easier, it's still a challenge to eat healthfully in restaurants. Sometimes you just feel you are swimming upstream against the fat-laden downstream current. But by putting the 10 Skills and Strategies and all the tips and tactics into action, you'll be on your way.

Good luck on your journey to healthier restaurant eating whether it's for health or medical reasons. My hope is that *The Restaurant Companion* will make your job easier without diminishing the pleasure of restaurant dining. It is also my hope that if all of us keep ordering healthier items and making special requests, restaurants will get the hint. Don't ever forget, every request creates consumer demand. So keep demanding and we'll create change together.

Hope S. Warshaw, M.M.Sc., R.D.

Foreword

Dining out, ordering out, and, indeed, eating any food prepared by others—apart from our own control—poses a major challenge to healthy eating. Given the difficulty of recognizing low-fat, high-fiber foods, it is no wonder that restaurant eating is commonly the downfall of many people trying to improve their health by eating right.

With *The Restaurant Companion,* the challenge of eating out can be transformed into an opportunity to learn about selecting optimal foods, to relax when eating out, and to enjoy life more through healthier dining habits.

Hope Warshaw has all the credentials for preparing this nutritional guide. She has devoted years to working with both individuals and groups to change their diet through healthy food selection and, thereby, avoid diet-related medical conditions such as diabetes, cardiovascular disease, hypertension, and obesity. She has focused this book on a major requisite for successful eating: how to choose wisely when dining in restaurants.

People need to vary their diets and enjoy eating without developing a tolerance—and craving—for foods that lead to an increased consumption of fat, sugar, and salt while reducing their interest in fruits and vegetables. Ironically, most people eat less than 20 types of food during any one season of the year. The end result is, of course, overeating and overweight, as well as missed opportunities to use diet to improve health and the enjoyment of life.

New restaurant experiences, new foods, and new eating patterns can break up this routine. Proper meal choices in restaurants can be healthy and enjoyable while providing a break from busy lifestyles. The unlimited opportunities for healthier eating made possible by the diverse restaurants around the country are brought out in *The Restaurant Companion.*

Indeed, this book is a great starting place for you and your friends to experience just how good—and how healthy—restaurant food can be when ordered by an informed consumer. It also provides an excellent opportunity to become acquainted with a host of ethnic cuisines that offer a wide variety of foods to replace our traditional eating patterns—standard meals that offer no new tastes or textures and usually employ foods with far too much sugar, oil, and protein. The new and unique approaches to healthier eating in *The Restaurant Companion* can also be used at the much-frequented fast-food spots, salad bars, sandwich shops—even when flying!

Soon, you will be adopting the healthy changes discovered in this book for your own diet and advocating them to family and friends. And with the confidence you gain by accepting the restaurant challenge, you may find yourself dining out more frequently and enjoying a wide variety of foods more.

> George L. Blackburn, M.D., Ph.D.
> Chief, Nutrition/Metabolism Laboratory,
> New England Deaconess Hospital
> Associate Professor of Surgery,
> Harvard Medical School

1

Healthier Eating Out
A will leads to a way

To say that eating healthy in restaurants is a challenge is an understatement. You might be one who believes that the expression "healthy restaurant meals" is oxymoronic. You might think healthy eating in restaurants is next to impossible. But by reading the pages ahead you'll learn to identify restaurant roadblocks and danger signs, from fast food to *haute cuisine*. You'll master many skills and strategies, tips and tactics for healthier eating out. As you turn the last page, you'll realize that healthy restaurant meals are quite possible. Remember, with a will there's a way.

Consider yourself in luck. You now have a permanent *Restaurant Companion* to guide you in myriad restaurants, whether they are Mexican, Middle Eastern, fast food, business lunch spots, fancy dinner clubs, or quick eateries at the mall. *The Restaurant Companion* can accompany you to restaurants or be consulted prior to crossing the threshold. Keep it in your glove compartment, desk drawer, briefcase, or purse for quick access. The book will prove helpful whether you just want to eat healthier or are modifying your eating plan for medical reasons.

The Restaurant Companion provides realistic advice and practical guidelines for eating in the wide variety of restaurants in America today. It covers eating places from inexpensive to costly, from casual to elegant. Most ethnic cuisines are included—from the ubiquitous Italian, Mexican, pizza, and Chinese to the less-frequented Indian and Thai restaurants. The authentically American establishments—fast-food stops, family-style places, and salad bars are also included. You'll find food options and strategies for eating healthier on airplanes, at ball games, at the mall, in snack shops, and other places you just happen to be when the hunger bell rings. In America, one rule applies: where there are people and activity, there's food.

Restaurant dining—no longer a special occasion

Eating in restaurants is less than 200 years old. Restaurants evolved from saloons, where men congregated, drank alcohol, and ate for free from a large buffet. Only women of ''ill repute'' accompanied men to such rough-and-ready places prior to our century. Tearooms became acceptable places for women. But even into the twentieth century, to eat out was for most people a memorable event, to celebrate a birthday or anniversary. In only a few generations, restaurant dining has gone from solely for the upper crust and reserved for special occasions to a daily happening.

Today, eating away from home is not only done in restaurants. You might eat in your car, when refueling your car, or at your desk. It's a fact of life: people are eating more meals out than ever before, either at a restaurant or purchased from a restaurant. That's why today's supermarkets are starting to look more like restaurants. Quick, convenient, ready-to-eat is our *modus operandi* when it comes to food choices today.

America eats out

According to the National Restaurant Association, in 1950 Americans spent 24 percent of their food dollar on food purchased away from home. The latest figure for 1993 is 43 percent. That's quite a change. The average American (eight years old and older) eats out almost four times a week, or 198 times each year. Lunch is the meal eaten out most frequently, with dinner next and breakfast least often. Men still dine out more frequently than women.

Fast-food places represent the largest segment of restaurants. When it comes to ethnic fare, Mexican, Chinese, and Italian are still America's favorites. Today, even when you peruse the menu in an "American" dining spot, you'll see the cross-cultural favorites of pizza, stir-fry, and chili. All told, eating out, taking out, and eating on the run are here to stay and heartily entrenched in today's convenience-focused world.

Who needs The Restaurant Companion?

While Americans are eating out more than ever before, there's also greater emphasis on health and disease prevention. The chants from health care providers, health associations, and the government's health agencies to manage weight, blood cholesterol, blood pressure, and blood glucose are broadcast in rapid fire. This book can help, as it was written for a wide array of people. It is beneficial for anyone who wants to adopt a healthier eating style. It also will help you if you need to modify your food choices due to specific medical problems, perhaps elevated blood cholesterol, high blood pressure, or blood glucose.

The Restaurant Companion can also help if you are trying to shed a few unwanted pounds. There's no reason to be scared away from restaurants when "dieting." For long-term weight control, it's simply necessary to learn how to dine healthfully in restaurants. So, when you find yourself in the middle of the menu battlefield, *The Restaurant Companion* is your weapon.

6 challenges to healthier restaurant dining

Becoming aware of the challenges to healthier restaurant dining is a first step in the right direction. Here are the six challenges:

1. Restaurant meals are often considered special occasions, where overeating is commonplace. The first challenge: move beyond this thinking. If you eat out four times a week, like most Americans, it will be difficult to achieve your health and nutrition goals if it's always an opportunity to overeat.

2. The second challenge is to take control. You are not in the kitchen preparing the food. Physical control is out of your hands and in those of the cook. You need to exert control with your mouth. Ask about ingredients, request certain items "on the side," and cross your knife and fork when your stomach shouts full!

3. Fats are the third challenge. In restaurants, fat is literally everywhere, from high-fat ingredients, such as cheese and butter, to high-fat food preparations, such as "deep-fried" and "smothered." Fats are also encountered at the table. In American restaurants, it might be butter for rolls; in a Mexican restaurant, it's chips for the salsa. Why so much fat? Because it's an easy way to make food taste good. Learning to be a good fat detective is an essential skill for healthier restaurant dining.

4. Portions are huge, often double the quantity you need. Unfortunately, a plate full of food in front of you is a set-up to overeat. Your challenge is to "outsmart" the menu and limit the amount of food placed before you. Ordering appetizer-size servings, splitting entrees, and taking home half the meal for tomorrow are just a few tips.

5. Challenge number five involves the reduction of protein. Protein (meat, poultry, and seafood) frequently takes up the largest section on the plate. American restaurants are the worst offenders. The question you ask yourself when gazing at the menu is, "Will I have beef, poultry, or seafood?" Few thoughts are given to the "sides"—potatoes, rice, green beans, or broccoli. The result: a 10-ounce piece of prime rib *un*balanced by a small

potato and few green beans. Yet today's nutrition recommendations suggest that protein is the food to eat in the *smallest* amount. To meet challenge 5, you'll learn strategies to make protein "the side dish" rather than the "main course." That's in sync with today's nutrition messages of less protein and more grains, vegetables, and fruits.

6. Controlling alcohol intake is challenge number six. It is consumed more often when dining out, especially in sit-down restaurants. Perhaps it's a beer with pizza, wine with an Italian dinner, or scotch prior to continental cuisine. Alcohol contributes quite a few calories with few nutrients, and it can diminish your resolve to abide by your healthier eating goals. Chapter 4, "What to Drink: Choosing Beverages," offers recommendations for drinking spirits and soft drinks when dining out.

Today's nutrition messages

Over the last 20 years, we've been bombarded by nutrition headlines that are often contradictory. Today, it's most important to follow the general guidelines of balance, variety, and moderation and not be confused or derailed by the nutrition "study of the week." The basic tenets—balance, variety, and moderation—are touted in the *Dietary Guidelines for Americans* (U.S. Department of Health and Human Services):

1. Eat a variety of foods
2. Maintain a healthy weight
3. Choose a diet low in fat, saturated fat, and cholesterol
4. Choose a diet with plenty of vegetables, fruits, and grains
5. Use sugar in moderation
6. Use salt and sodium in moderation
7. If you drink alcoholic beverages, do so in moderation

The United States Department of Agriculture brought us the now familiar Food Guide Pyramid. You'll note that the nutrition messages of the *Dietary Guidelines for Americans* are visually depicted in the Food Guide Pyramid. There's emphasis on using grains and starches as the foundation of your eating plan; try for 6–11 servings each day. Fruits and vegetables are prominently placed on top of the grains to note their importance; get at least 5 servings each day.

Meats, poultry, and other sources of protein are needed but should not be the main focus. Think of them as the ''side dish.'' Try for no more than six ounces of protein each day. Milk and dairy products are required, particularly because of calcium, but low-fat varieties are encouraged.

An important message at the tip of the Pyramid is to ''use fats and sweets sparingly.'' That means go light

Food Guide Pyramid
A Guide to Daily Food Choices

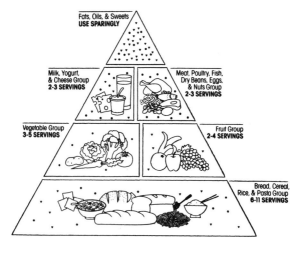

Fats, Oils, & Sweets
USE SPARINGLY

Milk, Yogurt, & Cheese Group
2-3 SERVINGS

Meat, Poultry, Fish, Dry Beans, Eggs, & Nuts Group
2-3 SERVINGS

Vegetable Group
3-5 SERVINGS

Fruit Group
2-4 SERVINGS

Bread, Cereal, Rice, & Pasta Group
6-11 SERVINGS

KEY
These symbols show fat and added sugars in foods.

● Fat (naturally occurring and added)

▼ Sugars (added)

on butter, margarine, and oils, and decrease fried foods and high-sugar and fat desserts.

All these messages dovetail with the nutrition directives of prominent health associations from the American Cancer Society to the American Heart Association, American Diabetes Association, and others. Everyone is singing the same song, and these nutrition strategies should be practiced to prevent disease or to treat it.

For those with diabetes

In May, 1994, the American Diabetes Association published its revised nutrition principles for diabetes. These recommendations blend well with the messages in *The Restaurant Companion* for eating away from home. However, you should establish your personal nutrition goals with a registered dietitian who has expertise in diabetes. Your personal guidelines should be in accordance with your blood glucose goals, other medical concerns, and lifestyle constraints.

Generally, people with diabetes are encouraged to eat a low-fat, low-saturated-fat, and low-cholesterol diet, as well as less animal protein. Today, people with diabetes, as all Americans, are encouraged to eat more carbohydrates such as grains, vegetables, and fruits.

Perhaps the most significant change in these new recommendations is their flexibility about sugars and desserts. Research over the last two decades has shown that foods high in sugar don't raise blood glucose faster than other complex starches. For that reason, people with diabetes can eat some sweets, with the knowledge that sweets are often high in fat and thus calories. It is still healthiest to keep sweets to a minimum, especially if weight and blood lipids are problematic.

Satisfy taste buds healthfully

As you start or continue your journey toward healthier eating in restaurants, think about finding your comfort zone, a balance between what's healthy and what will satisfy your taste buds. You must enjoy what you are eating or you will not continue this journey—that's just human nature. If you regularly go into restaurants and request items without sauce and eat salad without dressing, you'll end up feeling deprived and unsatisfied. In the end, you're not likely to continue the effort. It's critical to strike a balance between healthiness and enjoying the pleasures of food and eating. They can be one and the same.

This is not an easy task. Changing your habits takes time and commitment. But it is possible and you can do it. Remember: a will leads to a way. The premise of *The Restaurant Companion* is that you can eat in 99 percent of restaurants healthfully if you have the right mindset and put practical and realistic skills and strategies into action. Remember, practice makes perfect.

2

10 Skills and Strategies
for healthier restaurant eating

Whether you're lavishing for three hours over an expensive meal in a French restaurant, rushing through a fast-food franchise for a quick lunch, or eating at home, the principles of healthful eating are the same. The precepts are based upon the *Dietary Guidelines for Americans* and those promoted in the Food Guide Pyramid reviewed in Chapter 1. Remember, though, the challenges to healthier eating are greater when eating out than when eating in.

Here are the ten skills and strategies for healthier restaurant eating:

1. Develop a healthy mindset
2. Assess your whens, wheres, and whats of dining out
3. Select the restaurant carefully
4. Have an action plan
5. Be an avid fat detector
6. Order according to the Food Guide Pyramid
7. Practice portion control from the word go
8. Practice menu creativity
9. Order foods as you want them
10. Know when enough is enough

1. Develop a healthy mindset

Do any or all of these notions hold true for you?:

> Eating out means pigging out
>
> Eating out is a special occasion, a celebration
>
> Eating out means "blowing the diet" or "throwing caution to the wind"
>
> Eating out is how I reward myself
>
> I'm paying for it, so I have to eat it all
>
> It's just impossible to eat healthfully in any restaurant

If you answer yes to any of the above, then some mental gymnastics are in order. It's critical to determine your preconceived notions about eating out—"where you are coming from"—in order to work toward a healthy mindset.

After you have honestly assessed your attitudes, you are ready to establish new ones. Now you need to share with your dining partners your conviction that eating healthfully and abiding by your personal or medical nutrition goals has become a priority. Your resolve might impact the choice of restaurants and/or the choice of menu items selected if you order as a group. It is helpful to gain the support of people around you, but don't expect to get it all the time. There will be some, maybe your old "pig-out partners," who will not be pleased with your new attitudes. Be ready for their comments, goading you to deviate from your course. In your mind, change the value of the meal from a dollars-and-cents perspective to whether a meal meets your healthy objectives, pleases your palate, and enriches the whole dining experience.

To be successful, you must believe that dining out can be enjoyable and healthy at the same time. That is a critical first step. Until you readjust your attitude, you will have a difficult time putting the other nine skills and strategies, and many tips and tactics, into action.

2. Assess your whens, wheres, and whats of dining out

With a new attitude, the next step is to learn more about your current habits. Again, the more you learn about "where you are coming from," the more you will know about what behaviors to change. Answer the following questions to learn more about your whens, wheres, and whats of dining out.

Whens: In an average week, how many (estimate the number) meals and snacks do you eat away from home? (Don't forget to count the muffin and coffee eaten your car on the way to work, the meals in the workplace cafeteria, quick bites at the mall, snacks when filling your gas tank, etc.)

Are you surprised when you add them all up? How could you decrease the number of times you eat out?

Wheres: What types of restaurants do you frequent? (Divide them into ethnic, American style/family fare, fast food, pizza/sub shop, quick bites.)

Are you at one type of restaurant too frequently? Could you choose eating spots that offer healthier choices more frequently? What would be some healthier food stops?

Whats: What are your two typical orders in the two types of restaurants you most frequent? (After writing down the four typical meals, take two different color markers and circle all the high-fat items with one color, all the healthier items with the other color.)

Are there particular high-fat items that could be limited? Could you order smaller portions? Could you substitute lower-fat for higher-fat items?

Are there ways to swap protein for more grains, vegetables, and fruits?

Could you split any portions or share items to achieve a better-balanced meal?

There's no question that the more often you eat out, the more closely you need to monitor choices and portions. Also, you might need to monitor the frequency of eating out if your specific nutrition and/or medical goals require it. In another scenario, you might eat out only once a week and toe the line at home; thus you can allow yourself a bit more liberty in restaurants. However, if you have a medical condition that warrants keeping tabs on saturated fat or sodium and you eat out several times each week, you will need to be more diligent about choices and quantities.

By assessing your whens, wheres, and whats, did you realize that you are simply eating away from home more than is necessary? For instance, you may have found that you buzz by the local fast-food spot for a sausage and biscuit breakfast several days a week. Maybe a bagel or English muffin from home or an easy bowl of high-fiber cereal with low-fat milk before you leave would be a healthier choice and probably quicker. It would leave some change clinking in your pocket, too. Lunch in the company cafeteria or at a local sandwich or sub shop might be adding lots of fat as mayonnaise on a sandwich, chips on the side, and a cookie for dessert. Bring your lunch a few days a week, or at least a piece of fruit for the afternoon, to improve the health quotient of your eating plan.

Today, food is accessible practically everywhere, and that's one reason why you might eat out so often and shop and cook so little. If you found that you are eating out way more than necessary, here are some preplanning strategies:

Select a regular day to shop

Think about what foods you need to purchase to decrease the number of meals eaten out

Prepare a large casserole to last for several meals

Have foods in the pantry for quick meals, such as soups, pasta and tomato sauce, cans of tuna, and high-fiber cereal

3. Select the restaurant carefully

Once you've made the decision to dine out, choose a restaurant that has at least some healthier choices. Today, the choices are good 'n plenty. Don't find yourself in a place with a limited menu and/or enticing teasers. A fried-chicken or fish-and-chips fast-food spot is an example. There are no healthier choices, and it's a set-up to eat unhealthy foods. Because people are more concerned about nutrition today, most restaurants, even the fried-fish places, have a few baked offerings and healthier sides.

In many instances, you will be familiar with a restaurant's menu because you have eaten there many times before. Or maybe you've been told about the restaurant by friends or have heard of it through advertising. If you are traveling, you might choose a chain restaurant serving the menu you are familiar with. In the rare instance when you are completely unfamiliar with the menu, you might wish to call the restaurant to ask about your particular needs. However, most of the time that's unnecessary.

4. Have an action plan

Think before you act is the rule of thumb. Avoid finding yourself in a situation where your eyes are perusing the menu waiting to have your taste buds enticed. Since more times than not you are familiar with the menu offerings, preplan what you might order before you cross the threshold. Don't even look at a menu. This action will fuel your resolve and leave your taste buds in calm gear. If you want to split and/or share menu items, talk to your dining partners about their preferences prior to entering. Being the first to order is another helpful strategy. That avoids changing your planned order as the waiter scribbles orders from your dining partners.

On a broader scope, it's important to think about menu choices in the context of the whole day. Ask yourself the questions: have I eaten enough fruit and vegetables?; will I be eating more protein at another meal?; how much fat have I eaten today? A preplanning strategy that might help is ''nutrition banking.'' You can use this concept for whatever you might be monitoring—fats, carbohydrates, fruits, or vegetables. Nutrition banking teaches you to think about your food intake more than one meal at a time and, if necessary, more than one day at a time. For example, if you will be celebrating a special occasion at a fancy restaurant that evening, save up some available fat grams for sauce on an entree or a favorite dessert. Nutrition banking can also be done with exercise. Increasing exercise and calories burned adds more calories to the nutrition bank, a deposit of sorts.

When you practice preplanning strategies, don't fall into the trap of starving yourself prior to arriving at a restaurant. This practice is clearly a set-up to overeat. It usually backfires. For one thing, you will be extremely hungry, so your resistance to unhealthier foods will be weakened. Another factor is that rationalizing extras becomes a cinch.

5. Be an avid fat detector

Pinpointing fats in restaurants is your biggest challenge. Why so much fat? Fat is used to enhance taste and flavor, and it does its job well. However, while enhancing flavor, fat adds significant calories without adding any food volume (or ''bites''). A great example is a medium baked potato containing about 100 calories. Add to that one teaspoon of regular butter or margarine at 50 calories and two tablespoons of regular sour cream at 50 calories. You've added another 100 calories without adding any bites.

Fat is the most saturated form of calories at nine per gram. Volume being equal, carbohydrate and protein foods have half the calories at four calories per gram. Therefore, lowering fat intake, even just a little, can make a big impact on calories. Observe the following example of two menu selections from a sandwich shop menu:

High Fat/Calorie Lunch	**Lower Fat/Calorie Lunch**	
Cheeseburger on roll with lettuce and tomato	Ham sandwich on rye bread with mustard, lettuce, and sliced tomatoes	
French fries		
Regular soda	Pretzels	
	Low-calorie soda	
Calories:	1155	460
Fat (grams):	52	7
% Calories as fat:	41	14

This example shows that different choices from the same menu can make significant differences in calorie and fat content, yet not volume. Throughout *The Restaurant Companion* comparisons will be made between healthier and not-so-healthy choices. You'll be able to see how just a few simple changes can make a substantial nutritional difference.

Learning to be an avid fat detector will help put you in the driver's seat. To make this easier, we'll divide your training as a fat private eye into two sections: on the menu and at the table. "On-the-menu" fat creeps in as ingredients used in cooking and food preparation—butter, oil, cream, mayonnaise; as ingredients used in dishes—cheese, prime rib, pork spareribs. Certain preparation methods simply mean drenched in fat: deep fried, smothered, in creamy cheese sauce. Particular menu items—pasta with Alfredo sauce or chimichangas—by definition mean loaded with fat. Not only do you need to become acquainted with the high-fat items, but it will be important to learn about the ingredients, preparation methods, and menu descriptions that indicate low fat and healthy: herbs and spices, light wine or tomato sauce, pasta primavera (in sauteed vegetable sauce). Don't forget, feel free to ask waiters questions about unfamiliar ingredients, preparations, and menu descriptions.

Fat creeps in "at the table" in several ways. In sit-down restaurants, you might be greeted with rolls and butter if it's American; chips and salsa if it's Mexican; or garlic bread if it's Italian. So even before you order, the fat starts tallying up. Extra fats might be brought to the table in the form of sour cream, butter, margarine, mayonnaise, salad dressing, and cream for beverages. The best advice is, if agreeable to your dining partners, to reject the fats at the table. Maybe you keep the rolls but return the butter.

You're job as a fat detective becomes easy when using *The Restaurant Companion.* Each chapter on the different types of restaurants provides a list of "red flag" and "green flag" words. Red flag words are ingredients, preparation methods, and menu descriptions that are high in fat and calories. Green flag words are ingredients, preparation methods, and menu descriptions that are lower in fat and calories. In this edition we've made reviewing red and green flag words easier by separating ingredients from preparation methods and menu descriptions. We've also added "at the table" high-fat items to the red flag list.

6. Order according to the Food Guide Pyramid

From reading Chapter 1, you know the basic precepts of the Food Guide Pyramid. It's enlightening to contrast the nutrition messages of the Food Guide Pyramid with a typical high-fat restaurant meal as shown below. Many restaurant meals literally turn the Food Guide Pyramid upside down!

8-oz. steak	
Baked potato with butter (1 tsp) and sour cream (1 tbsp)	
Green beans topped with butter (1 tsp)	
Salad with Thousand Island dressing (2 tbsp)	
Apple pie à la mode	
Calories	1340
Protein (g)	76
Carbohydrate (g)	112
Fat (g)	66
% Calories as fat	44

Here's a typical steak and potato meal. The main focus is meat. The meal is heavy on fats: steak, and lots of it; butter and sour cream for the potato; more butter on the green beans; Thousand Island dressing on the salad, and ice cream on the apple pie, which already has fat in the crust. Here's how you can change this meal slightly for better health:

Split 8-oz. steak = 4 ozs.	
Baked potato with 1 tbsp sour cream	
Green beans (hold butter)	
Salad with 1 tbsp Thousand Island	
Split apple pie (hold ice cream)	
Calories	648
Protein (g)	40
Carbohydrate (g)	64
Fat (g)	26
% Calories as fat	36

As you work to change your restaurant eating habits, keep a visual picture of the Food Guide Pyramid in mind. When you stand at the counter of a fast-food restaurant or sit comfortably with a menu in hand, think about whether your order matches up with the Pyramid—right side up, that is!

7. Practice portion control from the word go

Large portions are simply a fact of restaurant dining. Your challenge is to "outsmart" the menu and control portions from the word go. Less food in front of you means you will eat less. We'll call that "out of sight, out of mind (or mouth)." There's an analogy here to healthier eating at home. If you leave certain "undesirables" on the supermarket shelf, you are much less likely to eat them than if they were inches away in the cupboard.

Throughout *The Restaurant Companion* you'll learn more tips about controlling portions in specific types of restaurants. Controlling portions from the start is also a strategy to avoid feeling deprived. Your goal is to eat smaller quantities of the foods you enjoy. Here are a few tactics:

> Steer clear of menu descriptions meaning large portions: jumbo, grande, supreme, king-size, feast, combo.

> Go for the menu descriptions meaning small servings: regular, petite, appetizer-size, kiddie, queen-size.

> Try to order half, lunch, or appetizer-size portions.

> Choose from the à la carte and/or side offerings section of the menu. Mix and match these to have small servings of a few items.

8. Practice menu creativity

Practicing menu creativity is the strategy that lets you continue to outsmart the menu. It's simply more tactics to boycott large portions. Choose items from the soups, salads, and appetizer listings. Use a cup of broth-based soup, such as chicken with rice or bean and barley, as a low-calorie filler, especially if your dining partners are partaking in high-fat appetizers. A side salad can be used similarly. Order the salad and then request that the waiter serve your appetizer as a main course. Or order two appetizers, one as an appetizer and the other as your main course. There are countless ways to mix and match with smaller portions.

Here are a few more ideas to practice menu creativity. Remember, no sign says "you must order an entree."

Split portions with your dining partner(s). Go ahead, order from soup to dessert, but split everything down the middle. In better restaurants, ask the waiter to split the portions in the kitchen and serve it on two plates.

Eat "family style." This is the serving style in Asian restaurants, but it can be used in any restaurant. Order one or two less entrees than the number of people dining, and pass the dishes around.

Share nutritionally complimentary dishes to eat in sync with the Food Guide Pyramid. For example, in an Italian restaurant, one person orders Pasta Primavera and the other others Chicken Marsala. The chicken dish will be at least 6–8 ozs. of chicken; that's enough protein for two. The pasta is enough for two and will provide two starch servings for each. A salad adds vegetables.

9. Order foods as you want them

Special requests are essential to get foods as you want them. A special request might mean asking for an ingredient to be left out—cheese, bacon, sour cream. Your request may be a substitution—baked potato rather than French fries or potato chips; mustard rather than mayonnaise. Maybe you just want an ingredient served on the side so you control the amount you use— salad dressing, butter, or guacamole. Perhaps your request will be a cooking instruction—broil the fish with a small amount of butter, or use very little oil in the wok. It's important to take the attitude that there's no harm in asking. The worst someone can say is no.

Special requests might make you feel like you are ruffling feathers. However, there are ways to approach special requests that will put you at ease and won't make your dining partners sink into their seats:

Be reasonable and realistic. Don't try to remake a menu item by requesting that certain ingredients be left off and others added.

Request simple rather than complex changes or additions.

Be pleasantly assertive. Let the waiter know what you want, using the "helping" words. Practice these phrases:

Do you think the chef will. . . ?
I'd really appreciate it if you could. . . ?
Can I have . . . on the side?
Would it be a problem to substitute . . . for . . ?

10. Know when enough is enough

You've already gotten the message that portion control is critical. Control portions from the start by ordering creatively, and control them once food is delivered by knowing when "enough is enough." If you know you'll get too much food, request a doggie bag to come *with* the meal. Immediately set aside the portion to take home. If that feels uncomfortable in some situations, try separating the portion and placing the take-home part on a small plate. Offer "tastes" to your dining companions.

Be clear about your definition of fullness. Often, you respond to external rather than internal cues. An external cue is food left on your plate. An internal cue is a full stomach. Learn to listen to your internal signals— how does your stomach feel when you have had enough to eat? Listen to this sensation as a message to put down your knife and fork rather than wait for the post-Thanksgiving-dinner-stuffed-turkey feeling.

Slow the pace of eating. This gives your stomach a chance to communicate with your brain that you are full. Lastly, take time to enjoy the taste of the food in your mouth. Remember, membership in the "clean plate club" is costly and unnecessary.

Enjoy the non-food pleasantries of restaurant dining. Frequently, you focus only on the food due to time constraints, hunger, or other stresses. Enjoyment of the surroundings is often missed. Train yourself to enjoy all aspects of the restaurant environment, even if it's just a few minutes of relaxation or conversation with a friend. Think about not cooking, putting away leftovers, or doing dishes. Enjoying the non-food pleasantries makes it easier to limit portions and eat healthfully.

3

How to Eat Out

with

The Restaurant Companion

*T*he *Restaurant Companion: A Guide to Healthier Eating Out* gives you a "hands-on" approach to making healthy restaurant choices. The book provides specific information on America's most popular eating places: Mexican, Chinese, Italian, fast food, American (family and dinner style), seafood restaurants, salad bars, and others. Less familiar ethnic restaurants are also included: Thai, Japanese, Indian, Middle Eastern, and more. This edition adds chapters on pizza, upscale dining, and Eating Just About Anywhere.

The chapters covering each cuisine present information in a parallel fashion. That's what makes this book easy to use. As you become familiar with the format, you'll be able to use *The Restaurant Companion* as a guidebook, referring to it prior to or while eating a specific cuisine.

This is the way each chapter is sectioned:

Get to Know the Cuisine
Before You Order
Menu Management
Green Flag Words
Red Flag Words
Special Requests
The Menu
Your Order, Please

Get to Know the Cuisine helps familiarize you with ingredients, techniques of cooking, and the particular serving styles unique to the cuisine. The chapters on ethnic restaurants also contain tidbits about the cuisine's history and how it has become "Americanized."

Before You Order provides you with information about the nutritional pros and cons of each restaurant's repertory. These guidelines help you navigate your way through each cuisine. Easy strategies help you keep fat and cholesterol intake on the light side, sodium down, and portions minimal. When reviewing these notes, keep your personal nutrition goals in mind. For instance, if you limit dietary cholesterol because of elevated blood cholesterol, pay special attention to comments about the cholesterol content of foods. You'll find specific notations about foods to order or limit if you want to modify other nutrients such as fat, sodium, or sugar. These suggestions are based on sound nutrition principles for weight loss or maintenance and/or management of diabetes, heart disease, and high blood pressure.

Menu Management provides specific suggestions about foods to order or limit to achieve healthier meals. Tips and tactics for choosing appetizers, soups, entrees, side dishes, and even desserts are given.

Green Flag Words gives you a list of ingredients, preparation methods, and menu items that signal you to "go ahead and order." Green Flag Words are relatively low in fat, saturated fat, cholesterol, sodium, and calories. In this edition we've made these lists even more user-friendly. You'll find two categories of Green Flag Words: one for ingredients (vinegar, wine); and the other for preparation methods (Cajun, poached) and menu descriptions or items (fajitas, marinara sauce). Review the list of Green Flag Words prior to eating the cuisine, and keep them in mind as you peruse the menu.

Red Flag Words give you a list of ingredients, preparation methods, and menu items that signal you to stop, look, and reconsider. Red Flag Words are relatively high in fat, saturated fat, cholesterol, sodium, and calories. In this edition we've also made these lists more user-friendly. You'll find three categories of Red Flag Words: the first is ingredients (butter, oil); and the second is preparation methods (deep fried, breaded and fried) and menu items (guacamole, sweet-and-sour shrimp). The third category is a new addition: "at the table," which lists items found at or brought to the table that add fat and calories. Fried tortilla chips and Chinese noodles are examples. Review the list of Red Flag Words prior to eating the fare, and keep them in mind as you search the menu.

Specials Requests help you get food "as you want it." They advise you on asking for special preparations and for the elimination, substitution, or addition of particular ingredients within the specific cuisine. A commonly used special request when ordering a salad is, "May I have the salad dressing on the side?" When ordering a Mexican salad, you might ask, "Can you hold the sour cream and put the guacamole on the side?" You might request that your salmon be grilled without added oil or butter, or you might say, "Please remove the Chinese noodles from the table." You'll see, as you read on, that special requests are simply part of healthier eating out.

The Menu provides a generic menu that lists the menu items most frequently found in that type of restaurant. As you know, if you go into a Chinese restaurant in San Francisco, Chicago, or Miami, you will find a similar menu. That's true for most ethnic cuisines. In chain restaurants, from coast to coast, you know only too well what menu choices to expect. The Menu represents the gamut of choices from healthiest to unhealthy, and it allows you a role-playing experience. Use it to practice preplanning your order or to review the items you will see when the real menu is placed in your hands.

A small check mark is used in front of the healthier, or "Preferred Choices." Preferred Choices are lower in fat, cholesterol, or calories. It is difficult to make black-and-white decisions about particular foods. Some are less healthy from the word go, such as pasta in Alfredo sauce. Others can be modified to be healthier, such as a Mexican salad, which can be served on a plate rather than in a fried tortilla shell, the sour cream can be left in the kitchen, and salsa can be used instead of dressing to lighten up further on fats. These factors are considered in the decision to check an item as a Preferred Choice.

Your Order, Please gives you "model meals." The five sample meals shown for each cuisine are based on different nutrition goals. They range from Low Calorie/Low Fat to Higher Calorie/Low Cholesterol to Low Sodium. The models provide realistic suggestions for what to order in each type of restaurant. The model meals should help you realize that eating out within the parameters of your health goals is easy. The five models are numbered 1 to 5 for quick identification from chapter to chapter. Following is a more detailed description of each model meal category. Match your nutrition goals with one of the categories; then you will know which model number to use as a guide throughout *The Restaurant Companion.*

1. Low Calorie/Low Fat

These meals, on average, contain 400–700 calories, with 30–40 percent of the calories from fat. They are based on a daily calorie intake of 1,200–1,600. If your target is 1,200 calories, observe the total calories of the meal. If you think it's too high, eliminate a food to put you closer to your calorie goal. We have attempted to strike a balance between encouraging you to try enticing and new taste treats and staying focused on nutrition goals. These model meals generally meet accepted guidelines for achieving a low-fat and low-saturated-fat diet. They are also moderate to low in cholesterol and sodium.

Low Calorie/Low Fat meals are appropriate for women and men seeking weight loss and for women who want to maintain their present weight. The sample meals meet the nutrition recommendations for people with diabetes who are following a meal plan between 1,200 and 1,600 calories per day. The meals meet the American Diabetes Association's 1994 nutrition principles for meal planning. The "guestimated" exchange values, which are provided, are based on the *Exchange Lists for Meal Planning* developed by the American Diabetes Association and The American Dietetic Association.

2. Low Calorie/Low Cholesterol

These model meals can be used interchangeably with ones designated Low Calorie/Low Fat. However, these maintain more focus on cholesterol content at 100–200 milligrams per meal. The meals contain an average of 400–700 calories and are based on a daily caloric intake of 1,200–1,600. These meals are moderate to low in saturated fat and sodium. As always, the items chosen encourage adventure in dining and trying new taste treats.

The Low Calorie/Low Cholesterol model meals are appropriate for men and women with heart disease and/ or elevated blood cholesterol who are encouraged to decrease weight and reduce dietary cholesterol and saturated fat intake. The meals also meet the American Diabetes Association's 1994 nutrition principles for meal planning. These meals can be used if you are striving either to maintain or achieve desired body weight or simply to eat healthier.

3. Higher Calorie/Low Fat

The model meals in this category are 600–1,000 calories. They are based on a daily calorie intake of 1,800–2,200. These meals are low in fat, at about 30–40 percent of the calories. They are also moderate to low in saturated fat and cholesterol. The meals can be used by large men who want to lose weight or by those who want to maintain weight and eat healthier. The sample meals are for readers with diabetes who are encouraged to follow a meal plan within the range of 1,800–2,200 calories per day. The meals meet the American Diabetes Association's 1994 nutrition principles for meal planning "Guestimated" exchange values for diabetes meal planning are provided.

4. Higher Calorie/Low Cholesterol

These model meals can be used interchangeably with the Higher Calorie/Low Fat meals. These meals are

600–1,000 calories. They are based on a daily calorie intake of 1,800–2,200. The individual examples contain 100–200 milligrams of cholesterol. They are moderate to low in saturated fat and sodium.

These meals can be used by individuals trying to lower blood cholesterol levels by following the American Heart Association's dietary guidelines and by readers simply trying to follow general nutrition recommendations for healthy eating and weight maintenance. The meals also meet the American Diabetes Association's 1994 nutrition principles for meal planning.

5. Low Sodium

These model meals provide suggestions for readers whose main priority is to achieve a low-sodium intake. The examples contain 1,000–1,500 milligrams of sodium per meal, which nicely matches guidelines for maintaining low- to moderate-sodium intake. These meals are based on a total sodium average intake of 2,000–3,000 milligrams per day.

For many people, maintaining low sodium intake is simply one nutrition goal, along with monitoring dietary cholesterol and/or fat. However, moderate- to low-sodium intake may be your only restriction if you have high blood pressure. Maintaining sodium consumption of 3,000 milligrams per day or less is recommended for the healthy public. These meals also meet the American Diabetes Association's 1994 nutrition principles for meal planning.

Estimated Nutrient Evaluation

For each of the model meals you will find an estimated nutrient evaluation. The total calories, grams of fat, protein, and carbohydrate (along with the percentage of the nutrient in parentheses) and percent of calories from alcohol (where appropriate) are given. Cholesterol and sodium quantities are also listed. To give you a frame of reference, the goals for daily intake of fat, protein, carbohydrate, cholesterol, and sodium are noted at the beginning of each model meal section.

The estimated nutrient data is based on a combination of sample recipes, computerized nutrient analyses from N-Squared Computing, First DataBank Division of The Hearst Corporation, 1111 Bayhill Drive, San

Bruno, CA 94066, and data from the nutrient composition tables developed by the USDA. Keep in mind that these are estimates based on usual amounts of ingredients and usual quality served. There are thousands of restaurants and thousands of cooks and chefs who prepare foods in different ways. Though much of the nutrition information is ''guestimated,'' some is exact. Information provided by all the fast-food restaurants and some chain restaurants is used. When exact information is used, it is so noted.

Over the last several years, the Center for Science in the Public Interest has provided nutrient analyses for a number of items from a variety of types of restaurants. These have been published in their newsletter *Nutrition Action Healthletter.* For copies of the articles, contact Center for Science in the Public Interest, 1875 Connecticut Ave., NW, Suite 300, Washington, DC 20009.

Now onto healthier eating in virtually all types of restaurants.

4

What to Drink
Choosing beverages

At a sit-down restaurant the first question usually asked is, "May I bring you something to drink?" At the fast-food counter, "and to drink?" might be the phrase. However the question is asked, you'll need to decide on fluids to help the food slide down. It might be non-alcoholic—soda, juice, or milk—or alcoholic—beer, wine, or a distilled spirit. Because the choice of beverages can raise your calorie count significantly, you need to know numbers for the gamut of liquids and be prepared with a plan and response to, "Something to drink?"

Since beverages are simply liquids, you might forget to tally the number of calories you gulp. Contemplate these numbers: 150 calories and next to no nutrition for 16 ounces of carbonated soft drink, "soda," and 150 calories for 12 ounces of regular beer. You swallow 100 calories with 6 ounces of fruit juice and 120 calories with 8 ounces of 2 percent milk, but at least you get a few vitamins and minerals with these two. Beverage choices deserve as much preplanning and thought as food selections.

Non-alcoholic drinks

Non-alcoholic drinks come in a wide variety, from the ever available soda, or "pop," and fresh ground coffee to the less plentiful juice and milk. Some pack in calories; others provide next to none. Non-caloric beverages can help fill you up. This is especially helpful for weight watchers trying to keep the calories low.

Carbonated Soft Drinks: The most frequently ordered cold beverage is soda. Sweetened with high-fructose corn syrup (the sweetener used in most carbonated and non-carbonated soft drinks) or sweetened with low-calorie sweeteners, soda is served in most restaurants. A rule of thumb: limit regular soda because it offers nothing but calories. The tables at the end of this chapter give the facts in black and white. A large (32-ounce) regular soft drink in a fast-food restaurant costs you 300 calories. That's a chunk, especially when you realize there's no nutrition. Think about saving calories for some extra "bites" and order a diet soda at 3 calories for a large serving.

New Age Drinks: Flavored seltzers, carbonated fruit drinks, and sweetened ice teas are coined "new age beverages." They're selling like wild fire and tally up to hundreds of calories each day if you choose not to twirl the bottle and take heed of the food label's nutrition facts. Their calories and lack of nutrition match regular soda.

Fruit Juice: Orange, grapefruit, and apple juices are healthy, vitamin- and mineral-dense beverages of choice. However, a 16-ounce jar can load on 240 calories. That's a lot when you are simply quenching your thirst and helping the food go down. Better than slurping juice, chew a piece of fruit for the munch and fiber. Grab a piece of fruit at the work cafeteria, pack one or two pieces from home each day, keep dried fruit in your desk or locker, or get a fruit fix before bed.

Mineral Water: If the restaurant has a bar, you'll be able to order healthy, no-calorie mineral water or club soda. You might try flavoring these with a twist or piece of lemon or lime. These are great thirst quenchers.

Water: Don't forget about good old, cheap, plentiful, healthy water. It's definitely non-caloric. One idea to make water a bit more enticing is to request a piece of lemon or lime. If you enjoy lemonade, you can easily make your own with wedges of lemon and low-calorie sweetener.

Milk: Most restaurants serve milk, but what kind is the question. As consumers continue to focus on fat, many restaurants stock low-fat or skim milk. The type of milk is often undefined on the menu. If you have questions, ask; try to drink skim or low fat. Skim milk rings in at 90 calories for 8 ounces, while whole milk has 150 for the same amount. The extra calories are nothing but unhealthy fat and cholesterol.

Coffee: One of America's favorite drinks, available morning, noon, and night, is coffee. More and more coffee is being sipped. Some view coffee as the last legal evil in life. For that reason, coffee shops are popping up on every other city block. Chapter 19, Breakfast, Coffee Shops, and Brunch, includes some information about coffee, donut, and bagel shops. Coffee is always available, caffeinated or decaffeinated. Whether you go for the kick or leave it out, coffee starts off with essentially zero calories. The calories creep in when scoops of sugar (16 calories per teaspoon) and half-and-half (40 calories per ounce, or 2 tablespoons) are stirred in. Use a low-calorie sweetener rather than granulated sugar, and try low-fat milk to lighten.

A hot beverage at fancier restaurants is espresso. Espresso usually follows the meal or accompanies a sweet treat. Some would define espresso as power-packed coffee. Espresso is very rich, dark, and thick coffee. It is served in a demitasse, about 3 ounces, with a twist of lemon to run over the brim and sugar cubes to cut the biting, bitter taste. It's a nice way to end a meal and, best yet, contains almost no calories, fat, or cholesterol.

Tea: More interesting teas are served today, both cold and hot. It's common to find Earl Gray, English Breakfast, or Darjeeling. You find tea either caffeinated or decaffeinated. Some herbal teas, which contain no caffeine, are available: lemon, orange and spice, or red zinger. Again, the scoops of sugar and/or half-

and-half should be traded for a low-calorie sweetener, whether the tea is hot or iced.

Alcoholic drinks

A few health considerations. Over the last few years, there have been strong warnings about the dangers of drinking and driving. Some people heed the warning of using a designated driver, or they imbibe alcohol in moderation. Beyond its hazard on the road, heavy alcohol use can exacerbate cancer of the mouth, esophagus, liver, and colon. When it comes to curtailing high triglycerides, a low-fat diet and very limited alcohol use is the order of the day. The positive health aspects of moderate alcohol consumption are stress reduction and a modest elevation of HDLs—good cholesterol. However, when you weigh the positives and negatives, moderation is the way to go. If you don't drink alcohol, for whatever reason, there is no health benefit worthy of encouraging you to start.

Perhaps the most negative aspects of alcohol are the excess calories and minimal or no nutrition. If you are looking to shed a few pounds, practice moderation if not abstinence. You simply can't afford the calories. If you are trying to eat 1,200 calories per day, there's not much room even for light beer at roughly 100 calories for 12 ounces. It's best to make a contract with yourself. Perhaps you will decide to drink alcohol only when dining out on weekends or with one or two restaurant meals per week. Concomitantly, you keep alcohol out of the house. Decide on your alcoholic beverage of choice and how many drinks are in your calorie and health budget.

Here are a few suggestions for limiting alcohol intake. Always make sure you have a non-caloric beverage by your side. That way you drink the non-caloric beverage to quench your thirst and you sip the alcohol to make it last longer. If your self-contract says one glass of wine or beer and you enjoy that with your meal, don't order it when you sit down. Ask for it just before your meal is delivered. Order a non-alcoholic beverage when your dining partners are initiating the meal with alcohol.

Beer: It might be labeled Singha in Thai restaurants, Dos Equis in Mexican dining spots, or Bud or Mich in the local bar and grill. Beer is a brewed and fermented drink. Its taste is created from blending malted barley and other starches and flavoring the brew with hops. Though it might be light or dark, gutsy or mellow, beer is beer from a calorie standpoint. And the calories add up fast. A 12-ounce can has about 150 calories, and how many people just drink one? Today, an available option is light beer. Most light beers have 100 calories for the same 12 ounces. It's a helpful alternative when trying to minimize calories.

Wine: Whether it's red, white, or rose, domestic, French, or Italian, wine contains about 120 calories for 6 ounces. If you like one brand better than the other, the word to the wise is drink what you enjoy. If you typically split a bottle of wine, you might want to reduce the quantity by ordering a half-bottle or simply two glasses. Today, more restaurants offer better wines by the glass.

Another calorie-conscious strategy is to order a wine spritzer with white, red, or rose. A wine spritzer is made with wine, club soda, and a twist of lemon or lime. Ask the bartender to mix it half and half rather than the usual three-fourths wine and one-fourth soda. What's great about a wine spritzer is that you get a nice tall, thirst-quenching drink with a small amount of wine. So, for the same number of calories as in one glass of wine, you can sip two wine spritzers.

Champagne: It's classified as wine and named after its place of origin in Champagne, France. Champagne is a celebratory beverage—toasting an occasion with a few sips. Champagne is slightly higher in calories than most wines, and the calories are dependent on its dryness. Drier champagne is slightly higher in calories. Champagne shows up at brunches, often in mimosas, where it is teamed with orange juice.

Distilled Beverages: Rum, gin, vodka, and whiskey are all classified as distilled spirits. Interestingly, like wine, they all have the same number of calories—about 100 per jigger (1½ ounces) for 80-proof liquor. Many people have the misconception that rum, scotch, and other slightly sweeter distilled spirits are higher in calories. That's not true. Don't get caught up in the misconception that wine and beer have less calories than distilled liquor, although you get more volume for your calories with wine and beer. The big problem with distilled spirits is that they are often mixed with other high-calorie ingredients. Consider a Planter's Punch (8 ounces at 400 calories) or a martini (6 ounces at 340 calories). It's best to limit drinks that are combinations of distilled spirits, liqueurs, fruit juice, regular soda, tonic water, or cream. Try ordering distilled spirits on the rocks, with a splash of water, club soda, or diet soda.

Liqueur and Brandy: The last category of alcoholic beverages is liqueurs, cordials, and brandies. Liqueurs and cordials synonymously describe beverages such as the familiar Kahlua, Amaretto, and Drambuie. You sip these straight-up or on the rocks as after-dinner drinks or in combination with other distilled spirits in mixed drinks. Brandy is created from distilled wine or the mash of fruit. The most familiar brandy is cognac. Liqueurs, cordials, and brandies ring in at about 150 calories per jigger (1½ ounces), a substantial number of calories for a small quantity.

Another way to enjoy liqueurs and get more ounces for your calories is to make a liqueur part of a coffee drink, such as Irish coffee or Kahlua and coffee. By adding a shot of liqueur to black coffee, you increase the volume substantially. Ask the waitperson to hold the usual whipped cream and sugar. Use one of these drinks in place of dessert to quench your sweet tooth. As others are downing their mega-calorie confections, you sip a 150-calorie, no-fat dessert.

Quenching Thirst: Non-alcoholic*†

Beverage Item	Amount	Calories	Fat (g)	% Cals. as fat	Protein (g)	Carbo-hydrate (g)	Cho-lesterol (mg)	Sodium (mg)
CARBONATED SOFT DRINKS–REGULAR								
Coca-Cola Classic®–small	16 oz	150	0	0	0	38	0	15
Coca-Cola Classic®–medium	21 oz	210	0	0	0	55	0	20
Coca-Cola Classic®–large	32 oz	300	0	0	0	82	0	30
Sprite–small	16 oz	140	0	0	0	37	0	35
Sprite–medium	21 oz	210	0	0	0	53	0	50
Sprite–large	32 oz	300	0	0	0	78	0	78
CARBONATED SOFT DRINKS–DIET								
Diet Coke®–small	**16 oz**	**1**	**0**	**0**	**0**	**0**	**0**	**20**
Diet Coke®–medium	**21 oz**	**2**	**0**	**0**	**0**	**0**	**0**	**25**
Diet Coke®–large	**32 oz**	**3**	**0**	**0**	**0**	**0**	**0**	**35**

Beverage Item	Amount	Calories	Fat (g)	% Cals. as fat	Protein (g)	Carbo-hydrate (g)	Cho-lesterol (mg)	Sodium (mg)
Diet Seven Up	**12 oz**	**4**	**0**	**0**	**0**	**0**	**0**	**22**
NEW AGE BEVERAGES–REGULAR								
Twister–Orange Peach	8 oz	120	0	0	1	29	0	20
Twister light–Orange Cranberry	**8 oz**	**30**	**0**	**0**	**0**	**7**	**0**	**20**
Arizona Ice Tea–Mucho Mango	8 oz	100	0	0	0	27	0	20
Arizona Ice Tea–ice tea	8 oz	95	0	0	0	25	0	20
Clearly Canadian–Wild Cherry	11 oz	120	0	0	0	31	0	15
Snapple–Fruit Punch	8 oz	120	0	0	0	29	0	5
Snapple–Orange-flavored tea	8 oz	110	0	0	0	27	0	10
Fruitopia–Raspberry Psychic Lemonade	8 oz	120	0	0	0	30	0	25
Nestea ice tea–Peach	8 oz	90	0	0	0	22	0	10

Beverage Item	Amount	Calories	Fat (g)	% Cals. as fat	Protein (g)	Carbo-hydrate (g)	Cho-lesterol (mg)	Sodium (mg)
NEW AGE BEVERAGES–DIET								
Quest–raspberry	**8 oz**	**2**	**0**	**0**	**0**	**0**	**0**	**40**
Nestea ice tea–unsweetened	**8 oz**	**0**	**0**	**0**	**0**	**0**	**0**	**10**
SPORTS DRINKS								
Gatorade	8 oz	50	0	0	0	14	0	110
Powerade	8 oz	70	0	0	0	19	0	55
FRUIT JUICES								
Orange	6 oz	80	0	0	0	20	0	20
Apple	6 oz	80	0	0	0	20	0	0

*Based on nutrition information provided by restaurants and obtained from N-Squared Computing.
†Healthier/lower-calorie beverages are noted in **bold.**

Quenching Thirst: Milk, Coffee, Tea*

Beverage Item	Amount	Calories	Fat (g)	% Cals. as fat	Protein (g)	Carbo-hydrate (g)	Cho-lesterol (mg)	Sodium (mg)
MILK								
Regular	8 oz	150	8	48	8	12	35	119
Low fat	8 oz	110	4	33	8	11	15	115
Skim	8 oz	80	0	0	8	12	5	130
COFFEE								
Black	8 oz	3	0	0	0	0	0	3
TEA								
Black	8 oz	1	0	0	0	0	0	0
Ice tea–unsweetened	16 oz	6	0	0	0	0	0	12
Ice tea–sweetened	16 oz	203	0	0	0	50	0	18

*Based on nutrition information provided by restaurants and obtained from N-Squared Computing.

Quenching Thirst: Alcoholic*+

Beverage Item	Amount	Calories	Fat (g)	% Cals. as fat	Protein (g)	Carbo-hydrate (g)	Cho-lesterol (mg)	Sodium (mg)
BEER								
Regular	12 oz	146	0	0	1	13	0	18
Light	12 oz	101	0	0	1	5	0	11
WINE								
White	6 oz	121	0	0	trace	4	0	n/a
Red	6 oz	129	0	0	1	3	0	114
CHAMPAGNE								
Champagne	6 oz	127	0	0	trace	4	0	n/a
DISTILLED LIQUOR								
Gin	1½ oz	98	0	0	0	0	0	0
Vodka	1½ oz	98	0	0	0	0	0	0
Whiskey	1½ oz	98	0	0	0	0	0	0

Beverage Item	Amount	Calories	Fat (g)	% Cals. as fat	Protein (g)	Carbo-hydrate (g)	Cho-lesterol (mg)	Sodium (mg)
LIQUEUR AND BRANDY								
Kahlua	1½ oz	178	0	0	0	24	0	5
Apricot Brandy	1½ oz	99	0	0	0	9	0	3
Cognac	1½ oz	110	0	0	0	0	0	1
MIXED DRINKS								
Daiquiri	6 oz	325	0	0	0	12	0	9
Kahlua and Cream	6 oz	567	27	43	5	36	n/a	159
Martini	6 oz	383	0	0	0	1	0	5
Piña Colada	6 oz	427	13	27	1	47	0	120

*Based on nutrition information provided from N-Squared Computing.
+Calories in alcoholic beverages not from fat, protein, and carbohydrate come from alcohol. Alcohol has 7 calories per gram.

5

Healthier eating out
Mexican Style

If you enjoy food hot, spicy, and heaped with
jalapeños, Mexican cuisine is likely number one
on your list of ethnic favorites. You're in sync
with many Americans. Today, Mexican food
tops the ethnic restaurant ranking. However, the
health quotient of Mexican restaurant food can spell
doomsday due to the high fat content. Mexican meals
conjure up notions of nachos topped with high-fat guacamole, cheese, and sour cream or combo plates of beef
tacos and cheese enchiladas served with refried beans
and Mexican rice.

The harsh reality of Mexican restaurants' fat tally was exposed by the Center for Science in the Public Interest (CSPI) (*Nutrition Action Healthletter,* July/August, 1994). Several "guilty" menu offerings are chimichangas, cheese quesadillas, and chile rellenos. The calories and fat broke your heart when the usual refried beans, Mexican rice, sour cream, and guacamole completed the plate.

There are healthier items: soft chicken tacos, chicken fajitas, and beef enchiladas. CSPI reinforced the same principles of *The Restaurant Companion:* you can improve the health quotient of many entrees by practicing the 10 skills and strategies for healthy restaurant eating.

Get to know the cuisine

Food aficionados say many foods we refer to as Mexican truly are not. Some people insist that chili con carne is a Texas invention. And you won't find a "Mexican" salad served in a fried tortilla shell in Mexico. Like most ethnic cuisines, Mexican food has been "Americanized," which means fat is allowed in from all sides.

Some people use the expression Tex-Mex to describe a type of Mexican food. These recipes and concoctions have roots in Mexican cooking, but the finished products don't resemble native dishes even though the basic ingredients—chilies, tomatoes, beans, and corn—and cooking methods remain the same.

Tracing the history of Mexican cuisine helps you understand its roots. The origins of Mexican cookery go back to Aztec and Mayan Indian civilizations, the early settlers. The foods eaten then still predominate today: beans, corn, and tomatoes. In the 1500s, the Spanish descended and spread their own food habits and preferences. They introduced more protein—pork, chicken, and beef. Other ingredients that became integrated were garlic, cinnamon, onions, rice, and sugar. Over the centuries there were also European influences in Mexican cuisine. In fact, Germans are supposedly responsible for teaching the Mexicans how to brew beer.

Tortillas, made from corn or wheat, are called the "bread" of Mexico. Tortillas are often stuffed with beef, pork, chicken, or cheese. Tacos, burritos, and enchiladas are examples of stuffed foods. These became popular for two reasons. First, small amounts of protein needed to be stretched to fill many mouths; and second, meats are tough, and cooking methods to soften them were used—marinating, braising, or stewing. Few dairy products are part of the Mexican diet. Coffee and cocoa are native and plentiful in Mexico and are common beverages.

Traditionally, Mexicans eat five meals a day. An early breakfast, *desayuno,* consists of coffee or cocoa with a roll. *Almuerzo,* the second meal, is bigger and analogous to an American brunch, where fruit, tortillas, eggs, and coffee are served. *Comida,* the main meal, is eaten in the afternoon, before the siesta. It can include up to six courses: appetizer, soup, chicken or fish, beans, dessert, and coffee. The last two light meals are called *merienda* and *cena.*

The proximity of Mexico to the United States impacts the influence of Mexican cuisine on food choices. There has and continues to be a large influx of Mexicans into the U.S. The Mexican-American population is still predominantly in the Southwestern border states.

The large and growing Mexican population in the U.S. contributes to the ever-growing number of Mexican restaurants and Mexican foods on American menus. Today, you find Mexican restaurants in almost every city. However, the abundance of Mexican eateries are still in the Southwest. Mexican fast-food stops now line America's highways, where you're sure to find tacos, burritos, and enchiladas.

Taco Bell, perhaps the best known Mexican chain, is getting on the health bandwagon, too, with their recently introduced ''Border Lights.'' This group of items, which includes chicken tacos, taco salad, and bean and beef burritos, contains half the fat of regular menu fare.

Maccheezmo Mouse is a small, but growing health-oriented Mexican fast-food chain based in Seattle. They're heavy on the carbos—rice and beans; light on protein; and they use lower-fat versions of high-fat toppers—cheese, sour cream, and salad dressing. Let's hope they spread east.

Numerous mid price-range Mexican chain restaurants exist and serve Mexican entrees such as fajitas or bowls of chili con carne. The fast-food and table-service Mexican chains represent the greatest ''Americanization'' of authentic Mexican cuisine. On the upscale side, independently owned Mexican restaurants offer a few more healthy choices such as arroz con pollo, mole poblano, and pescado (fish) de Veracruz (with tomato sauce). Special requests might be easier at these locales.

Whether it's authentic Mexican, Tex-Mex, or a Mexican salad in an American restaurant, Mexican food packs a lot of enjoyable punch. Even though you'll have to steer clear of the deep-fried and high-fat items, there are healthier choices waiting to be devoured.

Before you order

Dining out healthfully on Mexican food requires menu navigation. The three mainstay ingredients—corn, beans, and tomatoes—are healthy carbohydrates. They find their way into most offerings. Prior to adulteration, they are healthy; but once tossed into Mexican dishes, the result can be either a nutritional disaster or a wise choice. For instance, corn or wheat is the main ingredient in tortillas. In a soft taco, the flour tortilla contains just a bit of fat. But when a flour tortilla is deep-fried, it becomes a fat dense taco shell. So making healthy menu choices is key.

Another health benefit of Mexican food is the minimal focus on protein. Compare the small quantity of meat, one to two ounces, in one enchilada with the eight-to-ten ounce steak commonly served in American restaurants. The minimal protein gives Mexican meals an advantage in matching your intake to the Food Guide Pyramid goals.

Fat is, as always, the villain in Mexican restaurants. Not only are there many fried items, but many Mexican recipes traditionally call for lard or animal fat drippings. Both contain some cholesterol and saturated fat. With increasing emphasis on decreasing the use of animal fat, many chain restaurants, including Taco Bell, Del Taco, Chi Chi's, and Original El Torito's, tout their use of 100 percent cholesterol-free vegetable oil. Don't forget, that doesn't mean less calories or grams of fat; the oil just contains no cholesterol and less saturated fat. If the type of oil used is not broadcast on the menu, ask the waitperson to check with the chef.

Mexican food can also be high in sodium. Salt is used in many recipes, and a lot of the food preparation, such as the beef stuffed in a flauta, is done prior to placing your order. This makes it difficult to request "light on salt." However, if you order a dish like grilled chicken or fish in an upscale restaurant, you can request less or no salt. Chips, salsa, and cheese also add sodium. However, even though salsas and pico de gallo contain salt, amounts are small and you get some punch with no fat.

Menu management

The first foods to greet you, without request, are the "bet-you-can't-eat-just-one" chips and salsa. The basket is emptied before you know it, and the waitperson will gladly refill it. The corn tortilla chips are deep-fried and often salted (to boost the number of margaritas or beers you drink). You can exercise the utmost willpower and promise yourself to limit the number of chips you eat, or, easier yet, never let the basket reach the table. Compassionate dining partners or those with the same nutrition goals can help keep the chips at least an arm's reach away.

Salsa is the winning half of the partnership. Salsa, either red or green, is made with tomatoes, onions, garlic, chilies, cilantro, and salt. It has just about no fat and very few calories. Best yet, it makes a topping with plenty of pizazz. Use salsa rather than salad dressing on salads, and use it on entrees instead of the sour cream and guacamole. Pico de gallo, often found on Mexican menus, is basically chopped tomatoes and onions, and it can be used in the same way as salsa. Find it in the à la carte section of the menu.

As you gaze at a menu board or with the menu in hand, observe the appetizer listings. You'll find healthy choices, but they lurk behind many high-fat, fried items. Some healthier choices are gazpacho, ceviche, a cup of chili con carne or black bean soup. The appetizers to limit are nachos, super nachos, chili con queso, chips and guacamole, and quesadillas, which add insult to injury by combining at least two high-fat foods. If your dining partners order high-fat appetizers, start with a cup of chili, black bean soup, or a dinner salad. This takes the edge off your appetite and prevents indulgence in lethal appetizers. Remember to ask for salad dressing on the side, or try salsa.

Moving on to the main course, Mexican entrees frequently contain chicken, beans, corn- or wheat-based "breads," lettuce, tomatoes, onions, and chilies. All are healthy ingredients. Keep them in mind as you decide. Many high-fat and high-calorie ingredients are also found in Mexican entrees: cheese, sour cream, and chorizo (Mexican sausage). Use the Green Flag and Red Flag words (following) to familiarize yourself with

Mexican ingredients, cooking methods, and menu descriptions.

Chicken or beef enchiladas, burritos, or soft tacos are great choices. Fajitas have made their way onto many American menus and are a healthy choice. Choose among chicken, shrimp, beef, or combination fajitas. A bowl of chili con carne (hold the cheese, but load on the onions) is a good order with a complementary salad. A Mexican salad with either spicy chicken or beef is another healthy alternative. However, ask that the fried tortilla shell be left in the kitchen. At upscale Mexican restaurants you'll find a grilled chicken or fish dish served with spicy tomato sauce. It's always smart to ask that the high-fat add-ons be "held" or served "on the side"—sour cream, guacamole, cheese, and olives are a few.

Along with Mexican dinners come the starches— Mexican rice and *frijoles refritos,* better known to the English speaker as refried beans. Some restaurants might serve a side of black beans or rice and beans. Beans (usually pinto, kidney, or black) are high in carbohydrates and have the beneficial soluble fiber. Soluble fiber is known to lower cholesterol, triglycerides, and glucose. However, don't get too excited; the frequently served refried beans might be refried in lard. That likely negates beans' benefits. A side or à la carte order of black beans, Mexican rice, or soft tortillas are lower-fat choices.

Take advantage of à la carte orders. This enables you to pick and choose exactly what you want. If you watch your calories and fat intake, a chicken enchilada and bean burrito with a dinner salad might do the trick. Steer clear of combination plates unless you plan to split it down the middle. This is simply too much food and includes too many foods that should be boycotted.

The list of desserts in Mexican restaurants is minimal. A common Mexican dessert is the high-fat, high-sugar disaster sopaipillas, a deep-fried dough. Flan, a custard with caramel topping, is another familiar Mexican dessert. It's not a bad choice. However, if cholesterol is a problem, you should pass it up for a great cup of Mexican coffee.

Green Flag Words

INGREDIENTS:
shredded spicy chicken, beef, or
    ground beef
lettuce, tomatoes, onions
chilies
black beans
salsa, green or red
enchilada sauce
mole sauce
soft tortilla (corn or flour)

COOKING METHODS/MENU
DESCRIPTIONS:
pico de gallo
wrapped in a soft tortilla
fajitas
grilled
marinated
simmered
served with spicy tomato sauce
soft tacos
burritos

Red Flag Words

INGREDIENTS:
black olives
sour cream
guacamole
cheese (any way—topped, stuffed,
    covered, shredded)
chorizo (Mexican sausage)
bacon

COOKING METHODS/MENU
DESCRIPTIONS:
cheese sauce
cream sauce
served in a tortilla shell
served over tortilla or nacho chips
crispy
fried or deep-fried
layered with refried beans

AT THE TABLE:
tortilla chips
sour cream
guacamole

**Special
Requests
Mexican
Style**

Please hold (or serve on the side)
the sour cream.

Please hold (or serve on the side)
the guacamole.

Please serve my salad without the
fried tortilla shell (or nacho
chips) but bring an à la carte
order of soft tortillas.

Please remove the chips and salsa
from the table.

Please don't bring any chips and
salsa.

Please hold the cheese.

Would it be possible to get extra
salsa (or pico de gallo) on the
side?

Please put extra shredded lettuce,
tomatoes, and chopped onions
on the plate.

Would it be possible to substitute
shredded chicken for the beef?

Could this entree be split into two
portions in the kitchen?

Could I get this wrapped up to
take home?

The Menu: Mexican Style

Appetizers ✓**Tostada** chips with hot salsa
Tostada chips with guacamole
Nachos served with melted cheese
and jalapeños peppers
Super nachos (fried tostada chips
with layers of beans and spicy
ground beef, covered with melted
cheese, and topped with lettuce,
tomato, onion, and sour cream)
Chili con queso (melted cheese,
green chilies, and peppers served
with corn tortilla chips)
✓**Black bean soup,** cup or bowl
✓**Chili con carne,** cup or bowl
✓**Gazpacho** (spicy cold soup made
from a blend of fresh vegetables
and tomatoes)

Salads ✓**Dinner salad** of mixed greens,
cheese, tomato, and bacon bits,
topped with onions
✓**Mexican salad** of lettuce, tomato,
and red peppers, topped with two
kinds of cheese, served in a crisp
tortilla shell
✓**Mexican salad** of mixed greens,
diced tomatoes, and onions,
topped with shredded spicy
chicken or beef, shredded cheese,
sliced olives, and sour cream and
guacamole
✓**Taco salad** —a choice of spicy
ground meat or shredded chicken,
topped with refried beans, lettuce,
tomatoes, and onions, topped with
sour cream and guacamole and
served in a crisp tortilla shell

✓*Preferred Choice*
Some depending on special requests

Mexican Specialties

Each item can be served à la carte or with refried beans and Mexican rice

Chimichangas, beef or chicken (flour tortillas filled with spicy beef or chicken and Monterey Jack cheese, fried and topped with tomato sauce)

✓**Fajitas** (marinated beef, chicken, or shrimp grilled with onions, green peppers, lettuce, diced tomatoes, sour cream, and guacamole)—single or double order for two available

✓**Enchiladas** (corn tortillas stuffed with either ground beef or shredded chicken and topped with tomato sauce and shredded cheese and served with sour cream)

Tacos (fried flour tortillas stuffed with your choice of spicy ground beef, shredded chicken, or a seafood blend; loaded with shredded lettuce, diced tomatoes, and onions and topped with cheese)

✓**Burritos** (large flour tortilla filled with a choice of refried beans and cheese, spicy ground beef, or chicken; served with tomato sauce and topped with shredded cheese)

✓**Tostadas** (crisp corn tortillas covered with black beans, chili verde, and choice of chicken or beef filling and topped with lettuce, tomato, and onions)

Mexican Dinners

Served with refried beans and Mexican rice

Flautas con crema (crisp rolled tortillas stuffed with shredded chicken or beef, topped with a spicy cream sauce)

✓**Chili verde** (pork simmered with green chilies, vegetables, and Mexican spices)

✓**Mole pollo** (boned chicken breast cooked in mole sauce, hot and spicy)

✓**Camarones de hacha** (fresh shrimp sauteed in a red and green tomato coriander sauce)

Carne asada (grilled sirloin steak served in an enchilada sauce with chorizo and guacamole)

✓**Arroz con pollo** (boneless chicken breast served on top of spicy rice and vegetable sauce)

Side Orders
✓**Mexican rice**
Refried beans
✓**Black beans**
✓**Tortillas,** flour or corn
✓**Salsa**
✓**Pico de gallo**
Guacamole

Desserts
✓**Flan** (caramel-flavored custard)
Sopaipillas (deep-fried dough, tossed in sugar)

Now that you've seen what might be available on the Menu, find the Model Meal that best fits your nutrition goals. For an explanation of the Model Meals and their targeted nutritional values, see Chapter 3.

Your Order, Please

Healthy	30%	Calories as fat
Daily	20%	Calories as protein
Eating	50%	Calories as carbohydrate
Goals	300	mg/day Cholesterol
	3000	mg/day Sodium

Low Calorie/	**Chili con carne**
Low Fat	*Quantity:* 1 cup
Model Meal	*Exchanges:* 1 starch; 1 meat; 1 fat
	Dinner salad (hold cheese and dressing; order salsa)
	Quantity: 2 cups
	Exchanges: 2 vegetable
	Salsa for dressing
	Exchanges: Free
	Chicken taco, soft
	Quantity: 1
	Exchanges: 1 starch; 2 meat; 1 fat

Estimated	calories 480
Nutrient	fat 19g (35% of calories)
Evaluation	protein 31g (26% of calories)
	carbohydrate 47g (39% of calories)
	cholesterol 67mg
	sodium 1600mg

Low Calorie/	**Dinner salad** (hold the cheese
Low	and dressing; order pico de
Cholesterol	gallo)
Model Meal	*Quantity:* 2 cups
	Fajitas, chicken and shrimp (hold sour cream)

Quantity: 2 (1 oz. of chicken or
   shrimp in each)
Mexican rice
Quantity: ⅔ cup

Estimated Nutrient Evaluation	calories 570 fat 16g (25% of calories) protein 37g (26% of calories) carbohydrate 70g (49% of calories) cholesterol 120 mg sodium 1100 mg

**Higher
Calorie/Low
Fat Model
Meal**

Black bean soup
Quantity: 1 cup
Exchanges: 2 starches
Chili verde served with 2 flour
   tortillas
Quantity: 1½ cups
Exchanges: 2 starch; 3 meat; 2
   fat; 2 vegetable
Mexican rice
Quantity: ⅓ cup
Exchanges: 1 starch
Refried beans
Quantity: ⅓ cup
Exchanges: 1 starch; 1 fat
Mexican beer
Quantity: 12 oz

Estimated Nutrient Evaluation	calories 992 fat 30g (27% of calories) protein 42g (17% of calories) carbohydrate 119g (48% of calories) alcohol 8% calories cholesterol 96 mg sodium 2100 mg

Higher Calorie/Low Cholesterol Model Meal

Tostada chips
Quantity: 10
Salsa
Quantity: 3 tbsp
Burrito, bean and cheese (request extra lettuce and diced tomatoes, 1 cup)
Quantity: 1
Chicken enchilada (hold cheese)
Quantity: 1
Mexican rice
Quantity: ⅓ cup
Black beans (request as substitute for refried beans)
Quantity: ⅓ cup

Estimated Nutrient Evaluation

calories 780
fat 29g (34% of calories)
protein 37g (19% of calories)
carbohydrate 92g (47% of calories)
cholesterol 60 mg
sodium 2000 mg

Low Sodium Model Meal

Mexican salad with shredded, spicy chicken, black beans, lettuce, tomatoes, and onion
Quantity: 3–4 cups
Guacamole (on the side; hold sour cream)
Quantity: ¼ cup
Salsa verde for dressing
Quantity: 4 tbsp
Corn tortillas
Quantity: 2
Flan (split order)

Estimated Nutrient Evaluation	calories 720
	fat 25g (31% of calories)
	protein 50g (28% of calories)
	carbohydrate 70g (39% of calories)
	cholesterol 197 mg (125 from flan)
	sodium 950 mg

Learn the terms of Mexican cuisine

Arroz–Spanish word for rice. Mexican rice is made from long-grain white rice with sauteed tomatoes, onions, and garlic added for flavor.

Burrito–a wheat flour tortilla (soft, not fried) filled with either chicken, beef, or cheese in addition to refried beans; served rolled up and covered with a light tomato-based enchilada sauce.

Carne–Spanish word for meat.

Cerveza–Spanish word for beer.

Ceviche–raw fish, soaked or "cooked" in lime or lemon juice for many hours and served as an appetizer or light meal.

Chalupa–"little boat," a one-dish meal of cornmeal topped with meat or chicken, beans and cheese.

Chili–there are over 100 different types of chilies native to Mexico. They are of different shapes, sizes, and colors, and they vary in level of spiciness from mild to hot, hotter, and hottest. Chilies are available fresh or dried.

Chili con carne–usually simply called "chili" is a thick soup made with tomatoes, onions, peppers, beans, and ground or shredded beef; often served with raw chopped onions and shredded cheese.

Chimichanga–flour tortilla filled with beef, chicken, cheese, and/or beans; deep fried and served topped with tomato-based sauce

Chorizo–Mexican pork sausage, hot and highly seasoned.

Cilantro–leafy green herb with a strong flavor frequently used in Mexican cooking; also called coriander.

Enchiladas–corn tortillas dipped in enchilada sauce, lightly fried, and then filled with a choice of chicken, beef, or cheese and served topped with light tomato-based enchilada sauce.

Fajitas–sauteed chicken or beef served with sauteed onions and green peppers, shredded lettuce, tomatoes, and guacamole; served with flour tortillas. Usually roll your own at the table.

Flan–baked custard with a caramel top; contains sugar, eggs, and cream, whole or condensed milk.

Gazpacho–spicy, cold tomato-based soup that contains pureed or pieces of raw vegetables.

Guacamole–mashed avocado, onion, tomatoes, garlic, lemon juice, and spices; served as a topping, as a dip with chips, or on the side. Avocado is high in fat; approximately 80 calories per ¼ avocado, though it is mainly monounsaturated with no cholesterol.

Jalapeño–a type of chili often mistakenly referred to as a pepper. A very small, hot, green chili used to spice or top certain menu items.

Mole–refers to a "concoction," usually a spicy brown seasoning mixture for chicken or meats that contains a small amount of chocolate.

Pico de gallo–chopped tomatoes and onions relish.

Quesadillas–flour tortillas filled with cheese and chili mixture; tortilla is rolled and then fried.

Refried beans–pinto beans that have been cooked and then refried in lard and seasoned.

Salsa–hot red sauce made from tomatoes, onions, and chili; appears automatically on the table of most Mexican restaurants.

Salsa verde–very hot green sauce made from tomatillo, the Mexican green tomato, and other spices.

Taco–corn tortilla filled with meat or chicken, shredded cheese, lettuce, and tomatoes; the corn tortilla is fried in the shape of a "U." Soft taco is usually made with a flour tortilla and is not fried.

Tamale–spicy filling of either meat or chicken, surrounded by moist corn meal dough and wrapped in corn husks or banana leafs; they are then steamed.

Tortilla–the "bread" of Mexico, a very thin circle of dough made either from corn or flour; often corn tortillas are fried into taco shells or chips and served with salsa.

Tostadas–crisp, deep-fried tortilla chips, or the whole fried tortilla, which then may be covered with various toppings such as cheese, beans, lettuce, tomato, and/or onions.

6

Healthier eating out
Chinese Style

Chinese food is among the top three ethnic cuisines Americans enjoy in restaurants. Chinese foods and cookery were virtually unknown in America prior to the mid-1800s. Today, Chinese restaurants are commonplace, even in small American cities. Now, beyond simply Cantonese, the cuisine of different regions—Szechuan, Hunan, and Beijing—are served. There's more than egg rolls, chop suey, pork-fried rice, and fortune cookies lining the menus of Chinese restaurants. Chinese food is so well integrated into the melting pot of American cuisine that today the familiar Chinese stir-fry shrimp with vegetables pops up on American menus.

Get to know the cuisine

People from China began emigrating to the U.S. in the mid-1800s. During the later 1800s, thousands of Chinese arrived from Canton and settled on the West Coast, mainly in California. It's no surprise that the first generation of Chinese restaurants in America served Cantonese food, the most familiar to Americans. After World War II, another large influx of Chinese came to the U.S. They were from regions other than just Canton.

When Chinese initially came to the U.S., it was common for them to settle in enclaves known as ''Chinatown.'' Chinatowns grew in several large coastal cities: Boston, New York, San Francisco. These enclaves still thrive as social and cultural centers for ethnic Chinese as well as locales for Chinese markets with fresh and specialty foods and restaurants.

As is true of many cuisines, the style of cooking and the ingredients used can be traced back to the culture's roots. For instance, stir-frying, a common Chinese cooking method, was initially used because it conserved fuel. Foods were cut into small pieces to maximize their surface. Foods cooked quickly and used little fuel. A wide assortment of foods were used. There are the familiar shrimp, chicken, broccoli, and bean sprouts; and the less familiar lily buds and wood ears. The latter items were integrated into the cuisine because they were available, and the Chinese figured out how to make them edible.

Rice is the staple of southern China, whereas northern China is better known for wheat products. In American Chinese restaurants both rice and noodle dishes are on the menu. Seafood and animal protein—beef, pork, chicken, and duck—are always found. The by-products of soybeans create a whole array of ingredients, from tofu (bean curd) to black bean sauce and the all-important soy sauce.

Interestingly, little food in China is served raw. Salads are almost non-existent. Dishes might be cooked and then presented cold, but most Chinese foods are ladled up hot. A missing food group is dairy. Milk and dairy products are uncommon ingredients; no cream or shredded cheese are loaded on top. From a fat perspective, that's good news.

Regional variations in Chinese cuisine

Americans are most accustomed to Cantonese cuisine, but recently the number of Chinese restaurants serving Szechuan, Hunan, and Beijing cuisines has grown. Opinions vary as to whether there are three, four, or five regional Chinese cuisines. In reality, many more exist if you delve into the subtle differences. We'll describe a few of the most distinct regional cuisines. Many times, the name of the dish gives the origin away: Peking duck, Hunan crispy beef, and so on.

Canton is in southern China. Cantonese dishes are stir-fried with mild and subtle flavors. Black bean and oyster sauces are common. Seafood and pork are common protein foods. Rice and soybeans are plentiful in the region and therefore are staples.

Moving to the northern regions of China, you find Beijing (Peking), Shantung (Shandong), and Honan (not Hunan) cooking styles. Northern Chinese cooking styles were originally prepared for the palates of select citizens. Shantung is defined as the *haute cuisine* of Chinese cooking. Beijing dishes were served at the ancient imperial court in Peking. Even today Peking duck is a very special item, often requiring 24 hours notice for preparation. Sweet-and-sour, plum, and hoisin sauces are common. Liberal amounts of onions and garlic are trademarks of northern cooking.

The western region is the home of hot and spicy Chinese cookery. This is Szechuan and Hunan style cuisine. Chilies, garlic, and hot red peppers (which you don't want to bite) are used. On Chinese menus in America, hot and spicy dishes are often noted with a star or are printed in red. Not surprisingly, some similarities exist among Szechuan cooking and Thai and Burmese food, China's neighbors to the south.

Chinese restaurants in America

A broad range of Chinese restaurants exist, from fast-food stops in mall food courts to a growing number of elegant restaurants decked with linen napkins and fresh flowers. The fast-food menu is usually limited to egg rolls, spare ribs, sweet-and-sour dishes, and chow mein. The largest number of Chinese restaurants are mid-priced, and not fancy.

There are differences in Chinese food served in China and America, from the foods used to preparation and style of eating. No doubt, Chinese food has been "Americanized"—translated, that means fat added. Some ethnic foods are just not used in American-Chinese cooking because they are either not available or not appealing.

If you hang out at a Chinese restaurant long enough, you will observe the way the ethnics eat. Main dishes are at the table's center for all to share. Each person has a big bowl of steamed rice, which becomes a brief stopping place for food traveling from the center plates to the mouth. Lots of rice is eaten along with plenty of vegetables and only a small amount of protein. That sounds like a match-up with the goals of the Food Guide Pyramid.

Whether it is Cantonese, Szechuan, or Shanghai, Chinese food in America can be a healthy eater's nightmare or a dream come true. It depends on what you order and how much you eat. Compare two possible orders from the same restaurant: 1) a high-fat and high-calorie order of fried jumbo shrimp, egg drop soup, spicy beef with peanuts and scallions, and fried bananas; versus 2) lower-fat and lower-calorie steamed Peking raviolis, stir-fried sliced chicken with assorted vegetables, and steamed white rice. Use the 10 Skills and Strategies to make the healthier choice.

Before you order

A Chinese meal can easily match the nutrition goals for healthy eating. The biggest problem is the fat—mainly from deep frying and stir-frying. Several protein foods such as duck, beef, and pork can be high in fat, depending on the cut. Some high-fat cuts of pork are used, such as spare ribs. However, lean cuts are used as well, as in the roast pork appetizer. Menu items that are prepared "crispy" or "golden brown" should be scratched; sweet-and-sour dishes and General Gau's chicken are examples. Many appetizers are deep-fried.

The most common cooking technique is stir-frying in a wok. In fact, finding an oven in China used to be rare. Chefs use a lot of oil when stir-frying, so asking to limit the oil is a wise idea. A wok is also used for braising and steaming. Cooking in a wok is very fast, so foods and particularly vegetables retain color and vitamins and minerals.

Traditionally lard (pork fat) was used in Chinese cooking, but more vegetable oil is poured today. Peanut oil is sometimes used due to its high smoking point. The good news is that peanut oil is mainly monounsaturated fats. Monounsaturates help lower blood cholesterol. Sesame seed oil is also used, but just in small quantities for flavor. Sesame seed oil is mainly polyunsaturated, which also helps lower blood cholesterol, but it lowers the good cholesterol, HDLs, too.

Another villain of Chinese cookery is the high sodium. Many dishes contain both high-sodium soy sauces, light and dark, and MSG (monosodium glutamate). Other sauces such as oyster, black bean, and hoisin have good quantities of sodium. Just so you know, a tablespoon of soy sauce has 1,000 mg of sodium; the recommended daily limit is 3,000 mg. There are ways to work around the high sodium content. However, Chinese food might not be the optimal choice, at least on a frequent basis, if you have high blood pressure and watch sodium intake.

To limit sodium, stay away from Chinese soups. Find an appropriate appetizer or jump right into the entrees. Steamed white rice is a better choice than fried rice or lo mein. Dishes with a lighter sauce, both in color and texture, tend to have a lower sodium content than sauces such as black bean or hoisin. You can make special requests to limit sodium. Let the waitperson know about your sodium concerns, and ask to pass that message along to the chef. You can ask for less soy and no MSG. Don't forget, most Chinese entrees are prepared to order, so special requests are easy. Meats, however, are often marinating for hours in high-sodium sauces.

People with diabetes should be aware that there is sugar in many marinades and sauces. It might be white granulated, brown sugar, or honey. Some sauces, like plum and hoisin, are sweeter and likely to have a higher sugar content. Another consideration is the sweet sauce (duck sauce) placed on the table. Limit the amount used. The rules about sugars in diabetes meal planning have relaxed since the publication of the 1994 *Nutrition Recommendations and Principles* (*Diabetes Care*, May, 1994). Now the total amount of carbohydrate coming from starches and sugars is more important than just sugars.

Menu management

In Chinese restaurants chances are good that fried Chinese noodles will greet you at the table. Then, it's "something to drink?" Green tea, Tsing Tsao beer, or Planter's Punch are possibilities. Then, decisions, decisions—it's appetizer time. Many Chinese appetizers are simply off-limits because they are fried: fried shrimp, won tons, and chicken wings. Healthier appetizers are steamed Peking raviolis, roast pork strips, and teriyaki beef or chicken (if sodium is not a big concern). Think about skipping the high-fat appetizers and start off with a bowl of low-calorie soup. Hot-and-sour, sizzling rice, or delights of three are all good alternatives.

As many regions of China are near the ocean, it's usual to spot seafood on the menu. Shrimp, prawns, scallops, and whole fishes are common. Other healthy protein foods are chicken and tofu (bean curd). Peruse the menu and look for dishes with lots of vegetables. You might find assorted vegetables or broccoli and water chestnuts. If it's not obvious, ask if the dish has vegetables and what type. Better yet, try dishes from the vegetable column—spicy green beans or vegetarian delight. Complement a meat dish with a vegetable one.

On to the starches, rice and noodles. Both are always available, some healthy, some not. Obviously, white rice is tops. It's steamed with no added salt or fats. Fried rice has additional fat and soy sauce added. If you order fried rice, stick with the vegetable variety and avoid the fat and protein that comes with added pork or other meats. Similar advice holds true for lo mein and pan-fried noodles. The basic noodle is healthy, but the health quotient goes downhill as chefs add oils and high-sodium sauces.

Dessert in Chinese restaurants is low key. Often you don't even order it. Pineapple or orange sections and fortune cookies simply appear at the table. The limited desserts usually include pineapple chunks, lychee nuts, and ice cream. Opt for the pineapple or lychee nuts. You'll leave the table a bit healthier, and maybe wiser, if you read the fortune and discard the cookie.

Chopsticks are the eating utensils of choice, though forks and spoons are available if you are not adept with chopsticks. However, your lack of dexterity might be a blessing in disguise; it will slow your pace of eating. Go ahead and be daring, but put your napkin squarely on your lap.

No matter which or what type of Chinese restaurant you choose, you have a good sense of what you'll find on the menu before it's in front of you. So, in practicing strategy number 7, "portion control from the word go," think about your order before crossing the threshold. Don't allow your tastebuds a chance to fantasize. Contemplate sharing. In Chinese restaurants that's standard practice. Be careful to monitor your fullness—that's strategy number 10. Chinese restaurants are at the ready to ease taking leftovers home. That means tomorrow's lunch or dinner.

Green Flag Words

INGREDIENTS:
bean curd (tofu)
vegetables: broccoli, mushrooms, onions, carrots, cabbage water chestnuts, bamboo shoots, lily buds, wood ears, bean sprouts
fish, shrimp, scallops
chicken, roast pork
pineapple
soy sauce*, hoisin or plum sauce*
Chinese mustard
sweet (duck) sauce

COOKING METHODS/MENU DESCRIPTIONS:
brown sauce*
oyster or black bean sauce*
light wine sauce
lobster sauce
simmered or braised
steamed
stir-fried with vegetables
hot and spicy tomato sauce
served on sizzling platter
slippery white sauce or velvet sauce

*High in sodium

**Red Flag
Words**

INGREDIENTS:
duck
cashews or peanuts
pieces of egg
water chestnut flour
bits of pork, egg
Chinese noodles

COOKING METHODS/MENU
DESCRIPTIONS:
fried or deep-fried
battered or breaded and fried
deep-fried until crispy, crispy
served in bird's nest
sweet-and-sour

AT THE TABLE:
Chinese noodles

**Special
Requests
Chinese
Style**

Please remove the crispy Chinese
noodles from the table.
Please don't use MSG.
What type of oil is used for stir-
frying? (If lard or other
saturated fat, request that peanut
or other available non-animal
fat be used.)
Would it be possible to use less
oil in the preparation?
Would it be possible to use less
salt and soy sauce?
Can you substitute chicken in this
dish for duck?
Could you substitute (or add in
more) broccoli and leave out
the spinach?
Please don't garnish with peanuts
or cashews. (Or use small
amount)

Can you leave off the crispy fried
   won ton?
Could you add more vegetables to
   this dish?
Please serve this without the
   bird's nest.

The Menu: Chinese Style

Appetizers
Egg rolls (2)
Spring rolls (2)
✓**Steamed Peking raviolis** (6)
Fried Peking raviolis (6)
✓**Roast pork** strips
Barbecued spare ribs
✓**Teriyaki** beef or chicken on skewers
Jumbo shrimp, fried
Won tons, fried
Pu pu platter for two—contains egg rolls, spare ribs, fried shrimp, and teriyaki beef

Soups
✓**Hot-and-sour** soup
✓**Won ton** soup
✓**Sizzling** rice and chicken soup
✓**Sizzling** rice and shrimp soup
✓**Delights of three** (assorted Chinese vegetables and chicken, pork, and beef strips)
✓**Egg drop** soup

Poultry
✓**Velvet chicken** (breast of chicken, snow peas, water chestnuts, bamboo shoots in light sauce)
* **General Gau's chicken** (cubes of chicken coated with water-chestnut flour and eggs, deep fried until crispy, and coated with hot ginger sauce)
Sweet-and-sour chicken (chicken pieces battered and fried, topped with a thick sweet-and-pungent sauce, topped with pineapples)

✓*Preferred Choice*
Some depending on special requests
*Indicates a hot and spicy dish.

✓***Hunan spicy chicken** (spicy chicken with assorted vegetables)

✓**Chicken chop suey** (breast of chicken stir-fried with celery, Chinese cabbage, and other assorted vegetables)

Sweet-and-pungent duck (cubes of duck, dipped in batter, deep fried, and served with water chestnuts, cherries, and peas)

✓**Sizzling sliced chicken** with vegetables (sliced breast of chicken with assorted Chinese vegetables, served on a sizzling platter)

✓***Yu Hsiang chicken** (Strips of chicken stir-fried with bamboo shoots, water chestnuts, wood ears, lily buds, and Chinese cabbage)

Seafood   ✓***Shrimp with tomato sauce** (shrimp sauteed with fine-diced bamboo shoots and scallions, mixed in a hot and spicy tomato sauce)

✓**Shrimp with broccoli** and mushrooms (stir-fried shrimp with broccoli and Chinese mushrooms in light egg white sauce)

* **Spicy crispy whole fish** (a whole fish deep fried and coated with a hot, spicy sauce)

Shrimp and cashews (whole shrimp stir-fried with cashew nuts and water chestnuts)

✓***Szechuan** style fresh fish fillets (fish fillets sauteed with bamboo shoots and scallions, served with a hot and spicy sauce)

✓**Moo shi shrimp** (stir-fried shrimp with Chinese vegetables, served with Chinese pancakes and hoisin sauce)

Meats   ✓**Beef and broccoli** with black mushrooms (strips of beef sauteed with broccoli and black mushrooms in oyster sauce)

* **Szechuan orange beef** (beef coated with orange-flavored spicy sauce)

✓***Twice cooked pork** (pork with cabbage, green peppers, and bamboo shoots in hot bean sauce)

* **Hunan crispy beef** (beef deep fried and coated with a hot Hunan sauce, served surrounded by broccoli)

✓**Sizzling lamb** (lamb and vegetables in a light sauce, served on a sizzling platter)

✓**Roast pork** with vegetables (slices of pork stir-fried with assorted Chinese vegetables)

✓**Beef chow mein** (sliced beef stir-fried with diced cabbage, onions, sliced mushrooms, and other Chinese vegetables)

Vegetables ✓**Vegetarian delight** (ten kinds of crunchy vegetables stir-fried in a light sauce)

* **Yu Hsiang eggplant** (eggplant stir-fried with other Chinese vegetables)

✓***Spicy green beans** (green beans sauteed in hot and spicy Hunan sauce)

✓**Broccoli and black mushrooms** in oyster sauce (broccoli and mushrooms stir-fried with oyster sauce and topped with peanuts)

Indicates a hot and spicy dish.

Rice	✓**Steamed white rice** (small or large bowl)
	Beef-fried rice
	Pork-fried rice
	✓**Vegetable-fried rice**
	House special fried rice

Noodles	✓**Roast pork lo mein**
	✓**Chicken lo mein**
	✓**Vegetable lo mein**
	Pan-fried noodles with shrimp, pork, and chicken
	Pan-fried noodles with assorted Chinese vegetables

Desserts	✓**Pineapple chunks**
	✓**Lychee nuts**
	Vanilla ice cream
	~~**Fried bananas** served with sweet~~ syrup sauce
	Fortune cookies

Now that you've seen what might be available on the Menu, find the Model Meal that best fits your nutrition goals. For an explanation of the Model Meals and their targeted nutritional values, see Chapter 3.

Your Order, Please

Healthy	30%	Calories as fat
Daily	20%	Calories as protein
Eating	50%	Calories as carbohydrate
Goals	300	mg/day Cholesterol
	3000	mg/day Sodium

Low Calorie/
Low Fat
Model Meal

Hot-and-sour soup
Quantity: 1 cup
Exchanges: 1 vegetable, 1 fat
Yu Hsiang chicken
Quantity: 1 cup (split order)
Exchanges: 2 meat; 1 fat; 1
    vegetable
Shrimp with broccoli and
    mushrooms
Quantity: 1 cup
Exchanges: 2 meat; 1 fat; 1
    vegetable
Steamed white rice
Quantity: ⅔ cup
Exchanges: 2 starch
Fortune cookie
(Read fortune; skip cookie)

Estimated
Nutrient
Evaluation

calories 615
fat 27g (39% of calories)
protein 41g (27% of calories)
carbohydrate 51g (34% of calories)
cholesterol 150 mg
sodium+ 1300 mg

+Sodium values are based on usual preparation
methods determined from several Chinese cookbooks. If no MSG and less soy and other sauces
are requested, sodium intake can easily be lowered.

**Low Calorie/
Low
Cholesterol
Model Meal**

Beef with broccoli and black
    mushrooms
Quantity: 1 cup (split order)
Vegetarian delight
Quantity: 1½ cups
Steamed white rice
Quantity: ⅔ cup
Lychee nuts
Quantity: ½ cup

Estimated
Nutrient
Evaluation

calories 590
fat 25g (38% of calories)
protein 33g (22% of calories)
carbohydrate 59g (40% of calories)
cholesterol 52 mg
sodium 915 mg

**Higher
Calorie/Low
Fat Model
Meal**

Peking raviolis, steamed
Quantity: 2
Exchanges: 1 starch; 1 meat;
    1 fat; ½ vegetable
Moo shi shrimp
Quantity: 2 pancakes; 1 cup
    filling (split order)
Exchanges: 1 starch; 2 meats;
    1 fat; 2 vegetable
Vegetable lo mein noodles
Quantity: 1½ cups (split order)
Exchanges: 3 starch; 1 fat;
    1 vegetable
Tsing Tsao beer
Quantity: 12 oz.
Exchanges: 1 starch; 1 fat

Estimated Nutrient Evaluation	calories 911 fat 24g (24% of calories) protein 43g (19% of calories) carbohydrate 112g (49% of calories) alcohol 8% calories cholesterol 134 mg sodium+ 1300 mg

❹

Higher Calorie/Low Cholesterol Model Meal	**Sizzling rice** and chicken soup *Quantity:* 1 cup **Velvet chicken** *Quantity:* 1 cup (split order) **Szechuan fresh fish** fillets *Quantity:* 1 cup **Vegetable-fried rice** *Quantity:* 1 cup **Pineapple** *Quantity:* ½ cup
Estimated Nutrient Evaluation	calories 687 fat 23g (30% of calories) protein 43g (25% of calories) carbohydrate 77g (45% of calories) cholesterol 110 mg sodium+ 1700 mg

❺

***Low Sodium Model Meal**	**Peking raviolis,** steamed (use
	    sweet sauce and mustard)
	Quantity: 2
	Sizzling sliced chicken with
	    vegetables
	Quantity: 1 cup (split order)
	Beef chow mein
	Quantity: 1 cup
	Steamed white rice
	Quantity: 1 cup

*Request that no MSG and less soy sauce be used.

Estimated	calories 814
Nutrient	fat 33g (37% of calories)
Evaluation	protein 51g (25% of calories)
	carbohydrate 77g (38% of calories)
	cholesterol 135 mg
	sodium+ 1200 mg

+Sodium values are based on usual preparation methods determined from several Chinese cookbooks. If no MSG and less soy and other sauces are requested, sodium intake can easily be lowered.

Learn the terms of Chinese cuisine

Bean curd–known as "tofu" to Americans; made from soy beans and formed into blocks; used sliced or cubed in soups or dishes.

Black bean sauce–a thick, brown sauce made of fermented soy beans, salt, and wheat flour; frequently used in Cantonese cooking.

Bok choy–looks like a cross between celery and cabbage; also known as Chinese chard.

Five-spice powder–a reddish-brown powder, combining star anise, fennel, cinnamon, cloves, and Szechuan pepper; used in Szechuan dishes.

Hoisin sauce–a sweet and spicy thick sauce made from soy beans, sugar, garlic, chili, and vinegar.

Lily buds–dried, golden-colored buds with a light, flowery flavor; also called lotus buds and tiger lily buds; used in entrees and soups.

Lychees–crimson-colored fruit with translucent flesh around a brown seed, closely resembling a white grape.

Monosodium glutamate (MSG)–a white powder used in small amounts to bring out and enhance the flavors of ingredients.

Napa–also referred to as Chinese cabbage, it has thick-ribbed stalks and crinkled leaves.

Oyster sauce–a rich, thick sauce made of oysters, their cooking liquid, and soy sauce; frequently used in Cantonese dishes.

Plum sauce–an amber-colored, thick sauce made from plums, apricots, hot peppers, vinegar, and sugar, it has a spicy sweet-and-sour flavor.

Sesame seed oil–oil extracted from sesame seeds, it has a strong sesame seed flavor and is used as seasoning for soups, seafood, and other dishes.

Soy sauce–either light or dark, used in virtually all Chinese dishes. Light soy tends to be used with poultry and seafoods.

Sweet-and-sour sauce–thick sauce made from sugar, vinegar, and soy sauce. Meat, chicken, or shrimp served with this sauce is usually dipped in batter and fried.

Wood ear–a variety of tree lichen, which is brown and resembles a wrinkled ear; it is soaked before use.

7

Healthy eating out
Italian Style

I talian restaurants rate high on America's hit parade of ethnic favorites. That's a stat from the National Restaurant Association. Whether it's parmigiana, cacciatore, scampi, or primavera, a wonderful world of palate pleasers awaits you at Italian dining spots. As usual, some are healthy—fettucini primavera or linguine with white clam sauce; and some aren't—fettucini Alfredo or veal saltimbocca. Over the years, Italian dishes have been woven into the melting pot of America's food choices. Today, Italian foods aren't just standard fare at Italian eateries. You find the Italian specialties of baked manicotti and lasagna on some very American menus.

Today you can eat Italian food in a wide array of settings, from cheap eats to elegant four-star dining rooms. Several national chains specialize in Italian cuisine—Olive Garden, Papa Gino's, Pizza Hut, and the quickly growing California Pizza Kitchens are several biggies. In most cities and towns you'll find at least one family-run Italian restaurant serving home-cooked pasta coated with rich meat and tomato sauce, hard-crusted Italian bread, and carafes of Chianti. That's all laid out on a red-and-white checkered tablecloth. A few large cities boast areas where Italian restaurants congregate—Little Italy in New York City and North End in Boston.

Italian food goes upscale and expensive as well. An upscale Italian restaurant may gain fame with food from a particular region of Italy. In the last few years some Italian restaurants have lightened their offerings. ''Nouvelle Italian'' or ''continental Italian'' are appropriate tags. Heavy cream sauces are ousted, and they serve grain dishes such as polenta and risotto, offer grilled fish, and top dishes with artichoke hearts and sun-dried tomatoes.

Pizza could be the most commonly eaten Italian food. In fact, pizza probably ranks second in popularity to hamburgers in America today. Because of pizza's prominence, we've given pizza its own Chapter 14.

Get to know the cuisine

Interestingly, there's a difference between what Americans and Italians regard as Italian food, especially among traditional Italian chefs. Differences among the types of foods eaten, when meals are eaten, and even the order in which foods are served. Over the years, Italian food in America has been influenced by American taste buds and eating style. When some Americans think of Italian food, they conjure up images of spaghetti with tomato sauce and meatballs or veal parmigiana. These American-Italian favorites are examples of Southern Italian cooking. Some connoisseurs note that meatballs are an American invention and not even an Italian original.

As you delve into the details of Italian food, you quickly realize there are broad distinctions between Northern and Southern cooking. Southern cuisine is better known within our borders, represented by tomato sauces such as marinara and cacciatore. Northern Italian cuisine is gaining popularity and is more common in upscale restaurants. It focuses on wine, light cream, and butter sauces. Marsala and scampi are examples of Northern Italian dishes. Both Southern and Northern styles of Italian cooking have their healthy and unhealthy attributes.

Italian chefs might chuckle at this American polarized distinction between the South and North. In reality, Italian cooking styles, ingredients, and dishes have their origins in many corners of Italy. Polenta, for instance, came from the Po Valley. Heavy use of spinach, dried beans, and olive oil is typical of the Tuscany region. As usual, the roots of regional cooking are directly related to the predominant ingredients grown. As society grows increasingly mobile, regional cooking styles, like people, migrate from one region to the next. The result is cross-fertilization of regional Italian cuisines. As American chefs travel in Italy they taste regional cuisines and integrate their favorite ingredients, spices, and dishes into menus back home.

Over the last few years even our horizon of pasta has been widened. It's now common to see tortellini, fusilli, cannelloni, and angel hair pasta on menus. Beyond the many different shapes and sizes, you see tomato, spinach, sage, and whole-wheat pasta. (See ''Know Your Pasta'' at the end of the chapter.)

There are also big differences in eating style. In Italy, traditionally, the large meal is eaten midday. Historically, shops and businesses close midday, and people linger over their afternoon meal. The equivalent of the siesta in Mexico. The meal begins with an antipasto, which means ''before the pasta.'' The first course, referred to as *primo piatto,* is a pasta dish or soup, perhaps a minestrone. The *secondo piatto,* or second course, consists of meat, fish, or poultry and is plated with one cooked vegetable. Bread appears at this point. The salad, or *insalata,* comes along after the second course. Americans might think this is backwards. After the palate cleansing salad is eaten, a fruit and cheese platter is served. There's little attention to sweet desserts within the context of the meal. But, it's no secret, Italy is well known for its creamy *gelati* and other sweet treats.

Before you order

An Italian meal can range from healthy to nutritional disaster. It comes down to applying those 10 skills and strategies once again. Contemplate the following healthy Italian meal: for a filling starter, a cup of minestrone or stracciatelli; main course of linguini with white clam sauce; dessert of Italian ice; and a demitasse of espresso. At the opposite end of the spectrum, look at this high-fat heart breaker: two garlic-and-olive-oil-drenched dinner rolls; antipasto of cheeses, pickles, peppers, olives, and Genoa salami; main course of fettucini Alfredo; and, why not, a cannoli for dessert.

Italian restaurant meals miss the mark with vegetables and fruits. You see salads, marinated vegetables, a bit of eggplant (often fried), and, of course, plenty of tomato products. What you don't see are large side orders of broccoli, green beans, and other vegetables. Fruits are few and far between. You'll be lucky to find some fresh berries on the dessert cart.

Skill 7, "practice portion control from the word go," is a must in Italian restaurants. The strategy of sharing a few entrees can be quite helpful. Try creating a nutritionally balanced meal in line with the Food Guide Pyramid by complementing spaghetti with Bolognese sauce and veal piccata. You'll each get enough starch and 3–4 ounces of protein, rather than too much of either one. Remember to order one or two less entrees for the number of people dining. Don't forget to order extra plates. Split everything down the middle. Order from appetizers to desserts but split every item— mussels, marinara, tricolore insalata, fusilli primavera, chicken marsala, and spumoni.

As always, be a private eye when it comes to fat. In Italian cuisine, fat comes at you from all sides. It might be butter on bread, olive oil, cream, cheese, and other high-fat tasties on pasta and decadent desserts. Keep a watch for those Red Flag Words, and seek out the Green Flag items.

Menu management

As the menu is placed in your lap, the great crusty Italian bread with butter (or, more in vogue, extra virgin olive oil), garlic rolls, breadsticks, or focaccia (Italian flat bread) land on the table. Bread or lightly oiled breadsticks are best. The others simply bog you down in fat before you even place an order. If your nutrition goals allow it, try one piece of bread and ask for a small dish of tomato sauce to dip in. Then pass the bread as far away as possible—the kitchen would be best. Don't be afraid to be a trendsetter—your dining partners will thank you. Practice an out-of-sight, out-of-mind strategy.

Before we go further, let's get the olive oil story straight. It's used in heavy doses in Italian cooking, and the tradition goes far back. Olives are plentiful in Italy and therefore have been woven into many recipes. Recently, olive oil has been in the nutrition press. That's because monounsaturated fats are being touted for improving the ratio of good to bad cholesterol. Monounsaturated fats do this by helping to lower the bad cholesterol, LDLs, and not decreasing HDLs, the good cholesterol. Fatty ingredients that contain mainly monounsaturated fats have the added benefit of being cholesterol-free—olive, canola, and peanut oils, nuts, and avocados. These are good reasons to use olive oil in preference to other oils. However, olive oil contains the same number of calories (50 calories per teaspoon) as every other fat from butter to lard and hard shortening. So eliminate as much oil as you can.

If calories need to be on the low side, focus on a low-fat entree and green salad. If you have more calories and fat to "spend," contemplate an antipasto or broth-based soup. Healthy antipasto choices are few and far between. A few are squid, mussels, or clams in a lemon-garlic-herb-wine (any combination) sauce. Or maybe they are available in a marinara sauce (light tomato sauce). An antipasto of marinated vegetables—peppers, pickles, and olives—is an option but not if you're trying to keep a lid on sodium. Antipastos loaded with cheeses and Italian cold cuts come close to eating pure fat, and it's of the animal variety. Steer clear of the deep-fried mozzarella, calamari, and zucchini sticks.

Onto one of the healthiest reasons to eat Italian: pasta. Pasta is made from combining flour, water, and (optionally) eggs. Pasta is made into many different shapes and forms, some large, some small, some stuffed, some not. (See "Know Your Pasta" at the end of the chapter.) The age old negative nutrition news about pasta's fattening quality is a misconception. Pasta, on its own, has no fat. It's carbohydrate with a bit of protein. Choose angel hair, linguini, fusilli, fettucini, or ziti. Try the flavored pastas—spinach, squid ink, or tomato. The problems build when pasta is topped or stuffed with high-fat ingredients such as cheeses, sausage, cream, bacon, etc. Your challenge is to keep an eye out for the ''go-ahead-and-order'' words: herbs, spices, garlic, wine sauce, light tomato sauce, etc.

No need to sweat it; healthy pasta choices are always listed. Look for styles such as marinara, primavera (sauteed vegetables), red or white clam sauce, or Bolognese. Limit the stuffed items—ravioli, cannelloni, manicotti—because they are usually stuffed with cheese. Order one if it's stuffed with vegetables, but ask for details before you proceed. It might be topped with a cream sauce. If you carefully count calories and fat, pesto should be left alone. It's made with basil (that's a good start) but then three high-fat ingredients are piled on: pignoli (pine) nuts, olive oil, and lots of Parmesan cheese. Just because it's green doesn't mean it's healthy. If you've got a few extra calories and fat grams to spend, a bit of pesto spreads a long way.

In more authentic Italian restaurants, the pasta is listed as the first course, but don't feel compelled to order both pasta and an entree. Some menus will offer both full-size and appetizer or half-portions of pasta dishes. That's perfect for implementing portion control. Order a cup of soup, an antipasto of marinated vegetables or a salad, dressing on the side, of course, and a half-portion of pasta. If your dining partners are eating first and second courses, request the antipasto when their pasta is served and your pasta when their second course is served. The reverse is fine, too.

Two newer Italian taste treats to become commonplace in upscale restaurants are risotto and polenta—two grain dishes native to Italy. Both require a lot of elbow grease to ready them for the table. Risotto is a creamy, short-grain rice with stubby kernels. It traces its ancestry to the Po Valley region of Italy where it is grown in abundance. Unfortunately, chefs prepare risotto with lots of butter, cheese, and/or sausage. The taste might be great, but the fat, calories, and cholesterol will be high. If you wish to try it, look for risotto that blends spices and vegetables such as risotto with spinach and mushrooms or risotto primavera.

Polenta is like cornmeal pudding. Cornmeal, water, and salt are the three ingredients. Polenta is a staple in the Veneto region of Italy. It is served with sauces, many of which, as usual, load on the fat. Sometimes you'll see triangles of polenta that have been grilled. They're low in fat grams.

Insalata, the innocent sounding, crunchy greens, is filling and low calorie—maybe, depending on what's atop the greens. Look for salads made with radicchio (red leaves), arugula (strong-tasting greens), endive, tomatoes, broccoli, mixed baby field greens, spinach, beets, peppers, onions, and other raw or marinated vegetables. A few olives or the nouvelle sun-dried tomatoes aren't a problem. However, high-fat items lurk in some Italian salads: cheese, ham, bacon, and nuts.

Order dressing on the side and look for a light one. Better yet, try a bit of olive oil with vinegar or a few fresh lemon wedges. Some of the newer continental Italian restaurants use flavored vinegars—tarragon or rosemary. If you spot it on the menu, you know it's in the kitchen. Ask for some on the side to use alone, or stretch the dressing you've ordered. Caesar salad with egg, grated cheese, and anchovies is one to limit. The worst part is the Caesar dressing, now Americanized and often thick and heavy. Your options are to have it put on lightly, request it on the side, or request the cruet of vinegar on the side.

Moving onto the traditional *secondo piatto,* or main course, you might find *pollo, pesce,* or *carne,* that's poultry, seafood, or meat. Don't feel compelled to order a main course unless you split it or take half home. It's simply too much protein. Pasta, prepared healthfully, is a better bet any day of the week. Choose among grilled fish, scallops, or chicken breast. Again, as with pasta, the magic question concerns the preparation: is it tomato-based, in vegetable sauces, or in mushroom or wine sauce (without or with cream)? It's common to see different protein foods prepared with the same sauces. Limit the high-fat and high-sodium prosciutto ham, pancetta (Italian cured bacon), bacon, cheese, and cream sauces.

A popular Italian entree is veal. Misconceptions about veal exist. Many people believe that veal is relatively low in calories, fat, and cholesterol. True, lean veal cutlet is low in calories (40–50 per ounce cooked), but the cholesterol content is similar to lean beef (20–25 milligrams per ounce cooked). On the other side of the veal spectrum is veal breast, which is higher in fat (60–70 calories per ounce cooked). The main problem is that veal is most often prepared by dredging it in flour and then sauteing. If you have a few extra calories to spare, veal marsala, cacciatore, or piccata is acceptable. If calories are tight, stick with grilled fish or chicken in restaurants, and eat veal cutlet at home, where you can prepare it lean.

You'll be offered a side dish of pasta with a choice of tomato sauce or garlic and oil. Opt for the marinara sauce. Consider ordering pasta untopped, and mix it with sauce from your entree, which could be chicken cacciatore.

The end of an American meal might be a sweet dessert; that's not the style in Italy. However, Italian restaurants bend toward American ways. Italian menus list items such as spumoni, cannoli, tortoni, Italian ices, and fresh berries, of course, with liqueur and whipped cream to quench the sweet tooth. If you've allocated a couple of hundred calories and a bit of fat, think about splitting a dessert or choose the lower-fat Italian ices or berries. Another option is to end the meal as they do in Italy, with a demitasse of espresso.

If you have a few calories in the bank and a liqueur fits into your nutrition goals, request a jigger (1-½ ounces) of Amaretto or Kahlua for your coffee (about 150 calories); you'll ingest no fat or cholesterol and negligible sodium. This might provide just the finishing touch you're craving and save you from a decadent cannoli.

Green Flag Words

INGREDIENTS:
onions, peppers, and mushrooms
artichoke hearts
sun-dried tomatoes
capers
marinated vegetables
grilled chicken, fish, or seafood
herbs and spices
tomatoes
pasta—all types other than stuffed
    with cheese

COOKING METHODS/MENU DESCRIPTIONS:
lightly sauteed with onions and
    shallots
tomato-based sauces—marinara,
    Bolognese, cacciatore
tomato sauce and meatballs

white or red clam sauce
light red sauce
light red- or white-wine sauce
light mushroom and wine sauce
primavera (make sure without
    cream)
piccata (lemon sauce)

**Red Flag
Words**

INGREDIENTS:
eggplant or zucchini (if fried)
pancetta, or bacon
sausage—veal or pork
olive oil, butter
cheese—mozzarella, Gorgonzola,
    and others
Italian cold cuts—prosciutto,
    salami, bologna

COOKING METHODS/MENU
DESCRIPTIONS:
Alfredo
carbonara
saltimbocca
parmigiana—veal, chicken,
    eggplant
stuffed with cheese
creamy sauces—wine, mushroom,
    cheese
fried or deep-fried
manicotti
lasagna
cannelloni
stuffed shells

AT THE TABLE:
olive oil
butter
salad dressing
grated cheese

**Special
Requests
Italian
Style**

Please remove the olive oil

Could I have a small amount of tomato sauce to dip the bread into.

Would you ask the chef to remove the skin from the chicken.

Please hold the Parmesan cheese (or grated cheese), bacon, olives, pine nuts.

Hold the sauce on the pasta.

Please use only a small amount of sauce over the pasta.

Please serve the salad dressing on the side and bring some vinegar.

I'd like the appetizer-size pasta, and please bring that when you bring the other entrees.

Would you ask the chef to avoid using any extra salt.

Please remove my plate, I'm finished now.

I'll take the rest of this home in a doggie bag.

The Menu: Italian Style

Antipasto   **Antipasto for Two** —a
combination of marinated
mushrooms, artichoke hearts,
Genoa salami, and percorino
cheese
Prosciutto wrapped around melon
✓**Marinated calamari**
Garlic bread
✓**Marinated mushrooms**
Fried calamari
✓**Clams** steamed in white wine
Fried mozzarella sticks with
marinara sauce
✓**Marinated vegetable salad**

Zuppa   ✓**Tortellini in broth**
✓**Pasta e fagioli** (bean and pasta
soup)
✓**Minestrone**
Lentil and sausage

Insalata   ✓**Arugula and Belgian endive**
served with balsamic vinaigrette
dressing
✓**Insalata frutte di mare**
(marinated seafood, scallops,
shrimp, and calamari in a light
marinade, served on a bed of
greens)
✓**Insalata di casa** (house salad with
greens, tomato, and onion)
Caesar salad (greens with buttery
croutons, Parmesan cheese, and a
creamy Caesar dressing)

✓*Preferred Choice*
Some depending on special requests

Pasta	✓**Spaghetti** with tomato sauce and meatballs

✓**Spaghetti** with tomato sauce and meatballs

Cannelloni stuffed with ricotta cheese and spinach, topped with a light tomato sauce

✓**Ziti Bolognese** (tubular noodles topped with a light tomato sauce of sauteed meat, celery, carrots, and onions)

Fettucini Alfredo (thin, flat pasta served with a creamy cheese sauce)

✓**Angel hair with white clam sauce** (the thinnest and lightest pasta, served with a white-wine-based sauce containing whole clams)

✓**Fettucini with red clam sauce** (flat noodles served with light tomato sauce and whole clams)

Linguine with Gorgonzola (flat, thin pasta served with a creamy Gorgonzola cheese sauce)

✓**Fusilli primavera** (a spiral, long pasta topped with a blend of spicy sauteed seasonal vegetables)

Carne*

✓**Veal piccata** (medallions of veal lightly sauteed in a butter, lemon, and wine sauce)

✓**Veal cacciatore** (veal cutlet topped with tomato sauce and sauteed onions, mushrooms, and peppers)

✓**Chicken primavera** (breast of chicken lightly sauteed and topped with sauteed seasonal vegetables)

Veal saltimbocca (medallions of veal filled with prosciutto ham, sage, and mushrooms and topped with mozzarella cheese)

Chicken parmigiana (chicken cutlet baked with mozzarella cheese and tomato sauce)

✓**Chicken in wine sauce** (sauteed breast of chicken, roasted peppers, and mushrooms, with Burgundy wine, fresh garlic, and rosemary)

Pesce*

✓**Shrimp primavera** (sauteed shrimp and garden vegetables served on top of a bed of angel hair pasta)

✓**Shrimp marinara** (shrimp lightly sauteed in garlic and topped with tomato sauce)

Lobster in mushroom sauce (a creamy porcini mushroom sauce with large chunks of lobster tail)

✓**Scallops marsala** (sauteed scallops in a mushroom and marsala wine sauce)

Shrimp scampi (shrimp sauteed in olive oil, fresh garlic, white wine, lemon, and oregano)

✓**Sole primavera** (fillet of sole sauteed with an assortment of seasonal fresh vegetables, zucchini, peppers, and tomatoes)

*Above items served with a bowl of spaghetti topped with your choice of marinara sauce or olive oil and garlic.

Dolce

✓**Fresh raspberries with Kirsch and whipped cream**

Spumoni

Cannoli

✓**Italian ice**

Tortoni

Now that you've seen what might be available on the Menu, find the Model Meal that best suits your nutrition goals. For an explanation of the Model Meals and their targeted nutritional values, see Chapter 3.

Your Order, Please

Healthy	30%	Calories as fat
Daily	20%	Calories as protein
Eating	50%	Calories as carbohydrate
Goals	300	mg/day Cholesterol
	3000	mg/day Sodium

**Low Calorie/
Low Fat
Model Meal**

Arugula and Belgian endive salad (request balsamic vinegar on the side)
Quantity: 2 cups
Exchanges: 2 vegetable
Fusilli (request marinara or tomato sauce to top)
Quantity: 1 cup
Exchanges: 2 starch
Shrimp primavera (eat half)
Quantity: 1½ cups
Exchanges: 3–4 meat (lean); 2 fat; 2 vegetable
Espresso
Quantity: 1 cup
Exchanges: free

Estimated
Nutrient
Evaluation

calories 450
fat 11g (21% of calories)
protein 38g (34% of calories)
carbohydrate 51g (45% of calories)
cholesterol 160 mg
sodium 650 mg

**Low Calorie/
Low
Cholesterol
Model Meal**

Marinated mushrooms
Quantity: 1 cup
Ziti Bolognese
Quantity: 1½ cups
Parmesan cheese for above
Quantity: 1 tbsp
Coffee
Quantity: 1 cup or more

Estimated
Nutrient
Evaluation

calories 550
fat 20g (32% of calories)
protein 28g (21% of calories)
carbohydrate 65g (47% of calories)
cholesterol 55 mg
sodium 1100 mg

**Higher
Calorie/Low
Fat Model
Meal**

(Split entire meal; portions shown
    are already divided)
Italian bread
Quantity: 2 small pieces, hold
    butter or oil
Marinated vegetables (carrots,
    cauliflower, broccoli florets,
    Italian green beans)
Quantity: 1 cup
**Angel hair pasta with white
    clam sauce**
Quantity: 1½ cups
Veal piccata
Quantity: 4 ozs.
Fresh raspberries with Kirsch
    (hold whipped cream)
Quantity: ½ cup

Estimated Nutrient Evaluation	calories 937 fat 34g (33% of calories) protein 49g (21% of calories) carbohydrate 90g (38% of calories) alcohol 8% of calories cholesterol 140 mg sodium 1180 mg

Higher Calorie/Low Cholesterol Model Meal	**Tortellini in broth** *Quantity:* 1 cup **Insalata di casa** (dressing on the side) *Quantity:* 1 cup **Basil vinaigrette dressing** (on the side) *Quantity:* 1 tbsp **Veal cacciatore** *Quantity:* ½ portion (½ in doggie bag) **Spaghetti** (hold sauce and use that from entree) *Quantity:* 1½ cups **Coffee with Kahlua** (hold whipped cream) *Quantity:* 1 cup

Estimated Nutrient Evaluation	calories 870 fat 28g (29% of calories) protein 48g (22% of calories) carbohydrate 89g (41% of calories) alcohol 8% of calories cholesterol 100 mg sodium 1050 mg

Low Sodium Model Meal

Clams steamed in white wine
Quantity: 10 clams (½ order)
Linguini (request served without sauce)
Quantity: 1½ cups (split order)
Chicken in wine sauce (request limited additional salt)
Quantity: 4 ozs. (offer rest to companions)
Italian ice
Quantity: 1 cup

Estimated Nutrient Evaluation

calories 810
fat 29g (32% of calories)
protein 30g (15% of calories)
carbohydrate 107g (53% of calories)
cholesterol 170 mg
sodium 680 mg

Know your pastas

Pasta, meaning "paste" or "dough," is a staple in Italian restaurants. Pasta is created from flour (sometimes durum and sometimes all-purpose flour), water, and/or eggs. These ingredients create a wide variety of different pastas, from angel hair to ziti.

Unlike Italy of yesterday, many differently colored and spiced pastas are served in American restaurants today. There are whole-wheat, tomato, spinach, and artichoke, to name a few. It's hard to decipher all the shapes and names. Here is a basic primer to help you "Know Your Pastas" and have an easier time deciding which one to order.

Agnolotti–crescent-shaped pieces of pasta, stuffed with one ingredient or a combination of cheese, meat, and spinach.

Angel hair–the thinnest and finest of the "long" pasta family, it is quite light in consistency and often served with light sauces.

Cannelloni–large, tubular pasta, similar to manicotti, it is stuffed with one ingredient or a combination of cheese, meat, and spinach.

Capellitti–meaning a "little hat," these are small, stuffed pastas that look like little tortellini; often stuffed with cheese or meats.

Fettucini–flat, long noodle about ¼-inch wide (wider than linguine).

Fusilli–spiral-shaped long pasta, fusilli is round like spaghetti.

Gnocchi–little dumplings, in ½-inch pieces made from either flour, potato, or a combination of both; often topped with sauce.

Lasagne–the widest noodle among the long, flat pastas; found with either smooth or scalloped edges.

Linguine–flat, long noodle about ⅛-inch wide (thinner than fettucini).

Manicotti–long, tubular noodle about 2 inches in diameter, most often stuffed with cheese and/or meat and served with tomato sauce.

Mostaccioli–short, tubular noodle about 1½ inches long.

Penne–short, tubular noodle quite similar to mostaccioli and rigatoni.

Polenta–corn meal and water mixture, which is cooked, poured on a board to harden, and served with a sauce.

Ravioli–pasta squares, with corrugated edges, stuffed with cheese, spinach, or meats in combination or singly.

Rigatoni–short, tubular noodle quite similar to penne and mostaccioli.

Risotto–Italian short-grain rice that has a creamy consistency when cooked; often mixed with butter and cheese before serving.

Shells–noodles in the shape of conch shells, called *conchiglie* in Italian, and found in a variety of sizes; sometimes larger ones are stuffed, and most are served topped with tomato sauce.

Spaghetti–thin, round pasta (also called vermicelli); the most commonly known pasta in America.

Tortelini–small pastas, stuffed and joined at the ends to form a ring; a larger version of capellitti.

Ziti–a short, tubular pasta similar to mostaccioli.

8

Healthier eating out
Thai Style

As Asian cuisines go, Chinese has reigned supreme in America for years. But Thai food is quickly gaining ground. The increasing fame of Thai food and the sprouting number of Thai restaurants is good news for the health-focused. Soon Thai menu items such as basil rolls, tom yum koong, red curry, and pad Thai will be as familiar as the Chinese chicken chow mein, and moo shi pork.

Over the last ten years, an onslaught of Thai restaurants have opened, especially in large cities and particularly in coastal towns. William Clifford, a food writer describes Thai food as "the newest cuisine we've imported from the Orient. It's aromatic Thai, with trim vegetables, light sauces, and seasonings that tingle and tantalize.'' The author adds that ''some people have wondered if Thai food is only the latest oriental fad or whether its unique flavoring will ensure its place on America's international menu. The proliferation of Thai restaurants indicates that . . . Thai cooking is here to stay.''

Get to know the cuisine

Beyond quenching your yen for hot and spicy, Thai foods can fit today's healthy eating goals: light on fats and meats and heavy on vegetables, noodles, and rice. Overall, Thai food is a healthier choice than the food it's often compared with—Chinese. The similarities are the cooking technique of stir-frying, the central focus on rice and noodles, and common ingredients such as garlic, ginger, shrimp, chicken, onions, and mushrooms. However, Thai food differs substantially due to different flavorings and spices—curry, basil, and chili to name just a few. Taste-wise, Thai food more closely mimics Indian fare. Both India and China are Thailand's neighbors, thus the commonalities.

Both Thai and Indian cuisine are hot and spicy as well as ''aromatic.'' The common spices—coriander, cumin, cardamom, and cinnamon—are several that contribute to the aromatic flavor. These spices are blended into what Americans refer to as curry. Curry is truly a blend of spices. The use of chilies, which pack some punch, and tamarind, turmeric, and coconut milk are other resemblances between Thai and Indian cuisine.

The manner in which foods are cut up into small pieces and cooked quickly by stir-frying more closely mimics Thailand's eastern neighbor, China. Some food aficionados say there are also Malaysian influences in Thai cooking. Satay, a common Thai appetizer, has its roots in Malaysian cooking.

Thai cuisine, with its many influences, has its unique light flavors and spices. Thai cooks use nam pla, or fish sauce, similarly to the way Chinese chefs use soy sauce. Soy sauce is also drizzled in Thai cooking. Several different pastes—dried fish and spice combinations such as shrimp paste (*kapi*) or curry paste—are tossed in for flavor. Lemon grass (*takrai*), kaffir lime leaves (*makrut*), and basil (*horapa*) are common Thai spices. Sauces are lighter than in Chinese cuisine because little or no thickening agent, such as flour or cornstarch, is stirred in. (See "Spices, Seasonings, and Ingredients of Thai Cuisine" at the end of this chapter.)

Thai stir-frying is done quickly and on top of the stove in a wok or frying pan. Some fat is used. Appetizers and meats, like fried shrimp or chicken, are prepared by deep-frying. However, deep-frying is not the most common cooking method. Most often, dishes are stir-fried, steamed, braised, or marinated. Foods high in fat, as usual, are used to begin cooking, and they may end the cooking process, as when nuts are scattered on top.

In Thailand, it's typical to use lard or coconut oil. Both contain saturated fat; and lard, being animal fat, contains cholesterol. Some Thai restaurateurs say they use vegetable oil for stir-frying. Hopefully, this will eventually be true for all Thai restaurants. Coconut milk is used quite liberally. Coconut milk is loaded with calories and saturated fat. According to the USDA nutrient analysis, eight ounces of canned coconut milk contains 445 calories, about 97 percent of which are fat, and much of it is the artery-clogging, saturated variety. Therefore, you'll need to navigate around the coconut-milk-laden curry dishes.

Rice, as in many Southeast Asian cuisines, is a staple in Thailand. It's always served at the main meal. The rice used in Thai restaurants is a long-grain white rice. Interestingly, no salt is added when it's prepared. Noodles are also common, with the dish pad Thai the most well known.

A main meal in Thailand traditionally consists of soup, rice, a curry dish, assorted vegetables, a salad, and several sauces. In Indian style, it is common and acceptable for people to eat with their fingers. However, chopsticks are an optional utensil, and in certain parts of Thailand the fork and spoon are employed. Knives aren't seen because foods are presented in small pieces and don't need further mincing. The appearance of food is just as important as its taste. Dishes are aesthetically pleasing. In Thai restaurants time is taken to carve fruits and vegetables to decorate a serving platter.

Though there are some Thai foods and preparation methods to avoid, there are many palate and heart-pleasing entrees. Best news yet, sharing dishes and eating family style is Thai style. So fit in with the culture and practice Skill 7: "portion control from the word go."

Before you order

Due to its lighter qualities, Thai food is a healthy choice if you keep a watchful eye on fats and cholesterol and, as always, order by the Food Guide Pyramid. As you scan the menu, keep close tabs on the number of chili symbols, asterisks, or other notations alongside some dishes. These indicate hot and spicy. Three chilies may mean it's wise to have a glass of water within arm's reach. If you see a healthy pick but the number of chilies are a notch too high or low, just request that the chef turn the "heat" up or down. Keep in mind that the zip is fired by spices and flavorings with next to no fat or calories. So go ahead and be daring!

You'll have no problem keeping the carbohydrates up because rice arrives whether you want it or not. Another help in boosting the carbos are the many vegetable-focused dishes. You'll spot entrees that combine four, five, or six different vegetables as well as a few vegetarian dishes. Gear toward the veggies; that helps hold down the amount of meat, poultry, or seafood you'll eat.

Common protein foods are seafood—shrimp, scallops, squid, and clams. It's usual to see seafood combination dishes featuring all four. You'll also see plenty of chicken and duck listings. Limit duck if the skin is still attached. Beef and pork are used in many dishes. Both picks are fine, but mix them with seafood or vegetable dishes as the second or third entree choice when eating family style.

As mentioned, some saturated fat, perhaps lard or coconut oil, is used. Ask what type of fat is employed. If the response is lard or coconut oil, request that the chef use vegetable oil. But remember, vegetable oil doesn't reduce calories. It just lowers the saturated fat and cholesterol (in the case of lard).

As for limiting fat grams, keep an eye out for the Red Flag Words, most of which mean added fat. Fried, deep-fried, and crispy are telltale signs that you should move along in your menu search. To minimize fat, look for the stir-fried, steamed, sauteed, marinated, and grilled listings packed with vegetables. Stay light on fats by steering clear of coconut milk or cream. You'll find it in soups and curry entrees.

The sodium content of Thai food is not as high as in Japanese food, but it can still run high. The spicing and flavoring of Thai cuisine is not as dependent on soy sauce as other oriental cuisines. However, high-sodium soy sauce will find its way into main dishes, soups, and noodles. Some of the sauces, such as yellow bean paste, shrimp paste, and fish sauce, load on sodium. If your goal is to keep sodium on the low side, avoid the soups. Request that less salt and/or soy sauce be drizzled into dishes. Also, to further subtract sodium, request that no MSG be used.

People with diabetes should know that, similar to many Southeast Asian cuisines, a small amount of sugar is used in many dishes. Sometimes Thais use palm sugar.

Menu management

Satay, basil or vegetable rolls, and steamed seafood are healthier appetizers. However, be on guard for the sauces. Peanut sauce, served with satay is loaded with fat as it's made with smashed peanuts. Request a lighter sauce, for instance, the tamarind or sweet-and-sour sauce served with Thai rolls. That's Skill Number 8 in action: "practice menu creativity." As with many appetizers, American or Asian, many are deep-fried and fat-dense: Thai rolls, tod mun, stuffed chicken wings. However, portions are small. If you've got a few calories to spare and dining partners to share, nibble on a few tastes. If your dining partner is aligned with your healthy eating goals, just skip the appetizers and dive into the entrees.

Another option before jumping to the main course, is to stop by the soups. Soup is filling and takes the edge off a voracious appetite. Thai soups divide into two groups—healthy and ones to cast aside. Several clear broth soups, tom yum koong and pok taek, have a bit of protein and great taste from Thai spices such as lemon grass, chili paste, and lime juice. Their calorie counts are low, but sodium is high. One soup to avoid, due to its coconut milk, is tom ka gai, or chicken coconut. Read the soup's description to determine whether the base is clear or made cloudy with coconut milk. Stick with those you can see through.

Salads are unusual in Southeast Asian cuisines but are regulars on Thai menus. That's great for healthy eaters. Thai salads range from simple garden salads that focus on lettuce to beef, chicken, seafood, and combinations such as yam yai. That's a combo of shrimp, chicken, and pork. Dressings are light and made with Thai spices—lemon grass, chili, lime juice, and sometimes peanut sauce. A thick peanut sauce dressing is high in fat. Ask for it on the side, or request an alternative sauce or dressing you see on the menu such as tamarind or a light sweet-and-sour dressing. Think of a salad as an appetizer if others are digging into fried appetizers; or order a seafood or beef salad as your main course with a bowl of steamed rice. Split a salad with your dining partner(s) as one of the group's entree choices. A little roughage always helps fill you up and not out.

You'll find many healthy entrees in any Thai restaurant. Some load on the vegetables and are cooked in light sauces. Think about what protein foods you want: chicken, shrimp, scallops, fish, beef, or pork. Complement a protein-dense dish with one with veggies as its strong suit. Find a vegetable and tofu (bean curd) dish to help you stay light on animal protein and saturated fat. Remember the Food Guide Pyramid and pack on the carbos while going light on the meats. Spot those Red Flag Words: fried, deep-fried, crispy, and golden brown. They raise the fat grams count.

It's common to see peanuts, cashews, or peanut sauce as additions to Thai dishes. Request that nuts be left in the kitchen if the rest of the dish appeals. If calories are a prime concern, the lighter basil, chili, lime juice, and curry paste sauces are lower in calories.

The curry dishes add coconut milk, which adds lots of fat and it's the artery-clogging saturated variety. The best advice is not to overload on curry sauces, whether yellow, green, red, or mussaman. Order one curry dish to share among a group. Make an effort to minimize the amount of sauce spooned on. Curry dishes are packed with veggies and are light on meats—that's a plus.

Several rice and noodle offerings are up for grabs. Hands down, the best choice, which arrives with a prompt, is steamed white rice. It's long-grain, often with a sprinkling of jasmine grains. You can't beat it for healthiness. Fried rice is also available. It's a bit lighter in fat and color than most Chinese fried rice. Similarly, Thai fried rice comes in such varieties as vegetable, pork, seafood, or a combination. Stick with the vegetable. Without question, you up the fat and sodium content when you switch from white to fried rice. If you've got a few calories to spare, have some of each.

Pad Thai is the omnipresent Thai noodle dish. It's noodles, stir-fried with finely chopped peanuts, bean sprouts, egg, tofu, and scallions. A few shrimp are decked on top or hidden in between. Like fried rice, it gains fat and sodium in the cooking process. So use the same strategies; have some of it along with steamed rice. Several other (non-fried) noodle dishes have small amounts of shrimp, egg, and vegetables. Use the same strategies. Mee-krob, another famous Thai noodle dish, is on most menus. You might find it on the appetizer list, too, but don't look too hard—it's fried crispy to a golden brown.

The dessert listings in most Thai restaurants are minimal and easy to pass by. You might find lychee nuts, a common Southeast Asian fruit, and puddings or custards. The lychee nuts are fine, but a nice relaxing cup of coffee or tea might satisfy with less calories. Most Thai restaurants offer Thai ice coffee or ice tea. Don't be fooled into thinking these are just coffee or tea. They have plenty of sugar and milk or cream. If one of these quenches your sweet tooth and you've got the calories to spend, they're not a super-high-fat way to go.

Green Flag Words

INGREDIENTS:
basil or basil leaves
lemon grass
mint or mint leaves
lime juice
curry paste
chili, chili paste, crushed dried
    chili
Thai spices
fish sauce
sweet-and-sour sauce (used with
    appetizers)
bean thread noodles
napa (cabbage), bamboo shoots,
    black mushrooms (other
    vegetables)
scallops, shrimp, squid, chicken
bed of spinach or mixed
    vegetables

COOKING METHODS/MENU
DESCRIPTIONS:
stir-fried
sauteed
sizzling
braised
marinated
barbecued
clear broth soup
basil sauce
lime sauce
served in a pineapple shell
Thai salads

INGREDIENTS:
topped with peanuts, ground
    peanuts
topped with cashews
peanut sauce
coconut milk
red, green, yellow, mussaman
    curry
golden brown or fried duck

**Red Flag
Words**

COOKING METHODS/MENU
DESCRIPTIONS:
golden brown
fried
deep-fried
crispy
coconut milk soup
mee-krob (crispy noodles)
curry sauce

AT THE TABLE:
peanut sauce
soy sauce

**Special
Requests
Thai
Style**

Please put the dressing on the side of the salad.

Please hold the peanuts (or cashews) from this dish.

Can you prepare these dishes with no MSG?

What oil is used to prepare your foods? (If it's coconut oil or lard, ask that vegetable oil be used instead.)

Please minimize the salt and soy sauce; I'm carefully watching my sodium consumption.

Can I substitute scallops for shrimp or beef in this dish?

Could I have a bit more broccoli and less beef in this dish?

Please make this dish equivalent to three-chili hotness; I like lots of flavor.

Could I get the rest of this wrapped up to take home; I'd like to enjoy it for dinner tomorrow night?

The Menu: Thai Style

Appetizers   **Thai rolls** (delicate and crispy vegetable-filled spring rolls served with sweet-and-sour sauce)

✓**Satay** (beef or chicken marinated in coconut milk and curry, barbecued on skewers, and served with peanut sauce and cucumber salad)

✓**Basil rolls** (garden fresh vegetables rolled with basil leaves, served with sweet-and-sour sauce)

Tod mun (minced shrimp and codfish, mixed with Thai curry, and fried until golden brown; served with cucumber sauce)

✓**Steamed mussels** (steamed with lemon grass, sweet basil leaves, chili, and Thai spices; served with chili sauce)

Mee-krob (sweet crispy rice noodles with shrimp, chicken, and bean sprouts)

Vegetarian tofu (deep-fried tofu served with sweet chili sauce)

Soups   ✓**Tom yum koong** (Thai shrimp soup with lemon grass, chili paste, lime juice, and straw mushrooms)

Tom ka gai (chicken in coconut milk soup with mushrooms and lime juice)

✓**Crystal noodle** (clear soup with chicken, bean thread noodles, and vegetables)

✓*Preferred Choice*
Some depending on special requests

Fresh mushroom soup (with coconut milk, lemon grass, and diced chili)

✓**Pok Taek** (shrimp, squid, scallops, mushrooms with lemon grass, chili paste, and lime juice)

Salads   ✓**Thai salad** (green mixed garden salad with tofu and egg wedges, dressed with spiced peanut sauce)

✓**Pla koong** (spicy shrimp salad with onion, scallions, tomatoes, mushrooms, lemon grass, all tossed with chili and lime juice)

✓**Spiced beef salad** (charbroiled beef slices in chili paste, lemon grass, lettuce, tomatoes, mushrooms, and scallions tossed in spicy lemon dressing)

✓**Yam yai** (spicy combination salad of shrimp, pork, and chicken with lettuce, cucumber, onion, and tomato in light Thai spicy dressing)

Curry   The following curry dishes can be made with either chicken, beef, duck, shrimp, scallops, tofu, or vegetables.

✓**Green curry** (in coconut milk, with bamboo shoots, green peppers, string beans, green peas, and zucchini)

✓**Red curry** (in coconut milk, with bamboo shoots, red and green peppers)

✓**Yellow** (in coconut milk, with potatoes, onion, green pepper, and summer squash)

✓**Mussaman curry** (in coconut milk, with potatoes, onions, carrots, and peanuts)

Poultry   **Crispy duck** (fried duck, steamed with soy sauce, topped with fried spinach, and served with plum sauce)

✓**Thai chicken** (chicken sauteed with cashews, onions, mushrooms, pineapple, scallions, and chili; served in a whole pineapple)

Chicken in the garden (boiled, sliced chicken on a bed of broccoli, carrots, cauliflower, green beans, and asparagus; topped with peanut sauce)

✓**Sweet-and-sour chicken** (slices of chicken, pineapple, tomatoes, onions, and green peppers topped with a sweet-and-sour sauce)

✓**Chili duck** (sauteed roast duck with onion, hot pepper, mushrooms, scallions, and fresh sweet basil leaves with fish sauce)

Beef/Pork   **Spareribs curry** (red curry in coconut milk, with boneless spareribs, peas, string beans, snowpeas, hot pepper, tomato, and sweet basil leaves)

✓**Beef basil** (sauteed beef flavored with hot basil leaves, fresh hot pepper, mushrooms, and red pepper)

✓**Pork and string beans** (sauteed sliced pork tenderloin with string beans, snowpeas, red pepper, and cashew nuts tossed in spicy chili sauce)

Praram long song (fried beef with special curry sauce and peanuts over a bed of spinach)

✓**Chili beef** (sauteed sliced beef with baby corn, onions, mushrooms, and red and green peppers topped with chili sauce)

✓**Ginger pork** (sauteed pork in ginger with green pepper, onion, scallion, mushrooms, and chili paste)

Seafood   **Hot Thai fish** (deep-fried fish fillet topped with bamboo shoots, baby corn, mushrooms, eggplant, hot chili, and basil leaves with Thai spices)

✓**Garlic shrimp** (sauteed shrimp with fresh garlic, peppercorns, snowpeas, and napa; served on a bed of sliced cucumbers)

✓**Poy sian** (combination of seafood sauteed with straw mushrooms, napa, bamboo shoots, onions, and string beans)

✓**Scallops bamboo** (sauteed sea scallops, with bamboo shoots, snowpeas, baby corn, mushrooms, and scallions all mixed with Thai spices)

✓**Seafood platter** (sauteed assorted seafood, shrimp, scallops, squid, and clams, with celery, baby corn, and onions and a yellow bean sauce)

Vegetables   **Royal tofu** (deep-fried pieces of tofu with snowpeas, onions, scallions, and broccoli seasoned with a spicy chili sauce)

✓**Vegetable boat** (string beans, asparagus, zucchini, onions, and mushrooms stir-fried in Thai spices)

✓**Pad jay** (combination of napa, celery, onions, carrots, mushrooms, and bean sprouts topped with a sauce of Thai spices)

Rice and Noodles	✓**Fried rice** (rice fried with chicken, scallions, green peas, onion, and egg) ✓**Vegetable fried rice** (rice fried with assorted stir-fry vegetables) ✓**Steamed rice** ✓**Pad Thai** (noodles stir-fried with ground peanuts, bean sprouts, egg, tofu, and scallions, topped with shrimp) ✓**Pad gee** (noodles served with broccoli, pork, beef, or chicken)
Desserts	✓**Lychee nuts** **Fried banana** (deep-fried banana served with a sweet syrup sauce) **Tapioca** (coconut pudding) **Thai custard**

Now that you've seen what might be available on the Menu, find the Model Meal that best fits your nutrition goals. For an explanation of the Model Meals and their targeted nutritional values, see Chapter 3.

Your Order, Please

Healthy	30%	Calories as fat
Daily	20%	Calories as protein
Eating	50%	Calories as carbohydrate
Goals	300	mg/day Cholesterol
	3000	mg/day Sodium

❶

Low Calorie/
Low Fat
Model Meal

Tom yum koong
Quantity: 1 cup
Exchanges: ½ meat; ½ vegetable
Thai chicken (hold cashews)
Quantity: 1 cup
Exchanges: 2 meat (lean); 1 fat;
   1 vegetable
Poy sian
Quantity: 1 cup
Exchanges: 2 meat (lean); 1 fat;
   1 vegetable
Steamed rice
Quantity: 1 cup
Exchanges: 3 starch
Mineral water
Quantity: 12 oz
Exchanges: free

Estimated
Nutrient
Evaluation

calories 528
fat 16g (29% of calories)
protein 29g (22% of calories)
carbohydrate 65g (49% of calories)
cholesterol 153 mg
sodium 1210 mg

Low Calorie/ Low Cholesterol Model Meal

Pok taek
Quantity: 1 cup
Spiced beef salad
Quantity: 2 cups
Steamed rice
Quantity: 1 cup
Hot tea
Quantity: 2 cups

Estimated Nutrient Evaluation

calories 593
fat 21g (32% of calories)
protein 40g (27% of calories)
carbohydrate 61g (41% of calories)
cholesterol 100 mg
sodium 1069 mg

Higher Calorie/Low Fat Model Meal

Green curry with tofu
Quantity: 1½ cups
Exchanges: 2 fat; 3 vegetable
Scallops bamboo
Quantity: 1½cups
Exchanges: 3 meat (lean); 1 fat; 2 vegetable
Pad Thai
Quantity: 1 cup
Exchanges: ½ meat (lean); 2 fat; 2 starch
Steamed rice
Quantity: ⅔ cup
Exchanges: 2 starch
Coffee
Quantity: 2 cups
Exchanges: free

Estimated Nutrient Evaluation	818 calories
	fat 32g (35% of calories)
	protein 47g (23% of calories)
	carbohydrate 86g (42% of calories)
	cholesterol 64 mg
	sodium 1260 mg

❹

Higher Calorie/Low Cholesterol Model Meal

Satay, chicken
Quantity: 2 skewers
Ginger pork
Quantity: 1½ cups
Vegetable boat
Quantity: 1½ cups
Fried rice with vegetables
Quantity: 1⅓ cups
Light beer
Quantity: 12 oz

Estimated Nutrient Evaluation	calories 976
	fat 41g (38% of calories)
	protein 49g (20% of calories)
	carbohydrate 83g (34% of calories)
	alcohol 8% of calories
	cholesterol 136 mg
	sodium 1460 mg

❺

Low Sodium Model Meal

Yam yai salad
Quantity: 1½ cups
Sweet-and-sour chicken
Quantity: 1½ cups
Steamed rice
Quantity: 1 cup
White wine
Quantity: 6 oz

Estimated	calories 781
Nutrient	fat 21g (24% of calories)
Evaluation	protein 47g (24% of calories)
	carbohydrate 72g (37% of calories)
	alcohol 15% of calories
	cholesterol 138 mg
	sodium 820 mg

Spices, seasonings, and ingredients of Thai cuisine

Bamboo shoots–an oriental vegetable commonly found in Thai entrees; light in color, crunchy, and stringy in texture and very low in calories.

Basil–*horapa,* as it's known in Thailand, basil is used mainly in leaf form; there are several types of basil used in Thai cooking.

Cardamom–a member of the ginger family, the seeds are often used in curry mixtures and other dishes, as seeds or ground.

Chilies–various types used, depending on hotness of dish; red and green are common, used whole, chopped, or ground into paste for sauces.

Coconut milk–liquid extracted from grating fresh coconut, not the liquid from inside the coconut; used in marinating and in gravies for various dishes, especially curry sauces. High in saturated fat.

Coriander–dried coriander seed is the main ingredient in curry mixtures; the seeds or leaves are used; an essential spice in Thai cooking.

Cumin–another fragrant spice important to curry mixtures; used either as seeds or ground.

Curry–really a combination of spices, not a single spice as known in the U.S.; different spice and food combinations create the green, red, and mussaman curry mixtures.

Kapi–dried shrimp paste made from prawns or shrimp, commonly used to flavor many Thai dishes.

Lemon grass–*takrai,* as it's known in Thailand, is an Asian plant whose bulbous base is used to add a lemony flavor to many soups and main entrees.

Lime–*makrut,* in Thai, lime leaves or the juice of kaffir lime is commonly used in soups, salads, and entrees.

Nam pla–a fish sauce used like soy sauce in Thai cooking; this thin, salty brown sauce brings out the flavor of other foods.

Nam prik–called Thai shrimp sauce, it is used to flavor many Thai foods; made from shrimp paste, chilies, lime juice, soy sauce, and sugar.

Napa–also referred to as Chinese cabbage, it has thick-ribbed stalks and crinkled leaves.

Palm sugar–a strong-flavored, dark sugar obtained from the sap of coconut palms; it is boiled down until it crystallizes.

Scallions–also called spring onions, they are white, slender, and have long green stems; usually they are chopped into small pieces.

Soy sauce–used in many Thai dishes to cast a salty flavor; made from soy beans.

Tamarind–an acidy-tasting fruit from a large tropical tree; used for its acid flavor.

Turmeric–the spice that lends the yellow-orange color to commercial curry; part of the ginger family.

9

Healthier eating out
Japanese Style

Today, Japanese menu offerings conjure up dichotomous images. A sushi bar that slices fresh yellowfin tuna onto a pillow of su rice or crabmeat, avocado, and su rice wrapped around *nori* (seaweed) as California rolls versus the "Americanized" Japanese steak house, where the spotlight is on the aerobic chefs who cook and perform simultaneously. Or picture a Japanese restaurant where the familiar tempura, sukiyaki, and teriyaki and foreign-sounding agemono, yosenabe, and donburi are all menu options.

Between the popularity of sushi, the low-fat attributes of Japanese cuisine, and an increase in the number of Japanese restaurants, more people eat Japanese food today. That's especially true for the nutrition minded. And rightly so: Japanese food is one of the healthiest ethnic cuisines. It falls right in line with the Food Guide Pyramid—heavy on vegetables and starches, with white rice front and center, and light on seafood, meats, dairy products, and fats. The biggest thorn in the side of Japanese cuisine is its high sodium count.

Get to know the cuisine

When you first pick up a Japanese menu, you feel terribly confused by names of dishes and ingredients. Have no fear, it's easy to catch on and you'll quickly define the Japanese words for chicken (*tori*), beef (*gyuniku*), broiled (*yaki*), and so on. A glance at the "Seasonings, Spices, and Terms of Japanese Cuisine" at chapter's end will have you defining *nabemono* in no time.

In general, the Japanese living in Japan are healthy eaters, or at least have been in the past. They suffer less frequently than Americans from obesity-induced diseases such as heart disease, colon cancer, and diabetes. Studies that traced changes in eating habits of Japanese who emigrated to the U.S. over the last few decades showed that as Japanese immigrants adopted a Westernized high-fat diet, they also increased their risk of obesity-induced diseases.

At first glance, Japanese food preparation and presentation seem unique. Actually, some of the origins can be tracked to Chinese roots. Similarities appear in the core foods such as rice, soy products, and tea. European influences impact Japanese cooking as well. For instance, the original idea for tempura has its roots in Portuguese cuisine. The Japanese, however, learned to make a lighter and almost translucent batter. The Japanese dish tonkatsu is fried pork cutlet. It is said to imitate the German wiener schnitzel. Again, the Japanese interpretation is lighter and more delicate.

Though Asian and European influences on Japanese cuisines are evident, it remains a unique style of cookery and meal service. Japanese food preparation was described as "making the most of nature's seasonal offerings with utmost culinary artistry" by Shizui Tsuji, the author of *Japanese Cooking, A Simple Art.*

In Japanese culture, food does more than nourish the body. Harmony of foods is important, as is the role food plays in fueling the body and soul. It is also critical that food be served aesthetically. You only have to observe chefs rolling and serving sushi to appreciate the culinary artistry of Japanese preparation. The raw fish might be rolled with su rice and nori. Other ingredients, possibly avocado, roe, or egg are intertwined. The long roll is then sliced and decoratively placed on elegant serving pieces. Wasabi, soy sauce, and pickled ginger are accompaniments. The result is almost too beautiful to eat.

Different-sized plates, bowls, and sauce dishes are intended to please the diner's eye. Boxes, called *bentos,* may be used to serve a Japanese meal. Soups are dished up piping hot in china or lacquered bowls. The physical surroundings in a restaurant also receive attention. Beyond aesthetics, Japanese cookery is based on simplicity, purity, and sparseness of seasonings. These goals result in a cuisine that is light, delicate, and healthy.

Soybeans and its products are key to Japanese cookery. Soybeans are the basis for shoyu, the Japanese soy sauce. Miso, the fermented soybean paste, is a critical ingredient in soup, salad dressings, and entrees. Teriyaki sauce, which is familiar to Americans, is a combination of shoyu and mirin (sweet rice wine). Tofu, or soybean curd, is a significant protein source in the Japanese diet. Rice, called *gohan,* is a staple in Japan. It is the central feature of almost every meal. Rice is also the base of several important liquids, including mirin, sake, and Japanese rice vinegar.

Because Japan is surrounded by water, fish and shellfish are major protein sources in the Japanese diet. Poultry is eaten, but less frequently than seafood. Beef and pork, due to their expense and scarcity, were not commonly used. You might not think that when reading a Japanese menu in America. The poultry and red meat selections are just as predominant as seafood. That's ''Americanization'' for you.

Along with rice, vegetables contribute to the lightness of Japanese cuisine. It's usual to find vegetables such as bamboo shoots, napa (cabbage), mushrooms, scallions, and onions included in Japanese dishes. These vegetables are also central in Chinese cuisine. Pickled vegetables are common on Japanese menus. Pickling was used as a preservation method before the days of refrigeration.

Similar to many Southeast Asian cuisines, there is little use of dairy products. You don't see milk, cream, yogurt, or cheese. Many claim that is because many Southeast Asians are lactose intolerant, meaning they can't properly digest lactose, the milk sugar.

Nori, wakame, and kombu (also spelled konbu) are foreign-sounding ingredients to Americans but common items in Japanese cooking. All are seaweed. Kombu is used to make dashi, the soup stock, and nori is used to roll and form maki sushi and rice rolls. Many other flavoring agents have a role, such as wasabi and bonito (fish) flakes. The prominent use of seaweed illustrates the constraints of Japan's once limited food supply. Everything possible, including seaweed, was converted to available food.

Minimal seasoning ingredients and simple cooking techniques define Japanese cookery. Dashi, the basic soup stock; shoyu, the Japanese soy sauce; miso, the fermented soybean paste; and mirin, the sweet rice wine, are the mainstay seasoning ingredients. One or more of these are used to flavor soups, teriyaki and sukiyaki sauces, and other dishes. The downside of these sauces is that they are quite high in sodium. If that is your concern, observe the sodium content of the model meals later in the chapter.

In Japan the dinner meal includes rice (of course), a soup, and pickled vegetables. The main dish is frequently fish or shellfish that is broiled, steamed, or dried. All dishes are traditionally presented together. If any item is held back for the end of the meal, it is soup. This contrasts to Japanese meal service in the U.S. Our custom prevails—appetizer first, then soup and salad, followed by rice and the main course(s). Notice: dessert hardly deserves a mention.

Before you order

Japanese foods, preparation, and style of eating make it one of the healthiest cuisines to enjoy when you eat out. It features such carbohydrates as rice, noodles, and vegetables, and it minimizes fat with low-fat cooking methods. Also, small portions are standard. The only drawback is the heavy use of high-sodium flavorings and sauces. With some adaptations, you can savor Japanese food.

The sodium level adds up with the soy-based ingredients. Marinades and sauces, whether for teriyaki, sukiyaki, or shabu-shabu, are mixtures of shoyu, dashi, mirin, sugar, sake, and a bit of kombu. Here are a few strategies to keep tabs on the sodium. If you order a dish like teriyaki, you know that the protein (meat or fish) has been soaked in the high-sodium sauce. However, if you order shabu-shabu, you can control the amount of sauce because the cooking is done table-side and the sauce is on the side.

Choose appetizers that aren't marinated or cooked in high-sodium ingredients. Try a steamed item or sashimi or sushi, then limit dunks in the soy and enjoy the flavor-packed wasabi and pickled ginger. Have a salad rather than soup, and ask for vinegar or lemon wedges. Pour little or no miso dressing. White rice with minimal added salt is the starch of choice in Japanese restaurants. Fresh fruit, a rarity in restaurants, is available. Fruit has next to no sodium.

Japanese food gets the gold star as a cuisine that uses minimal fat. The Japanese use healthy cooking techniques: broiling, grilling, boiling, steaming, braising, or simmering. None of these cooking methods introduces much fat. It's usual to see foods pickled or raw, such as sushi and sashimi. Rarely, with the exception of tempura, katsu, and agemono, are foods fried. Stir-frying is not an Asian cooking technique used in Japanese cooking. Several so-called *nabemonos,* or one-pot meals, might be cooked before your eyes. If so, ask the chef to go light on the sauces. Sukiyaki, yosenabe, and shabu-shabu are all nabemonos. Monitor the menu for the Red Flag Words indicative of added fats.

The only fat you need to end up with is the fat from ingredients. To keep that fat down, order fish, shellfish, or poultry rather than beef or pork. The typical portion, whether it's fish or beef, is usually more in line with healthy guidelines than in a typical American meal. That helps keep the fat, saturated fat, and cholesterol content down, too.

If oil is drizzled at all, it's mainly the non-cholesterol variety—cottonseed, olive, or peanut. A small amount of sesame seed oil might be used for its wonderful nutty flavor. Large amounts of lard and coconut oil are not used in Japanese cooking. However, a bit of lard, for flavor, might be rubbed on a pan before cooking.

Sugar is a regular in Japanese food preparation. That's true for many Southeast Asian cuisines. Sugar is used in sauces and marinades. You also find it in su, the vinegared rice used to make sushi. Su rice is flavored with vinegar, salt, and sugar. You won't know it contains sugar because menus describe it as vinegared rice, and it doesn't taste sweet. For people with diabetes, most sauces and dishes won't contain more than several teaspoons of sugar. You can make an effort to minimize your use of sauce and gravy to keep the empty sugar calories down to a dull roar. Dip lightly and don't spoon in lots of gravy from dishes such as sukiyaki, donburi, or other sauced dishes.

The raw seafood dishes, sushi and sashimi, are gaining popularity in the U.S. They have become "in" foods in some cities and among some age and social groups. Sushi and sashimi have a long heritage in Japanese dining. Freshness is of utmost importance. Creativity in assembling sushi is also an essential detail. The adjective "beautiful" is not an overstatement to describe a well-decorated platter of sushi or sashimi. Sushi and sashimi generally come with vinegared rice (su). The rice is either in, around, or under the fish.

Sushi is served with wasabi, a strong, green-colored horseradish paste, and soy-based dipping sauce. Four basic types of sushi are created. Oshi is pressed sushi rice served with a marinated or boiled piece of seafood. Nigiri is a common variety, in which the vinegared rice is hand-shaped and the fish rests on top. Maki combines sushi rice with fish and other items such as avocado, egg, or vegetables, all rolled into a seaweed-clad cylinder, which is sliced and served. Chirashi sushi is presented with the rice scattered and the seafood served in or on the su rice.

Sashimi is served more simply but with no less attention to freshness and beauty. Sashimi is raw, sliced fish served with wasabi, pickled ginger, and soy sauce. Tuna, salmon, lobster, clams, and bream are often used for sashimi. Calorically speaking, both sushi and sashimi are smart choices. You can order them as appetizers or as main courses. Complement sashimi with a bowl of steamed rice and tossed salad with miso dressing. The result will be a low-fat and low-sodium Japanese meal.

There are health concerns about eating raw fish. Due to the rise in raw fish consumption in the U.S., an increase of fish-borne illness has been observed. One disease that develops from bad raw fish is anisakiasis. It is a parasitic roundworm that lives in larval form in fish, most often in the internal organs. On occasion, the roundworms find their way into the flesh of the fish. If the fish is not cleaned well, refrigerated, and cooked properly, in rare instances it can cause severe stomach pain, nausea, and vomiting. Anisakiasis results from eating infected raw fish because the parasite has not been killed by the heat of cooking. A word to the wise: make sure your raw fish is fresh, your restaurant serves a lot of it, and you feel confident that they handle it carefully.

Menu management

A number of healthy appetizers are on Japanese menus. Firstly, you'll find sushi and sashimi. Other good choices are barbecued, steamed, or pickled foods. Appetizers often have dipping sauce as a partner. That's high in sodium. Avoid the few fried items—tempura, agetofu (fried bean curd), and fried dumplings.

Light and delicate soups are a mainstay. The simple clear broth called suimono has a base of dashi and bits of vegetables or meat. The miso soup, also quite light, has a few vegetables and/or pieces of tofu tossed in. The Japanese udon, or noodle soups, are dashi-based and have a few more calories from the noodles. Su-udon is plain broth with noodles. Other varieties of udon have stir-fried beef, vegetables, or tempura items added. Stick with the su-udon or yaki-udon. Soup is a great, filling start to put a dent in your appetite.

You'll find salads in Japanese restaurants, either tossed greens, tofu, or seafood. In Japan salads are called *sunomono* or *aemono*. They are vinegared or otherwise dressed vegetables and seafoods served in small quantities in elegant little bowls. The dressing is miso, a combination of the regular Japanese seasonings.

The majority of Japanese entrees are low in fat and potentially low in saturated fat and cholesterol if you choose wisely. Several styles of food preparation are usually stated on the menu. You can have different protein foods prepared in different ways. For example, you can order chicken, beef, or salmon prepared teriyaki style. Or you can have these foods as nabemonos, the one-pot meals. Sukiyaki, yosenabi, and shabu-shabu are members of the nabemono group. Nabemonos keep you more in line with Skill 7, eating according to the Food Guide Pyramid, than, say, teriyaki. Nabemonos go heavy on vegetables and light on protein. The technique of sharing comes in handy. Share a teriyaki and a sukiyaki or yosenabe. That way, you'll have vegetables plus the great taste of two dishes.

Donburi is a rice dish topped with broiled or fried meat, fish, or poultry plus eggs and soy sauce. Obviously, donburi is best topped with broiled items rather than breaded and fried ones. Donburi, due to the whole eggs, should be avoided by cholesterol watchers, or simply request that the egg be left off.

Rice, a short-grain variety, is the staple automatically served with most dishes. It's starchier and stickier than the Chinese long-grain rice. It's served plain and blends well with all the Japanese sauces and flavors. Noodles are another starch, but not as predominant as rice. Either udon (wheat noodles) or soba (buckwheat noodles) are served. Udon noodles are found in the udon soups. Both types of noodles are great—lots of carbos and no fats. Just for variety you might want to try either udon or soba noodles instead of rice.

Dessert in Japan is typically fresh fruit. You'll see a short list of desserts: fresh fruit, ice cream, and maybe yo kan, a sweet bean cake. It's unusual to find fresh fruit at restaurants, so take advantage of this opportunity in Japanese places. Green tea and sake are the national beverages of Japan. Tea is sipped plain, with no sugar, lemon, or milk. Tea is held in such high esteem in Japan that it has its own ceremony, called *kaiseki,* which is an important ritual. Sake is a fermented beverage, fragrant and colorless. It contains a bit higher alcohol content than most wines, 15–17 percent. Sake is more often sipped warm than cold. It is served in a small bottle, *tokkuri,* and poured into individual cups, *sakazuki.*

Green Flag Words

INGREDIENTS:
clear broth
vinegared, seasoned, or su rice
    (vinegar, salt, and sugar added)
vinegar sauce*
soy sauce*
teriyaki sauce*
miso dressing*
dipping sauce*
udon noodles
seafood
chicken

COOKING METHODS/MENU
DESCRIPTIONS:
steamed (mushimono)
sauteed
nabemono (one-pot meal)
braised
simmered (nimono)
marinated
pickled
broiled (yaki)
barbecued
grilled (yakimono)
on skewers
boiled
served in broth*
with vegetables
salads

INGREDIENTS:
fried bean curd

COOKING METHODS/MENU
DESCRIPTIONS:
deep-fried, battered and fried,
    breaded and fried
tempura
agemono
katsu
pan-fried

AT THE TABLE:
soy sauce*

**Red Flag
Words**

*high in sodium

Special Requests Japanese Style

Could you serve the salad with the dressing on the side?

I'm carefully watching my salt intake; can you use less sauce in preparing this dish?

Could you substitute shrimp, scallops, or chicken for the beef in this dish?

Could you leave the egg out of the sukiyaki (or donburi)?

I couldn't finish all this; may I get it wrapped up to take home?

The Menu: Japanese Style

Sashimi and Sushi*

✓**Sashimi, tuna** (fillet of fresh raw tuna)

✓**Sashimi, salmon** (fillet of fresh raw salmon)

✓**Sashimi, combination** (fillet of fresh raw seafood, tuna, salmon, and lobster)

✓**Chirashi sushi** (fresh raw seafood served on seasoned rice)

✓**Maki sushi** (fresh raw tuna and vinegared rice rolled in seaweed)

✓**Sushi combination** (3 nigiri and 3 maki sushi)

*Served with soy sauce, wasabi, and pickled ginger

Appetizers

✓**Yutofu** (hot bean curd boiled with napa, served with special sauce)

✓**Ebi-su** (shrimp in vinegar sauce)

✓**Shumai** (steamed shrimp dumplings wrapped in thin noodle skin)

Tempura appetizer (shrimp and vegetables dipped in batter and lightly fried)

✓**Yakitori** (two skewers of chicken broiled with teriyaki sauce)

Agedashi tofu (fried tofu in tempura sauce)

✓**Oshinko** (Japanese pickled vegetables)

✓**Ohitashi** (fresh spinach boiled and served with soy sauce)

✓*Preferred Choice*
Some depending on special requests

Soups	✓**Suimono** (clear broth soup)
	✓**Miso** (soy bean paste soup with tofu and scallions)
	✓**Su-udon** (plain Japanese noodle soup)
	Tempura-udon (Japanese noodle soup with tempura)
	✓**Yaki-udon** (Japanese noodle soup with stir-fried vegetables)
Salads	✓**Tossed salad** served with miso dressing
	✓**Tofu salad** served with miso dressing
	✓**Seafood sunomono** (seafood with cucumber, seaweed, and shredded garnish with vinegar sauce)
Entrees†	**Tempura** (lightly battered and fried; served with tempura dipping sauce)
	Shrimp
	Vegetable
	Combination shrimp and vegetable
	Teriyaki (broiled and served with teriyaki sauce)
	✓Chicken
	✓Beef
	✓Salmon
	✓Seafood combination
	Agemono (battered in breadcrumbs and deep-fried)
	Tonkatsu (pork cutlet)
	Chicken katsu
	Shrimp
	Nabemono (one-pot cooked dinners)
	✓Sukiyaki, chicken (sliced chicken, tofu, bamboo shoots, and vegetables simmered in sukiyaki sauce)

✓Sukiyaki, beef (thinly sliced
    beef, tofu, bamboo shoots,
    and vegetables simmered in
    sukiyaki sauce)
✓Yosenabe (noodles, seafood,
    and vegetables simmered in
    a special broth)
✓**Shabu-shabu** (sliced beef and
vegetables with noodles cooked
and served at the table, with
dipping sauces)
Donburi (served on a bed of rice
with special sauce)
    ✓Oyako (sauteed chicken, egg,
        and onion)
    Katsu (deep-fried breaded
        pork, egg, onion)
    ✓Unagi (broiled eel)

†Entrees served à la carte with steamed white rice or soba
noodles.

Desserts   ✓**Fresh fruit**
            Ice cream, ginger or vanilla
            Yo kan (sweet bean cake)

Now that you've seen what might be available on the
Menu, find the Model Meal that best fits your nutrition
goals. For an explanation of the Model Meals and their
targeted nutritional values, see Chapter 3.

Your Order, Please

Healthy	30%	Calories as fat
Daily	20%	Calories as protein
Eating	50%	Calories as carbohydrate
Goals	300	mg/day Cholesterol
	3000	mg/day Sodium

Low Calorie/ **Sashimi, tuna**
Low Fat *Quantity:* 1 serving
Model Meal *Exchanges:* 3 meat (lean)
Dipping sauce for above
Quantity: 2 tbsp
Exchanges: free
Yaki-udon soup
Quantity: 1 cup
Exchanges: 1 fat; 1 vegetable;
1 starch
Steamed rice
Quantity: 1 cup
Exchanges: 3 starch
Tofu salad (dressing on the side)
Quantity: 1–2 cups
Exchanges: ½ meat (lean); 1–2
vegetables
Miso dressing for above (on the
side)
Quantity: 2 tbsp
Exchanges: free

Estimated	calories 528
Nutrient	fat 9g (16% of calories)
Evaluation	protein 40g (30% of calories)
	carbohydrate 71g (54% of calories)
	cholesterol 76 mg
	sodium 1490 mg

Low Calorie/ Low Cholesterol Model Meal

Shumai
Quantity: 1 order
Yakitori
Quantity: 2 skewers
Miso soup
Quantity: 1 cup
Steamed rice
Quantity: 1 cup
Tossed salad (dressing on the side)
Quantity: 1–2 cups
Miso dressing for above (on the side)
Quantity: 1–2 tbsp

Estimated Nutrient Evaluation

calories 434
fat 4g (9% of calories)
protein 34g (31% of calories)
carbohydrate 65g (60% of calories)
cholesterol 106 mg
sodium 1850 mg (lower by using vinegar or lemon wedges on salad)

Higher Calorie/Low Fat Model Meal

Ohitashi
Quantity: 1 order
Exchanges: 1 vegetable
Siumono soup
Quantity: 1 cup
Exchanges: 1 vegetable
Teriyaki, salmon (split order)
Quantity: 4 oz
Exchanges: 4 meat (lean)
Donburi, oyako (split order)
Quantity: 1½ cups
Exchanges: 1 meat (medium); 3 starch

Steamed rice
Quantity: ⅔ cup
Exchanges: 2 starch
Fresh fruit
Quantity: 1 small piece
Exchanges: 1 fruit

Estimated Nutrient Evaluation	calories 719 fat 18g (23% of calories) protein 54g (30% of calories) carbohydrate 84g (47% of calories) cholesterol 251 mg (mainly from egg in Donburi) sodium 1700 mg

Higher Calorie/Low Cholesterol Model Meal	**Yutofu** *Quantity:* 1 order **Su-udon soup** *Quantity:* 1 cup **Sukiyaki, beef** (split order— request no egg) *Quantity:* 1½ cups **Yosenabe** (split order) *Quantity:* 1½ cups **Steamed rice** *Quantity:* 1 cup **Sake** *Quantity:* 4 oz

Estimated Nutrient Evaluation	calories 913 fat 26g (26% of calories) protein 55g (24% of calories) carbohydrate 87g (38% of calories) alcohol 12% of calories cholesterol 106 mg sodium 2050 mg (to lower, avoid soup and limit sauce on entrees)

Low Sodium   **Sushi combination**
Model Meal   *Quantity:* 1 order
                 Tossed salad (request vinegar or
                    lemon wedges)
                 Quantity: 1–2 cups
                 Shabu-shabu (use minimal
                    dipping sauce)
                 Quantity: 1½ cups
                 Soba noodles
                 Quantity: 1½ cups

Estimated   calories 672
Nutrient   fat 19g (25% of calories)
Evaluation protein 45g (27% of calories)
            carbohydrate 81g (48% of calories)
            cholesterol 147 mg
            sodium 870 mg

Seasonings, spices, and terms of Japanese cuisine

Bonito–a fish important in Japanese cuisine, a member of the mackeral family; bonito flakes are an important ingredient in the basic stock called dashi.

Daikon–giant white radish; grated daikon is mixed into tempura sauces.

Dashi–an important element in Japanese cooking, dashi is the basic stock made with water, kombu (seaweed), and bonito flakes.

Gyuniku–beef.

Kombu–a Japanese seaweed central to the basic stock, dashi; also used in sauces and as a wrapper for certain dishes.

Mirin–Japanese rice wine, which is used more in sauces than consumed as a beverage; a central ingredient to the sauces and flavors of Japanese cuisine.

Miso–a fermented soy bean paste that comes in various types, thicknesses, and degrees of saltiness; used in soups, sauces, and dressing—a basic ingredient in Japanese cooking.

Nabemeno–one-pot meals.

Nori–a seaweed often toasted prior to using; has a strong flavor and is used to wrap maki sushi.

Sake–fermented rice wine, sake is the national alcoholic beverage of Japan, most often served warm; it is also used as an ingredient in sauces.

Shitake mushrooms–an abundant mushroom in Japanese cookery, it has a woody and fruity flavor; used fresh or dried.

Shoyu–Japanese soy sauce, with light or dark varieties used; it is made from soy beans, wheat, and salt and is an essential ingredient in Japanese cooking.

Teriyaki sauce–sauce used to broil; made from shoyu and mirin, it means "shining broil."

Tofu–soy bean curd, a major source of protein in the Japanese diet; used in soups, salads, and entrees.

Ton–pork.

Tori–chicken.

Vinegar–in Japan, made from rice and lighter and sweeter than the vinegar Americans are used to.

Wakame–a seaweed used for its flavor and texture; available dried.

Wasabi–grated horseradish that is fragrant and less sharp in taste; one of the strongest spices used in Japanese cooking, it is commonly served with raw fish.

Yaki–broiled.

10

Healthier eating out
Indian Style

Raita, tikka, papadum, and biryani are terms that represent just a sampling of taste sensations in Asian Indian restaurants. Certainly not the familiar ring of burger, fries, and Coke. The first challenge to enjoying healthy Indian cuisine is acquiring the food language. Beyond the new world of food names, you'll find menu listings spelled differently on different Indian menus by one or several letters. It may be "vandaloo" or "vindaloo," "samosa" or "samoosa." An Indian menu can, to say the least, be confusing. To get up to speed, we'll tell you about unique ingredients and seasonings, cooking methods, and menu offerings. In no time, you'll be a pro at picking and choosing the healthiest items from an Indian menu.

Get to know the cuisine

One simply has to look at India's location on a map for clues about the tastes of Indian cuisine. Though Indian food has unique qualities and cooking techniques, it resembles the cuisine of its neighbors Pakistan, Sri Lanka, Thailand, Burma, and, to a lesser degree, the more distant China. To Americans, Indian spices and ingredients seem similar to Thai food. The hot and tasty spices used in curries are regulars in both countries. Rice is also a prominent feature of both cuisines. Basmati rice is the variety of choice in Indian restaurants. This long-grained, aromatic rice is unique to India and is of premium quality.

India contains Himalayan mountains and major rivers such as the Indus and Ganges. Various religions are practiced. Hinduism, Islam, and Buddhism are the three most common. Food practices reflect the geography and a region's predominant religion. For example, vegetarianism is often practiced by Buddhists; pork products are avoided by Moslems. In fact, very few pork products are used in Indian cooking. Hindus do not eat beef due to their belief in the sanctity of the cow.

Beyond religious mandates, the foods native to different regions of India also vary. Northern Indian food is not as hot as southern cuisine, which makes use of chilies and peppers. The North uses more wheat products, teas, and eggs, whereas the South features more rice, vegetables, and coffee. More seafood is consumed in the South, proximal to the sea. Expect to find hot pickles and chutneys served in the South. Yogurt is a common ingredient in both northern and southern cookery.

The food served in Indian restaurants in America bends toward northern regional cuisine and includes many foods you simply expect to find on Indian menus: the appetizers samosa and pakora; entrees such as chicken vandaloo and vegetable curry; and the accompaniments mango chutney and raita. If you ate Indian food in a traditional Indian household, it would be hotter and spicier. There has been some ''cooling down'' for the American palate. As with many ethnic cuisines, Indian food is influenced by the

American taste bud and style of eating—it has been Americanized.

Indian restaurants are growing in number and popularity in the U.S. Not surprisingly, this correlates with the growing Indian population within our borders. A small influx of Indians immigrated in the early 1900s, and a second wave came in the 1960s and 1970s. Asian Indians, like people of many cultures, found America a great country for education and personal growth. In the last 20 years a large influx of Indians emigrated from rural India, whereas earlier immigrants came from the cities. Indians now make their homes in American cities from California to Massachusetts. Like many newer and less well-known ethnic cuisines, it's more common to spot Indian restaurants in large urban centers.

Common cooking methods are stewing, frying, and roasting tandoori style. It's usual to fry appetizers and breads and to stew main dishes such as masalas and bhunas. A limited amount of food preparation is done in the oven since many of these cooking techniques evolved before ovens existed. The tandoor, still in use today to prepare tandoori style, is a clay oven that uses charcoal.

There is a morning meal and afternoon tea. The evening meal in an Indian household is eaten between 7:00 and 9:00 p.m. At the evening meal a rice dish and a curry entree made either with vegetables, legumes, meat, or seafood are served. Breads such as poori or chapati are always part of the main meal, along with some accompaniments, perhaps raita, dahl, and pickles. Fruits may follow the meal. There is little emphasis on sweet desserts.

The main meal is served family style. Small bowls containing curry dishes, raita, chutneys, and others are placed on the *thali,* a large metal platter. The breads and the small bowls on the thali are put in the middle of a low table, and everyone takes their portion. Each person has their own bowl of rice, just like Chinese style. Eating with fingers of the right hand is acceptable, and bread is used somewhat like a scoop.

Some Indian restaurants let you place one order for a family-style meal called *thali.* The meal comes with several dishes, rice, choices of breads, raita, and papadum. This is a good way to order with a group. You get to taste lots of foods in small portions. Be aware of the contents, however. Make sure you have a choice of bread and can select the much lower-fat chapati rather than the high-fat poori. Ask the waiter to hold the butter, which is often applied to bread in the kitchen.

It is more common for Indian restaurant to serve American style. You can order a complete dinner or à la carte. You are better off ordering à la carte to decrease the quantity of food you eat. Soup comes first and appetizers follow. Next the breads, rice, and entrees. Typical of Americanization of a foreign cuisine, there is major focus on the entree choice—will it be chicken, lamb, or seafood? Sharing several dishes family style is the optimal ordering strategy.

Vegetables and legumes play an important role in Indian cooking, so it is easy to minimize the protein content of your meal. The tradition of bringing several bowls of accompaniments to the table is commonplace. You'll see hot and spicy onion relish, chutney, and dahl delivered to your table without request. Mango chutney and raita might also arrive.

Charmaine Solomon, author of *The Complete Asian Cookbook,* defines spices as the "soul" of Indian cooking. What we know as curry, a single spice available in the U.S., is unknown in Indian cooking. Actually, curry means "sauce." The main dishes in Indian cooking use a variety of spices to provide what we call the curry flavor. A garam masala, or fragrant mix of ground spices combined in varying quantities, produces the wonderful tastes of Indian cuisine. Some spices in the garam masala are cardamom, coriander, cumin, cloves, and cinnamon. Several are called "fragrant" spices. In southern regional fare you'll find peppers and chilies added to raise the "heat." Mint, garlic, ginger, yogurt, and coconut milk are other common ingredients. (See "The Spices, Seasonings, and Ingredients of Indian Cuisine" at the end of the chapter.)

Another distinctive item at Indian meals is basmati rice. You'll find rice on an Indian menu listed as pullao, or pilau. Plain pullao is served along with the main dish, although peas pullao or pullao with paneer (cheese), peas, and nuts are offered in the rice column. Basmati rice is the main ingredient in biryani. This is a rice dish that also contains a choice of chicken, beef, or shrimp with vegetables and dried fruits. It's a good choice because it's low in protein and high in carbohydrates.

Before you order

As with most ethnic cuisines, there are pros and cons to Indian cuisine. If you have some basic facts, read the menu descriptions carefully, and ask questions as necessary, you'll navigate around an Indian menu just fine. Indian food is healthy if you work to keep fat down, protein low, and push complex carbohydrates.

The pros of Indian food include an accent on carbohydrates and deemphasis of protein. Basmati rice is a staple of Indian cuisine. Bread is an important component, but watch out for the fried varieties. Legumes, good sources of soluble fiber and non-animal protein, include lentils and chickpeas and are often found in main dishes or accompaniments such as dahl. Remember, soluble fibers lower blood cholesterol and triglycerides. Vegetables are found in most entrees—curry dishes, biryani, and pullao. Common vegetables are spinach, eggplant, potatoes, and peas. Onions, green peppers, and tomatoes are found in stewed entrees. Yogurt is an ingredient used in sauces.

Another pro that helps you keep calories and fat low is the availability of chicken and seafood. Beef and lamb dishes are found on the menu but can easily be detoured around. Dishes with pork are rarely found on Indian menus. Small quantities of protein are usually used, relating back to their minimal availability in times past. If you share a chicken or shrimp masala and complement that with bengan bharta (tandoori-roasted eggplant), neither of you will eat much more than two to three ounces of protein. That's about right. Then order a biryani or pullao to further boost the carbos. These practices keep the protein, fat, and cholesterol low.

Like most cuisines, fat is lurking in many crevices. Fat finds its way into Indian foods by way of cooking methods. Ghee, clarified butter, is a common ingredient. Frying and sauteing vegetables for stews are usual cooking methods. For example, appetizers such as samosa and pakora are fried. Many breads, such as paratha and poori, are fried or layered with butter.

The first step in cooking many Indian dishes is to saute onions and other ingredients in oil or ghee. Oils cooked with are sesame and coconut oil. Sesame is mainly a polyunsaturated fat. However, coconut oil is the most saturated fat known. It is difficult to determine exactly which oil or combination of oils is used in most Indian restaurants. Coconut milk is used much less frequently than in Thai cuisine. Coconut milk adds calories, fat, and saturated fat. Look for the words coconut milk, coconut cream, or simply shredded coconut as part of menu descriptions.

Keep sodium within bounds by careful menu navigation. Avoid the soups, which are high in sodium. Entrees have small amounts of salt added, but if you keep portions small, you'll end up consuming minimal sodium. Obviously, there are different recipes and varying quantities of salt used in cooking.

Many items are prepared to order. Request that no salt be added to your dishes. This is similar to requesting no MSG in a Chinese restaurant. That request is met with ease. Though salt is used in many Indian recipes as a flavor enhancer, Indian food does not depend on it. Other frequently used spices are sodium-free, so you can get lots of taste and next to no sodium. Due to the spiciness and highly seasoned quality of Indian foods, you don't need salt at the table. Actually, it's uncommon to find a salt shaker in an Indian restaurant.

Menu management

A healthy appetizer is a rarity. Most are deep-fried: samosas, turnovers stuffed with peas and potatoes, then fried; cheese, chicken, or vegetable pakoras, all fried; and fried shrimp with poori. One item doubling as an appetizer and bread is papadum, a thin wafer made from spicy lentils. It is baked and quite light—the best of the appetizer choices. If you have calories to spare, sample one appetizer. Share it with your dining partner. If you're with a group and you order several appetizers or a combination plate, decide what's healthiest and take one piece or half each of two pieces.

Two soups that you may order as a nice opener and filler are mulligatawny and lentil soup. They are both seasoned with Indian spices and quite tasty. They are mainly carbohydrates, low in fat and calories. Creamy soups such as poppyseed and coconut should be avoided.

Ordering bread can present some difficulties, but there are several healthy choices. Papadum, also seen abbreviated as "papad," is the crisp baked lentil wafer. Chapati is a flat disc of unleavened bread resembling pita bread. Nan is a leavened bread made with white flour. Two more are kulcha, a baked bread stuffed with vegetables, and roti, a bread made with whole-wheat flour and baked. Poori, a light, puffed, fried bread, and the varieties of paratha, a multi-layered bread with butter, should be left alone for obvious reasons.

Moving onto the entrees, you'll find that similar cooking styles are used for chicken, fish, shrimp, beef, and lamb dishes. To keep total fat, saturated fat, and calories on the decline, stick with fish, chicken, or shrimp and order these cooking preparations: masala, a combination of Indian spices with sauteed tomatoes and onions; bhuna, another style similar to masala; saag, which has spinach and spices; and vandaloo, a mixture of Indian spices with potatoes. Preparations done in the clay oven are called tandoori and tikka. They are healthy, too. Steer away from the malai and korma dishes, which are creamy.

In most restaurants you'll get plain pullao (basmati rice) without asking. If you want a more elaborate rice dish, order biryani. Biryanis are listed under rice dishes but work well as an entree to stack the carbohydrates. They are made with chicken, lamb, beef, shrimp, or just vegetables. A chicken masala, for instance, nicely complements a shrimp biryani. That way, you keep the protein and fat content down.

Vegetable dishes can be a main course. From a nutritional standpoint, that's great. Vegetable dishes pile on a variety of chickpeas, lentils, potatoes, spinach, cauliflower, onions, and/or tomatoes. Often they are in curry or cheese (paneer) sauces. Paneer, what we refer to as cheese in Indian food, is not like cheese in America. Paneer is made from milk and lemon juice. The milk is curdled by the lemon juice to create the thick "cheese."

A fun and unique part of Indian cuisine are the accompaniments and condiments. Raita, a combination of plain yogurt, cucumbers, and onions (though it can also contain tomatoes or fruit) is quite healthy. Its role is actually to cool the mouth from hot curry tastes. Dahl is the low-fat, spicy, lentil-based side sauce that is served warm. Onion chutney, sometimes called relish, might arrive without request. It is quite low in calories and adds zip. Mango chutney is very popular in U.S. Indian restaurants. It is quite sweet and contains small pieces of mango and sugar. Other chutneys such as mint and tamarind are regulars. Pickles are another frequent accompaniment. They are prepared with a variety of low-calorie ingredients and hot spices. Accompaniments are eaten in very small quantities and most are quite low in fat, so let them be an added treat when eating Indian.

Desserts are deemphasized in India and can remain that way when you eat Indian cuisine. You'll find koulfi, a rich ice cream with nuts, and several custards and puddings, kheers. It's best to skip dessert or order one for the table.

You'll find a few low-calorie to no-calorie beverages on the menu. Low-calorie soda, water, coffee, and tea are regulars. Darjeeling, an Indian tea, is nice to sip for a different flavor. A unique non-alcoholic beverage is lassi. It is a sweet drink made with yogurt and rosewater, usually available plain or blended with mango. It's a healthy choice for a sweet dessert if others are indulging. Several Indian beers are usually offered, Kingfisher and Golden Eagle, as well as beers and wines from around the world.

It's easy to choose a healthy meal in an Indian restaurant. Simply watch out for the fats, fried foods, and overeating. Menus usually give you a brief description of the offerings. If you don't have enough information, ask questions. Portion control is not difficult because the size of most dishes is small, and you can eat family style. Don't over-order, and don't gorge on the basmati rice or the several accompaniments delivered without even saying ''I'll have. . . .''

Green Flag Words

INGREDIENTS:
skinless chicken
shrimp
baked leavened bread
papadum
vegetables
lentils and chickpeas
potatoes
matta (peas)
Indian spices—curry, garam
    masala
basmati rice (pullao)

COOKING METHODS/MENU
DESCRIPTIONS:
tikka
tandoori
cooked with or marinated in
    yogurt

cooked with onions, tomatoes,
　spinach, peppers, potatoes, or
　peas
masala
paneer
marinated or cooked in Indian
　spices
Indian hot spices
garnished with dried fruits
chutneys—mango, mint, etc.
pickles
raita
dahl (lentils)
kebabs

INGREDIENTS:
ghee
nuts—almonds, pistachios, etc.
molee (coconut)
coconut milk

**Red Flag
Words**

COOKING METHODS/MENU
DESCRIPTIONS:
fritters
fried, deep-fried
dipped in batter, chickpea batter
korma (cream sauce)
stuffed and fried
creamy curry sauce

**Special
Requests
Indian
Style**

Please bring my soup when you bring the appetizers for the others.

Please bring my salad when the others have their appetizers.

Please bring the accompaniments raita, dahl, and onion chutney.

If a special rice is ordered, request that the plain pullao not be brought.

My order will be à la carte, not a complete dinner.

Please don't garnish with nuts.

Is it possible to prepare my dish without adding any salt?

Please don't use extra salt in the preparation.

I'll have a cup of Darjeeling tea with my meal.

We'd like an extra plate so we can split/share these dishes.

The Menu: Indian Style

Appetizers   **Cheese pakoras** (homemade cheese deep-fried in chick pea batter)
Samosa (vegetable turnover, stuffed and fried)
Fried shrimp with poori (shrimp with onions and peppers fried with spices)
✓**Papadum** (also seen as papad) (crispy, thin lentil wafers)
Chicken pakoras (chunks of boneless chicken marinated in spicy sauce, then fried)
Shami kebab (ground meat patty, fried)

Soups   ✓**Mulligatawny** (lentil, vegetables, and spices)
Coconut soup (coconut cream and pistachio nuts)
Poppy seed soup (almond, poppy seed, milk, and coconut cream)
✓**Dahl rasam** (pepper soup with lentils)

Breads (Roti)   **Paratha** (shallow-fried multi-layered bread made with butter)
Poori (light, puffed fried bread)
✓**Chapati** (thin, dry whole-wheat bread)
Aloo paratha (paratha stuffed with potatoes, made with butter)
✓**Nan** (leavened baked bread topped with poppy seeds)
✓**Kulcha** (leavened baked bread)

✓*Preferred Choice*
Some depending on special requests

Chicken (Murgi)	✓**Chicken tandoori** (marinated in spices and roasted in a tandoor, or clay oven)
	✓**Chicken tikka** (roasted in charcoal oven with mild spices)
	✓**Chicken saag** (boneless chicken cooked with spinach)
	✓**Chicken vandaloo** (boneless chicken cooked with potatoes and hot spices)
	Chicken kandhari (chicken cooked with cream sauce and cashews)
	✓**Chicken masala** (roasted chicken cooked in spices and thick curry sauce)
Shrimp/ Fish	**Shrimp malai** (cooked with cream, mushrooms, and coconut)
	✓**Shrimp bhuna** (cooked with green vegetables, onions, and tomatoes)
	✓**Fish masala** (boneless fish marinated in a spicy yogurt sauce)
	✓**Shrimp curry** (cooked in a thick curry sauce)
	✓**Fish vandaloo** (boneless fish cooked with potatoes and hot spices)
Beef/Lamb	✓**Lamb bhuna** (pan roasted with spices, onions, and tomatoes)
	✓**Lamb saag** (cooked with spinach in a spicy curry sauce)
	✓**Beef vandaloo** (beef curry cooked with potatoes and hot spices)
	✓**Kheema matter** (minced lamb and peas cooked with fresh herbs)
	Beef korma (beef curry cooked with cream)

Rice (Pullao)	✓**Shrimp biryani** (shrimp cooked with basmati rice and garnished with dried fruits)
	✓**Vegetable biryani** (basmati rice cooked with green vegetables and garnished with dried fruits)
	✓**Plain pullao** (basmati rice cooked with saffron)
	✓**Peas pullao** (basmati rice cooked with peas)
	✓**Shrimp pullao** (shrimp cooked with basmati rice)
Vegetables	✓**Vegetable curry** (green peas, tomatoes, and cauliflower)
	Vegetable korma (mixed vegetables cooked with cream, herbs, and cashews)
	✓**Saag paneer** (spinach cooked with homemade cheese)
	✓**Matter paneer** (homemade cheese and green peas curry)
	✓**Aloo chole** (chick peas cooked with tomatoes and potatoes)
Accompaniments	✓**Raita** (rayta) (yogurt with grated cucumbers, onions, and spices)
	✓**Mango chutney**
	✓**Mint chutney**
	✓**Onion chutney** (diced onions with hot spices)
	✓**Tamarind sauce**
	✓**Dahl** (lentil sauce)
	✓**Tamata salat** (diced tomatoes and onions with hot spices and lemon)
Desserts	**Koulfi** (rich ice cream with almonds and pistachios)
	Mango koulfi
	Gulab jamun (fried milk balls soaked in sugar syrup, served warm)

Ras malai (homemade cheese in sweetened milk)

Now that you've seen what might be available on the Menu, find the Model Meal that best fits your nutrition goals. For an explanation of the Model Meals and their targeted nutritional values, see Chapter 3.

Your Order, Please

Healthy	30%	Calories as fat
Daily	20%	Calories as protein
Eating	50%	Calories as carbohydrate
Goals	300	mg/day Cholesterol
	3000	mg/day Sodium

❶

Low Calorie/ **Nan**
Low Fat *Quantity:* ¼ loaf
Model Meal *Exchanges:* 1 fat; 1 starch
Shrimp biryani
Quantity: 1½ cups
Exchanges: 2 meat; 1 fat; 1 vegetable; 2 starch
Raita
Quantity: 3 tbsp
Exchanges: ½ vegetable
Onion chutney
Quantity: 2 tbsp
Exchanges: ½ vegetable
Tamata salat
Quantity: ½ cup
Exchanges: 1 vegetable
Darjeeling tea
Quantity: 2 cups
Exchanges: free

Estimated   calories 480
Nutrient   Fat 13g (25% of calories)
Evaluation   protein 29g (25% of calories)
              carbohydrate 60g (50% of calories)
              cholesterol 128 mg
              sodium 950 mg

Low Calorie/ Dahl rasam soup
Low *Quantity:* 1 cup
Cholesterol **Fish masala**
Model Meal *Quantity:* 1½ cups
Plain pullao
Quantity: 1 cup
Raita
Quantity: 3 tbsp
Mango chutney
Quantity: 2 tbsp
Pickle
Quantity: 1 tbsp

Estimated   calories 540
Nutrient   fat 14g (23% of calories)
Evaluation   protein 30g (22% of calories)
             carbohydrate 74g (55% of calories)
             cholesterol 60 mg
             sodium 1400 mg

Higher **Samosa**
Calorie/Low *Quantity:* 1 piece
Fat Model *Exchanges:* 2 fat; 1 starch
Meal **Chicken tandoori**
Quantity: 4 oz (split order)
Exchanges: 4 meat (lean); 1 fat
Peas pullao
Quantity: 1½ cups
Exchanges: 3 starch
Saag paneer
Quantity: 1 cup
Exchanges: 1 fat; 2 vegetable;
   ½ milk
Mint Chutney
Quantity: 2 tbsp
Exchanges: free

Dahl
Quantity: 3 tbsp
Exchanges: ½ starch

Estimated Nutrient Evaluation	calories 852 fat 36g (38% of calories) protein 49g (23% of calories) carbohydrate 83g (39% of calories) cholesterol 93 mg sodium 1700 mg

Higher Calorie/Low Cholesterol Model Meal

Papadum
Quantity: 1 slice
Lamb Bhuna
Quantity: 1½ cups
Plain pullao
Quantity: 1 cup
Vegetable curry
Quantity: 1 cup
Tamata salat
Quantity: ½ cup
Mango chutney
Quantity: 3 tbsp
White wine
Quantity: 6 oz

Estimated Nutrient Evaluation	calories 949 fat 33g (31% of calories) protein 40g (17% of calories) carbohydrate 93g (39% of calories) alcohol 13% of calories cholesterol 102 mg sodium 1200 mg

Low Sodium Model Meal

Samosa
Quantity: 1 piece
Chicken tikka
Quantity: 4 oz
Plain pullao
Quantity: 1 cup
Aloo chole
Quantity: ¾ cup
Raita
Quantity: 3 tbsp
Mango chutney
Quantity: 3 tbsp
Singha beer
Quantity: 12 oz

Estimated Nutrient Evaluation

calories 890
fat 32g (32% of calories)
protein 42g (19% of calories)
carbohydrate 85g (38% of calories)
alcohol 11% of calories
cholesterol 80 mg
sodium 900 mg

The spices, seasonings, and ingredients of Indian cuisine

Bombay duck–this term does not describe a bird but rather fish served sauteed, fried, or dried, along with curries and rice; not often seen in U.S.

Cardamom–expensive spice native to India, in the ginger family. Either the whole cardamom pod or only seeds are used; one of the most common spices found in garam masalas (curry mixtures).

Cinnamon–delicate spice commonly found in spice combinations used in curries and rarely as the ground spice typically used in the U.S.; stick cinnamon with more intense flavor is used in India.

Clove–another commonly used spice in curries, it is the dried flower bud of an evergreen tropical tree found in Southeast Asia.

Coconut milk–not the liquid found inside the coconut, it is a creamy fluid extracted from the flesh of the coconut.

Coriander–fragrant spice often the main ingredient in curries; either ground coriander or the whole leaf is used.

Cumin–another fragrant spice important to curry dishes; used as either seeds or ground.

Curry–The word means ''sauce,'' and many spices, individually roasted, make up the curry mixture, known as garam masala.

Fennel–another spice used in curries; a member of the cumin family and on occasion referred to as sweet cumin.

Ghee–clarified butter; contains none of the milk solids.

Malai–a thick cream made by separating and collecting the top part of boiled milk; used in entrees for a thick, creamy sauce.

Mint–used to add flavor to curry dishes and also as a main ingredient in mint chutney and mint sambal; used in biryani and as a dipping sauce for appetizers.

Paneer–referred to as homemade cream or cottage cheese and made from milk curdled with lemon juice and strained through cheese cloth. Paneer is used in vegetable and rice dishes. For vegetarians, it is a complete protein source.

Poppy seeds–ground to a powder and used in curry dishes to thicken the gravies.

Rose water–flavoring agent used in Indian desserts; extracted from rose petals by steaming and then diluting the essence.

Saffron–known as the most expensive spice in the world, small quantities are used in Indian cooking. Obtained by drying the stamens of saffron crocus, saffron strands are thread-like and deep orange in color.

Tamarind–used for its acidic quality, it is a fruit from a large tropical tree; a commonly used Indian spice or food.

Turmeric–spice which lends the yellow-orange color to commercial curry. Part of the ginger family and commonly used in Indian cooking.

Yogurt–called *dahl* in India, a common ingredient in Indian cooking; always plain and unflavored.

11

Healthier eating out

Middle Eastern Style

Pita bread, hummus, baba ghanoush, tabouli, and kalamata (olives) are familiar foods to Americans who enjoy Middle Eastern cuisine. These are regulars on Middle Eastern, Armenian, Israeli, and Greek menus. Middle Eastern restaurants are not as plentiful, especially in the heartland of America, as Italian or Chinese dining spots, but the number is rising. Over the last century, more Middle Easterners have emigrated to the U.S.

and, as usual, this pattern results in more Middle Eastern restaurants. Middle Eastern foods and restaurants offer Americans another interesting and potentially healthy cuisine to join our ever-expanding options.

Let's define Middle Eastern cuisine. There are strong similarities among foods native to Greece, Syria, Lebanon, Iran, Iraq, Turkey, Armenia, and Israel. Commonalities also exist among Middle Eastern foods and those indigenous to several North African countries—Morocco, Egypt, Tunisia, Algeria, and Libya. Individual qualities shine through, but there are more similarities than differences. You'll see differences in the spelling of Middle Eastern foods on restaurant menus. For instance, hummus, the chickpea and tahini spread, is also spelled ''homos,'' ''hummos,'' and ''hoomis.'' Pronunciation of words also varies with accents falling on different syllables.

Get to know the cuisine

A brief look into the history of the Middle East, one of the oldest civilized areas of the world, reveals reasons why the foods are so similar. As Claudia Roden writes in *A Book of Middle Eastern Food,* ''the history of this food is that of the Middle East.'' There were times when Greeks and Romans ruled the area. Then the Middle East was long dominated by Turkish rule. Early in the nineteenth century, France and Britain had their stint at controlling parts of the Middle East. Today, most Middle Eastern countries are independent.

The Middle East has been, and continues to be, a hot bed of political and religious unrest. The search for political stability, education, and economic opportunity are reasons Middle Easterners emigrate to the U.S. Two waves of emigration have occurred. The first was from the late 1800s to the early 1900s, and the second took place after World War II. Immigration of Middle Easterners continues today. It is common to find immigrants in the restaurant business. The result is an increasing number of authentic Middle Eastern restaurants.

Whether the food is called Greek, Israeli, Armenian, Moroccan, or just plain Middle Eastern, these foods are served at a gamut of restaurants. You'll find Middle Eastern restaurants, simple or more upscale, that are dedicated to serving just traditional foods. The items baba ghanoush, lamb shish kebabs, kibbeh, and the very sweet dessert baklava always appear on the menu.

Middle Eastern foods are even found in mall eateries. You'll find places serving gyros or souvlaki wrapped in pita bread with lettuce, tomatoes, and onions and topped with tzateki sauce. Or you might see fast-food stops serving the Middle Eastern regulars falafel, fattoush (salad), or tabouli. Middle Eastern foods are now integrated into "American" restaurants in the form of pita bread sandwiches, gyros, Greek salads with feta cheese, kalamata olives, and rice pilaf.

As usual, the foods that play a predominant role in Middle Eastern cooking are those naturally plentiful in that region. Wheat, grains, legumes, olives, dates, figs, lamb, and eggplant are a few central ingredients. Rice, combined with several ingredients to make rice pilaf, is served in Greece and the Middle East. Whereas couscous, made with cracked wheat, is more indigenous to North African countries. Tabouli, the cracked wheat or bulghur salad with raw tomatoes and onions, is most familiar in Lebanon, though it's served throughout the Middle East.

Pita, or pocket, bread, as it's called in America, is well integrated into American culture. Pita is a flat, round bread only slightly leavened. Due to the very hot oven in which it is cooked, steam is created. This results in a hollow center, a "pocket," which makes it perfect for stuffing. It also lends itself to rolling. In American sandwich spots you might find hummus with grilled vegetables or tuna salad spread into the pita pocket then rolled up for an easy eat. A benefit of pita bread is that it is low in fat and calories. As Ken Haedrich explains in an article titled "Pita Principles" in the *Country Journal,* "Once almost unheard of in this country outside of Middle Eastern enclaves, pita emerged in the eighties as the repository for almost anything edible, from burgers, sprouts, and salad to more traditional Middle Eastern fillings like hummus, tabouli, and kibbeh."

Stuffed dishes are common. The best known are dolmas, stuffed grape leaves, but stuffed cabbage and stuffed eggplant are also regulars. The stuffing can be either a meat or meatless (vegetarian) mixture. Chickpeas, fava beans, and other healthy legumes are used. Chickpeas and fava beans are pureed together to make falafel, or ta'amia. Chickpeas are mashed and mixed with tahini (sesame seed paste) to make the familiar hummus.

Because olives are plentiful, olive oil is the oil of choice. It is used more predominantly in cold dishes.

Olives, both green and black, are also frequent additions. Greek olives are salty because they are soaked in brine. There are several varieties of Greek olives, a common one being kalamata olives.

You'll see little seafood in Middle Eastern cuisine. Other than legumes and grains, lamb is the most familiar protein. Beef is also served but to a lesser degree than lamb. Eggs are incorporated into soups such as avgolemono, egg and lemon sauce, pasta dishes, and spinach and cheese pie (spanikopita).

Milk is not drunk in the Middle East due in part to the high incidence of lactose intolerance. Yogurt is frequently used, served plain as a side dish or mixed with garlic, mint, and salt. You'll see yogurt in dressings for salads, in soups, or as a sauce base, such as tzateki, the sauce on gyros and souvlaki sandwiches. The role of yogurt, as in Indian cuisine, is to act as a refresher, or soother, from the spiciness. Two cheese, feta and kasseri, are common. They are served alone or incorporated into appetizers, salads, and entrees.

Phyllo (also called filo and fila), which literally means leaf, is the paper-thin Middle Eastern dough. It's used to make spinach and cheese pie and sweet desserts such as baklava. Phyllo dough is made from flour, egg, water, and a bit of oil or butter. However, when phyllo dough is readied for a recipe, the layers are separated and one by one slathered with butter. This technique quickly raises the fat quotient.

Another historical trait common to Middle Eastern cooking is that many dishes are created from few ingredients. The same vegetables, eggplant, onions, and tomatoes, are found in raw vegetable salads, in meatless casseroles, with ground lamb, and stuffed into grape leaves.

The geographic locale also has an impact on ingredients, spices, and flavors of the foods served. Commonly used spices are parsley, mint, cilantro, and oregano. Others include spices that are also mainstays in Indian cooking—cumin, coriander, cinnamon, and ginger. Long ago, the Middle East was a major link on the spice route between the Far East and Europe and Europe and Africa.

Today's cooking methods reflect those passed down through generations. They reflect the absence of modern conveniences such as ranges and refrigerators. It's common to see foods grilled, such as shish kebab; fried, as is falafel; ground as is kibbeh; or stewed such as lamb and vegetable stew with couscous. Marinating is a favorite way to eat vegetables and meat. You'll see pickled vegetables, too, originally a method of food preservation. All of the cooking methods are quite simple.

The main meal in the Middle East is at midday. It is usually a meat stew or meat in a stuffed item, which might contain ground beef and/or lamb, vegetables, and legumes. In addition, there is always a grain, perhaps rice pilaf, couscous, or tabouli, depending on the country; bread, often pita; a salad or raw vegetable combination; and yogurt as a side dish. The meal is concluded simply with a bowl of fresh fruit set on the table, family style. The sweets or pastries are served several hours after the meal, with the familiar strong Greek or Turkish coffee. Baklava, kataif, and rice pudding are common Middle Eastern desserts.

Middle Eastern restaurants, quick-eating spots, and upscale establishments offer a truer rendition of the foods from their homeland than do other ethnic cuisines. So, if you visit the Middle East, you will see similar foods and preparation methods. That is not as true for cuisines such as Chinese or Mexican that have undergone greater "Americanization."

Before you order

Middle Eastern food is a good match with today's healthy eating goals. It's easy to keep the carbos up and the protein and fat down. Vegetables abound, both raw in salads and cooked in tomato-based sauces. Legumes are widely used, adding more healthy carbohydrates. Higher-fat red meats are served more than chicken and fish, but the saving grace is that servings are small. Meats are often combined with grains or vegetables to make the meat stretch farther. That's great because there's less meat, fat, and calories in the dish.

Fats, of course, are your enemy. Fat creeps into Middle Eastern foods in myriad ways. So keep your eye out for these as you peruse the menu. Olives, rich in fat, are indigenous to the Middle East; therefore, olives and olive oil show up in appetizers, salad dressings, salads, marinades, and sauces. The oils used in frying are corn or nut oils. It's important to avoid fried foods such as falafel. Eggplant entrees can be high in fat because eggplant absorbs huge quantities of oil in cooking.

Butter is traditionally used in several recipes, such as spinach and cheese pies, other foods made with phyllo dough, baklava, and kataif. Fat also creeps in from seeds and nuts used in cooking. Tahini, ground sesame seed paste, is basically all fat, the polyunsaturated variety. Tahini is used in hummus and baba ghanoush, and it might turn up in salad dressings and sauces. Pine nuts (pignoli) are in some casserole dishes (sheik el mahshi is an example); and walnuts are in desserts such as baklava. Eggs are found in appetizers, soups, spinach pie, omelets, and thick sauces. Limit the obvious sources if you monitor cholesterol closely.

The sodium content of the Middle Eastern meal doesn't need to skyrocket, especially if you are aware of the real danger foods. Several Middle Eastern regulars that are high in sodium include feta and kasseri cheeses, kalamata olives, and lokaniko (sausage). Salt is consistently used in Middle Eastern cooking but not in huge quantities. In addition, many of the flavorings and spices are very low in sodium, items such as garlic, lemon, dill, parsley, mint, onion, and yogurt.

Menu management

The appetizers, or mezza, as they are called, are traditionally eaten leisurely. Several items are listed as both appetizers and entrees—dolmas, falafel, and spanikopita. Some appetizers are high in fat and best limited—spanikopita, falafel, dolmas, taramosalata, and cheese casserole. Baba ghanoush and hummus contain tahini, which boosts the fat. You'll find appetizers served with pita bread and in small quantities. If you can hold back, small amounts are fine.

The best way to keep fat and calories down is to hop over the appetizers and move directly to salad. You'll find several offerings, including Greek or house salad that are lettuce-based with cucumbers, tomatoes, onion, and the high-sodium ingredients cheese and olives. Don't forget to order dressing on the side. You might find fattoush with cucumbers, tomatoes, onions, and toasted pieces of pita bread. It might be dressed prior to serving because it usually marinates for a while. Tabouli, the cracked wheat salad, and tomato and cucumber salad are also regulars and very healthy unless they are doused in oil.

Soup entries are few and far between. Lemon-egg soup, avgolemono, is a regular. It's light and relatively low in calories. If cholesterol is a concern, it's best skirted. You might find a healthy lentil, vegetable, or yogurt-based soup on the menu, all of which are quite healthy.

Middle eastern entrees are usually combination dishes. There's kibbeh, with meat, cracked wheat, vegetables, and spices; and kafta, ground beef with onions, parsley, and spices. If desired, it's easy to eat vegetarian when eating Middle Eastern food. Order stuffed eggplant or an appetizer and several à la carte salads. Grilling, stove-top cooking, and baking are the preparation methods of choice.

A very familiar entree is shish kebab. Its origins relate to when Ottoman armies camped outdoors and had to cook quickly. They devised the method of skewering vegetables and meats together. In most restaurants you can order shish kebab with lamb, beef, chicken, and occasionally shrimp. Sometimes a combination is available. The meats are marinated in olive oil, lemon, wine, and spices, then grilled on a skewer with vegetables.

Eggplant is an ingredient used in several dishes, mousaka being a familiar one—an eggplant and tomato sauce casserole with white sauce topping. Or you might find sheikh el mahshi—stuffed eggplant with meat. It's important to realize that eggplant absorbs lots of oil, and that prior to cooking eggplant is sometimes salted to remove the bitter taste. Mousaka, due to the high fat content from the white sauce, is best avoided.

Gyros meat, a spicy combination of lamb and beef, and souvlaki, which is lamb, are often available wrapped in pita bread or served on platters. Both usually come with lettuce, tomato, onion, and a spicy sauce called tzateki. Tzateki is made either with sour cream or yogurt. The best advice: ask at each restaurant to find out if it's low-cal yogurt or high-fat sour cream. Gyros and souvlaki are good choices, but try to eat more bread and vegetables than meat.

Lah me june is the Mid-East's answer to pizza. It's dough topped with ground meat, parsley, tomatoes, onions, and Middle Eastern spices. This is a good choice because it's low in protein and high in carbos. Omelets made with feta cheese or lokaniko (sausage) and three eggs are offered on Middle Eastern menus. These are best avoided. Adding cheese or sauce to three eggs is enough cholesterol for several days, not to mention the fat load.

Dinners in Middle Eastern restaurants are usually served with a small salad, pita bread, rice pilaf, and/or a steamed vegetable. All of these offer relatively low-fat additions to your meal. Don't feel compelled to order an entree. Unless you can split or complement two dishes by sharing, that might be too much food and a set-up to overeat. Order à la carte appetizers, salads, and side dishes that can be combined to make a healthy meal and allow you to taste more foods. Another approach is to split—from appetizer to dessert—hummus and pita, lentil soup, couscous with lamb stew, and rice pudding.

Dessert is traditionally just a bowl of fruit, but not so in Middle Eastern restaurants in America. You'll have the sweet choices of baklava, kataif, and rice pudding. If you have indulged in baklava, you know it is one of the richest desserts known to humankind. Baklava is made with phyllo dough, plenty of butter, walnuts, sugar, and spices. A few bites are enough to quench your sweet tooth for a week or so. The other half of enjoying sweets in the Middle East is sipping a cup of Turkish coffee. It might be called Greek coffee as well. It all resembles espresso—strong and concentrated. Small portions are served in demitasses. The coffee alone might be a new taste treat and, best yet, it has next to no calories.

Green Flag Words

INGREDIENTS:
lemon juice
herbs and spices, Middle Eastern spices
parsley or onion
mashed chickpeas
fava beans
eggplant
with tomatoes, onions, green peppers, and/or cucumbers
spiced ground beef or lamb
gyros meat
souvlaki
cracked wheat (tabouli)

COOKING METHODS/MENU DESCRIPTIONS
lemon dressing
tomato sauce
stuffed with ground lamb or meat
stuffed with rice and meat

grilled on a skewer—kebabs
marinated and barbecued
charbroiled or charcoal broiled
stewed
simmered
baked

INGREDIENTS:

Red Flag Words

caviar*+
tahini—ground sesame seeds
sesame seed paste or puree
olive oil, pure olive oil
egg
kalamata olives*
Greek olives*
feta cheese*
kasseri cheese*
lokaniko*

COOKING METHODS/MENU
DESCRIPTIONS:
phyllo dough and foods made
    with it
tarator sauce
lemon and butter sauce
dolmas, dolmatis
cheese pie
spanikopita
topped with creamy sauce
bechamel sauce (white sauce)
in pastry crust
pan fried
golden fried

AT THE TABLE:
butter
olive oil
olives

+high in cholesterol
*high in sodium

**Special
Requests
Middle
Eastern
Style**

I'll have the appetizer portion, but I would like that served when you serve the others their entrees.

Please bring the dressing for my salad on the side.

Please serve the tzateki (or other sauces) on the side.

Please bring my salad when you bring the appetizers for the others.

We're simply going to have salad and share a few appetizers.

Can you leave the feta cheese and olives off the salad; I'm watching my sodium consumption?

Could you bring my cup of soup when the others are having appetizers?

Please bring an extra plate because we're going to do some sharing.

Could I get a doggie bag when you bring the entrees because I'd like to put half away for tomorrow?

The Menu: Middle Eastern Style

Appetizers ✓**Hummus bi tahini** with pita bread (mashed chickpeas blended with tahini, lemon juice, and spices)

✓**Baba ghanoush** with pita bread (smoked eggplant mashed and combined with tahini, lemon juice, garlic, and other spices)

Taramosalata with pita bread (caviar blended with lemon juice and olive oil)

Kasseri casserole (kasseri cheese fried with a lemon and butter sauce)

Spanikopita (spinach and feta cheese pie made with phyllo dough)

✓**Dolma** (cold grape leaves stuffed with a spicy combination of rice, onions, and tomatoes)

✓**Dolma** (hot grape leaves stuffed with a spicy combination of ground lamb, rice, and onions)

Falafel (blend of chickpeas and fava beans, fried and served with tarator or tahini)

✓**Ful Medames** (fava beans and chickpeas blended with spices and seasonings)

✓**Cold combination** (tabooli, hummus bi tahini, and baba ghanoush)

Hot combination (falafel, spanikopita, and dolma)

✓*Preferred Choice*
Some depending on special requests

Salads   ✓**Greek salad** (lettuce, tomato,
cucumbers, onions, feta cheese,
and olives, served with a spicy
light lemon and olive oil dressing)
✓**Middle Eastern salad** (lettuce,
onions, cucumbers, tomato, mint,
parsley, and spices, served with a
spicy olive oil and vinegar
dressing)
✓**Tabouli** (cracked wheat combined
with parsley, tomatoes, cucumbers,
lemon, and a spicy dressing)
✓**Fattoush** (lettuce, peppers,
scallions, onions, tomatoes, and
pieces of toasted pita bread, tossed
and served with a light garlic and
lemon dressing)
✓**Tomato and cucumber salad**
(diced cucumbers and tomatoes
marinated in a spicy, light
dressing)

Soups   ✓**Avgolemono** (chicken-broth-based
soup with eggs and lemon)
✓**Lentil soup** (lentils simmered
with zucchini, celery, onions,
potatoes, and Middle Eastern
spices)

Entrees*   ✓**Shish kebab** (chunks of beef,
lamb, or chicken marinated and
spiced, skewered with tomatoes,
onions, and peppers and grilled)
Mousaka (layers of eggplant,
ground lamb, and cheese topped
with béchamel sauce)
Spanikopita (spinach and cheese
pie made with phyllo dough)
✓**Kibbeh,** baked (cracked wheat
mixed with spicy ground meat and
stuffed with sauteed onions and
pine nuts)

✓**Gyros,** available in a pita or on platter (combination of seared, spicy lamb and beef, served with lettuce, tomato, onions, and tzateki sauce)

✓**Sheik el Mahshi** (baked eggplant, stuffed with ground lamb, pine nuts, onions, Middle Eastern spices, and tomato sauce)

✓**Souvlaki,** available in pita or on platter (marinated and grilled meat, served with lettuce, tomato, onions, and tzateki sauce)

Pasticchio (baked macaroni with ground beef and eggs, topped with a creamy sauce)

Fried kalamaria (squid)

Dolma (stuffed grape leaves, with ground lamb, rice, onions, and spices)

Falafel (fava beans and chickpeas blended with spices and served with tahini or tarator sauce)

✓**Lah me june** (Armenian pizza, topped with ground meat, parsley, tomatoes, onions, and spices)

✓**Kafta** (beef ground with parsley, onions, and other spices and served grilled)

✓**Couscous** (a wheat grain steamed on top of a spicy lamb and vegetable stew)

Omelet (three eggs combined with choice of feta cheese, lokaniko, chicken livers, or any combination)

*Each entree is served with a choice of Middle Eastern salad or steamed vegetable and rice pilaf

Side	✓**Tabouli**
Dishes	✓**Rice pilaf** (long-grain rice seasoned with butter and saffron)
	✓**Steamed vegetable** combination
	Feta cheese
	Kalamata (olives)
	✓**Pita bread**
Desserts	**Baklava** (pastry made with layers of phyllo dough, nuts, and sugar)
	Kataif (pastry made with shredded dough, nuts, and sugar)
	✓**Rice pudding**
	Assorted Middle Eastern pastries
	✓**Turkish coffee**
	✓**American coffee**

Now that you've seen what might be available on the Menu, find the Model Meal that best suits your nutrition goals. For an explanation of the Model Meals and their targeted nutritional values, see Chapter 3.

Your Order, Please

Healthy	30%	Calories as fat
Daily	20%	Calories as protein
Eating	50%	Calories as carbohydrate
Goals	300	mg/day Cholesterol
	3000	mg/day Sodium

Low Calorie/ **Tabouli salad**
Low Fat *Quantity:* ¾ cup
Model Meal *Exchanges:* 1 fat; ½ vegetable; 1
    starch
Gyros plate or platter
Quantity: 3 oz
Exchanges: 3 meat (med.); 1
    vegetable
Pita bread
Quantity: ¾ pita
Exchanges: 2 starch
Low-calorie carbonated beverage
Quantity: unlimited
Exchanges: free

Estimated	calories 560
Nutrient	fat 20g (32% of calories)
Evaluation	protein 36g (26% of calories)
	carbohydrate 59g (42% of calories)
	cholesterol 75 mg
	sodium 1000 mg

❷

Low Calorie/ Low Cholesterol Model Meal

Ful Medames (split order)
Quantity: ½ cup
Greek salad (dressing on the side)
Quantity: 1–2 cups
Dressing (request extra lemon wedges)
Quantity: 1 tbsp
Lah me june (Armenian pizza)
Quantity: 8-in. round
Turkish coffee
Quantity: unlimited

Estimated Nutrient Evaluation

calories 612
fat 24g (35% of calories)
protein 34g (22% of calories)
carbohydrate 66g (43% of calories)
cholesterol 75 mg
sodium 120 mg

❸

Higher Calorie/Low Fat Model Meal

Fattoush (dressing on the side)
Quantity: 1–2 cups
Exchanges: 2 vegetable; ½ starch
Dressing (on the side)
Quantity: 1 tbsp
Exchanges: 1 fat
Sheik el Mahshi (split order)
Quantity: 1½ cups
Exchanges: 1 meat (med.); 1 fat; 2 vegetables
Kibbeh, baked (split order)
Quantity: 1 cup
Exchanges: 1 meat (med.); 1 vegetable; 1 starch
Rice pilaf
Quantity: ⅔ cup
Exchanges: 1 fat; 2 starch

Retsina wine
Quantity: 6 oz
Exchanges: account for calories
    but don't omit exchanges

Estimated   calories 826
Nutrient   fat 30g (33% of calories)
Evaluation   protein 31g (15% of calories)
             carbohydrate 78g (38% of calories)
             alcohol 14% of calories
             cholesterol 50 mg
             sodium 1110 mg

Higher   Hummus bi tahini
Calorie/Low   *Quantity:* ⅓ cup
Cholesterol   Pita bread
Model Meal   *Quantity:* ½ pita
             Tomato and cucumber salad
             Quantity: ½ cup
             Rice pilaf
             Quantity: 1 cup
             Shish kebab (combination lamb
                 and chicken)
             Quantity: 2 skewers (about 4 oz
                 meat)
             Light beer
             Quantity: 12 oz

Estimated   calories 866
Nutrient   fat 27g (28% of calories)
Evaluation   protein 43g (20% of calories)
             carbohydrate 93g (43% of calories)
             alcohol 9% of calories
             cholesterol 100 mg
             sodium 1260 mg

Low Sodium Model Meal

Baba ghanoush
Quantity: ½ cup
Pita bread
Quantity: ½ pita
Middle Eastern salad (hold olives and feta cheese; request lemon wedges or vinegar)
Quantity: 1–2 cups
Kafta (eat half)
Quantity: 3–4 oz
Rice pilaf
Quantity: 1 cup
Steamed vegetable combination
Quantity: ½ cup
Mineral water
Quantity: unlimited

Estimated Nutrient Evaluation

calories 821
fat 33g (36% of calories)
protein 39g (19% of calories)
carbohydrate 92g (45% of calories)
cholesterol 88 mg
sodium 1010 mg

12

Healthier eating out
Fast Food Burgers & Fries

"Fast food"—the expression alone conjures up thoughts of burgers, fries, and soda. But since *The Restaurant Companion's* first edition, many restaurant foods have gained speed. Pizza, subs, and Mexican food can be eaten lickety-split after driving through, faxing your order, calling for delivery, or simply dashing in for an express meal. Because so much food is faster today, we've devoted more space to the subject. This chapter focuses on the fast-food chains whose main gig is burgers and fries, though their menus have widened with grilled chicken in a sandwich or on a salad; roast beef sandwiches; and baked potatoes. You'll find separate chapters on other "fast foods": Fast Chicken (Chapter 13); Pizza (Chapter 14); Seafood (Chapter 17); and Breakfast, Coffee Shops, and Brunch (Chapter 19). Chapter 4 tells you about the beverages served in fast-food restaurants.

Get to know the cuisine

Is there a healthy fast-food meal? Or is that another one of those oxymorons in light of all the cheese, red meat, special sauces, and French fries? Not at all; today a healthy fast-food meal is possible. The fast-food world has responded to American's nutrition concerns. In the mid '80s fast-food restaurants added baked potatoes and salads. In the late '80s grilled chicken sandwiches were unveiled along with leaner burgers. All along, however, the string of new fat-dense items never ceased—bigger burgers with bacon and cheese, jumbo fries, and combo meals. We're now in an era of nutrition backlash, the "why bother eating healthy" attitude. We've grown from large to extra large, to jumbo and giant. We can't blame this trend on the restaurants. They listen to consumers by monitoring sales, and it's not the salads and grilled chicken sandwiches that keep them counting the greenbacks. They've responded by just leaving a few "big seller" healthier options on the menu.

The fast food business began in the '40s and '50s. Growth was rapid through the '70s and '80s as society sped up. As long as the goal of getting things done quickly with no time for cooking continues, fast food will have a place in America's heart. The dollars spent on fast food continue to rise, as do the many customers around the country, and for that matter around the world.

Over the years, as some Americans have become more health conscious, fast-food restaurants have been criticized for their food quality. Large chains have spent millions convincing nutrition-conscious Americans that they use healthy foods, such as 100 percent pure beef or products from nationally recognized food manufacturers. They do use quality foods; that's not the problem. The problem is too much fat. The fat creeps in as foods are battered or breaded and fried or topped with cheese, bacon, and special (mayonnaise-based) sauces. This makes fast food calorie-, fat-, and sodium-dense. Even though there's a scattering of healthier options, the vast majority of foods posted on the menu board are nutritional disasters. The companies continue to spend big bucks developing and advertising many unhealthy offerings.

An advantage of fast-food restaurants is that nutrition content is not a secret. They've gone out of their way to give you the nutrition facts. See the table ''Fast Food Chains (Burgers and More) Sampler—Healthy and Not So Healthy'' at chapter's end for nutrition information on a representative sampling of popular fast-food choices. Some companies even publish diabetes exchanges. Ask for the nutrition sheet when you get to the counter, or write or call the corporate headquarters.

Most of you will, at least on occasion, swing by the hallowed halls of a fast-food chain. Sometimes you can't beat it. The meals are quick, a known entity, accessible, and relatively inexpensive. You can navigate the menu board and come up with healthy fast-food combinations as long as you pick and choose using the 10 skills and strategies for healthier eating.

Before you order

Fast food is higher in fat, saturated fat, and sodium and lower in carbohydrate than desirable. Also, the protein choices are mainly red meat, fish, or chicken (fried, broiled, or grilled). Even the nutritious potato is drenched in toppings to become a bit of carbohydrate surrounded by lots of fat. Vegetables are hard to find. You don't see much that's green and crunchy in an order of burger, fries, and shake although a side or garden salad can help complement a burger with something other than fries. Fruit, other than juice, is one food group that barely shows its face. Some people might try to pass off the deep-fat-fried fruit pies as a fruit serving—don't buy it. Today, you can purchase low-fat or skim milk at some chains.

Try to minimize the fried foods or at least offset one fried food with a grilled or non-fried item. For example, opt for a small order of French fries with a no-frills hamburger, grilled chicken, or roast beef sandwich. Or complement an order of fried chicken pieces with a plain baked potato or garden salad. Obviously, you're better off avoiding all fried foods, but that's easier said than done.

Beyond simply counting the fat grams from fried foods, you need to be concerned about the type of fat used. Prior to being chastised, fast-food restaurants fried in shortening with a bit of beef fat. That added a small amount of cholesterol. Due to the cholesterol controversy, most have switched to partially hydrogenated vegetable-based shortening. That's good for reducing cholesterol. Now, the count is usually zero. Remember, though, that change doesn't lower calories. Don't be duped by believing that the healthy-sounding expressions ''cholesterol-free'' or ''vegetable oil shortening'' mean any less calories.

Now there's a new fat concern: trans-fatty acids. These are some fats in hydrogenated or partially hydrogenated margarine and shortening. Hydrogenated fats have been processed to create a more solid fat. For instance, liquid corn oil is hydrogenated to create a solid corn-oil margarine. The process of hydrogenating introduces trans-fatty acids. A few studies accuse trans-fatty acids of raising blood cholesterol. The shortening used in some fast-food restaurants is partially hydrogenated and contains some trans-fatty acids. Once again, the message is clear. Reduce total fat consumption and you will accomplish all goals: less total fat, cholesterol, saturated fat, and trans-fatty acids.

You can pick up fast-food fats in yet other ways. Think about the add-ons to hamburgers, roast beef, or chicken sandwiches—cheese, bacon, special sauce or just plain mayonnaise. All are just about 100 percent fat. Even with the healthier options of salads and baked potatoes, fat is added with salad dressing or cheese. Consider the pre-packaged chicken salads that ring in around 150 calories. The packet of salad dressing contains four tablespoons and around 250 calories. So if you drizzle on the whole packet, you've tripled the calories and made a healthy item into a high-fat meal. The same is true for the no-fat baked potato that gets the fat-dense cheese sauce, sour cream, and/or bacon bits added. A positive aspect of the healthier food choices—grilled chicken sandwiches, salad, and potatoes—is that you're in the driver's seat, controlling what's added by using special requests or just by not overdoing it with things like salad dressing, cheese sauce, or sour cream.

The high sodium content of fast-food meals is another pitfall. The sodium needle rises as foods are coated in salty batters or as pickles, special sauces, bacon, cheese, and salad dressing are added. Not to mention the salt itself. Consider the Whopper® with cheese at close to 1,300 milligrams of sodium. That's about half your daily need. Interestingly, French fries are often blamed for adding sodium, but small orders ring in at a bit over 100 milligrams. It's not unusual to see a fast-food meal quickly rise to 2,000 milligrams of sodium. Common sense tells you to minimize the high-sodium ingredients—salad dressing, cheese, special sauces, and bacon bits. These changes also reduce fat content.

Practicing the art of preplanning is easier in fast-food restaurants. You aren't greeted with a menu to peruse. You know only too well what's on the menu board whether you're in California or Connecticut. So decide what you'll order before crossing the threshold. That's Skill Number 4—have an action plan. The smells and visual cues might torment you to vacillate, but hold firm. If you have a willing mate, give him or her your order prior to walking in and offer to snag a table. That way you avoid the cues that might lead you astray.

Portion control from the word go—Skill Number 7—is also a bit easier. First, you don't wait to eat. It's order and chow down. There's no bread and butter on the table or high-fat appetizers to watch your dining partners consume. Also, dessert gets next to no attention. Secondly, the portions, as long as you order smartly, are small. Look for the words that mean small—regular, junior, small, or single. Skirt around the words meaning large portions—giant, super, jumbo, double, triple, big, extra large. A single hamburger has between two and three ounces of meat, just about the right portion when eating according to the Food Guide Pyramid—Skill Number 6.

Special requests are difficult, though not impossible. If you remember back a few years, Burger King's slogan was "special orders don't upset us." The biggest problem with special requests is that individualized orders are not a fast-food restaurant's forte—uniformity is. So be patient if you want different. Weigh the advantages and disadvantages, the time it takes, and the difficulty of your request.

Lastly, monitor your pace of eating. Granted, getting the job of eating done quickly is the main goal of your fast-food stop. And the environment of a fast-food restaurant fosters a quickened pace. Take at least 15–20 minutes for a meal. Avoid drive throughs; there's nothing positive about them. You eat quickly and can't focus on eating, so you hardly taste the food as it goes down.

Little changes add up to a big nutrition difference, whether it's ordering small French fries rather than jumbo or a junior burger rather than the triple decker. The chart, pg. 177, "Little Changes Add Up to a Big Nutrition Difference," gives examples of how simple changes easily create healthier fast-food meals.

Menu management

Here's a quick review of the main menu offerings. Check out the chart "Fast Food Chains (Burgers and More) Sampler—Healthy and Not So Healthy" (pg. 179) for exact nutrition information on a representative sampling of these foods, and note the healthier choices in **bold** before stepping up to the counter to place your order.

Hamburgers and Cheeseburgers: When going for the burgers, consider the size. Ordering a regular, single, or other smaller burger is a good start. Then watch how it's topped off. Limit the cheese, bacon, ham, and special (mayonnaise-based) sauce.

Grilled Chicken Sandwich: See Chapter 13.

Roast Beef Sandwiches: Apply the same message. Go for the smaller size, regular, or junior and hold the usual cheese or cheese sauce topping. Apply low-calorie toppers yourself—ketchup, barbecue sauce, or mustard.

Other Sandwiches: Whether it's beef gyros at Jack in the Box or ham 'n cheese at Arby's, go for the smaller size and limit the high-fat and sodium toppers.

Fish Sandwiches: There's just nothing nutritionally positive about fish sandwiches. Unfortunately, the health virtues of fish are quickly destroyed by breading and frying. As if that weren't enough fat, a dollop of mayonnaise-based tartar sauce and cheese is often added.

Baked Potatoes: You start with a healthy bet and have the option of eating it healthfully or adding fats—sour cream, butter, bacon bits, or cheese sauce. The fillers that are wiser choices—chili, broccoli, and chives—are usually combined with high-fat add-ons. So special requests are the way to go. Try chili with just a tad of cheese and broccoli with a smidgen of cheese sauce or sour cream.

Salads: A variety of salads are available at most fast-food restaurants, from the common chef salad and grilled chicken to the rarer taco and Caesar salads. The healthier choices for a main meal are the chicken and chef salads. The garden and side salads are great to complement a hamburger or a roast beef or grilled chicken sandwich. The taco salad runs a bit higher in fat due to the chips. But salads are all relatively healthier choices, although any salad can be destroyed if the whole packet of dressing is emptied. Here are some thoughts: try a reduced or low-calorie dressing, but keep in mind that it also has calories. Best yet, try a fat-free dressing if available. If you use a regular dressing, especially a creamy one, dilute it with vinegar or lemon wedges or a bit of water. Most importantly, use as little as you can. See Chapter 13 for more discussion on fast-food salads with chicken and Chapter 21 for more details about salad dressings.

Fried Sides: What's fast food without the fries? No need to skip the fries or onion rings entirely. You'll note from the nutrition chart that the small fries have about half the calories of the large size and half the fat grams. Small is the key with fries; or find a dining partner willing to share a large order.

Shakes: The shakes pack a lot of calories from carbohydrates, but they are low in fat. Perhaps a shake on occasion would satisfy a sweet tooth or add a nice complement to a small hamburger, a sandwich, or a salad. Order an extra cup and split it.

Desserts: As the nutrition chart details, fast-food desserts range in calories quite a bit, from a low 120 for a McDonald's vanilla yogurt cone to a high of over 300 for the fried fruit pies. Pick one of the lower-calorie desserts and treat yourself now and then.

Beverages: Refer to Chapter 4 for a detailed discussion on best bets for beverages. The goal is to avoid the sugar-laden carbonated soft drinks and go for the no-calorie diet drinks, unsweetened iced or hot coffee or tea, or just good old water. Choosing skim or low-fat milk or fruit juice will cost you a few calories, but they're healthy choices packed with nutrients.

Green Flag Words

INGREDIENTS:
lettuce, tomato, onion
grilled chicken
hamburger (single)
roast beef
baked potato
salad
light, reduced-calorie, or fat-free
    salad dressing
chili
low-fat frozen yogurt
low-fat milk

COOKING METHODS/MENU
DESCRIPTIONS:
grilled
French dip sandwich
single, junior, regular

Red Flag Words

INGREDIENTS:
fried chicken
croissant
mayonnaise-based sauces (tartar,
    special)
bacon
cheese (any type)
cheese sauce
sour cream
salad dressing (regular)

COOKING METHODS/MENU
DESCRIPTIONS:
fried, deep-fried
French fries
onion rings
fish sandwich
fried desserts
jumbo
super
double, triple

**Special
Requests
Fast Food
Style**

Please hold the special sauce (mayonnaise, tartar sauce, etc.).

Please hold the cheese (and/or bacon)

Can I have an extra cup so we can split the milk shake (or juice)?

Can I have a few extra ketchups?

Can I have some honey-mustard sauce (or barbecue sauce) to use on my grilled chicken sandwich?

Your Order, Please

Healthy 30% Calories as fat
Daily 20% Calories as protein
Eating 50% Calories as carbohydrate
Goals 300 mg/day Cholesterol
3000 mg/day Sodium

---

❶
Low Calorie/ **Cheeseburger**
Low Fat **Garden salad** with reduced-
Model Meal: calorie French dressing (2 tbsp)
McDonald's **Iced tea** (unsweetened)
Vanilla frozen yogurt cone

Estimated calories 600
Nutrient fat 22g (32% of calories)
Evaluation protein 25g (16% of calories)
carbohydrate 79g (52% of calories)
cholesterol 185 mg
sodium 1150 mg

---

❷
Low Calorie/ **Chef salad** with reduced-calorie
Low Italian dressing (2 tbsp)
Cholesterol **Vanilla shake**
Model Meal:
Hardee's

Estimated calories 628
Nutrient fat 24g (34% of calories)
Evaluation protein 34g (22% of calories)
carbohydrate 69g (44% of calories)
cholesterol 70 mg
sodium 1410 mg

❸
Higher   **Hamburgers** (2 regular)
Calorie/Low   **French fries** (small)
Fat Model   **Orange juice**
Meal:
Burger King

Estimated   calories 920
Nutrient   fat 30g (29% of calories)
Evaluation   protein 32g (15% of calories)
              carbohydrate 127g (56% of calories)
              cholesterol 60 mg
              sodium 1100 mg

❹
Higher   **Baked potato** with chili and
Calorie/Low   cheese (request light on cheese)
Cholesterol   **Deluxe garden salad** with fat-free
Model Meal: French dressing (2 tbsp)
Wendy's

Estimated   calories 770
Nutrient   fat 30g (35% of calories)
Evaluation   protein 28g (15% of calories)
              carbohydrate 97g (50% of calories)
              cholesterol 45 mg
              sodium 1200 mg

❺
Low Sodium   **Light roast beef sandwich**
Model Meal: **French fries** (small)
Arby's   **Side salad** with honey-French
                     dressing (1 tbsp) add vinegar or
                     lemon wedges
                  Milk (2%)

Estimated	calories 766
Nutrient	fat 34g (40% of calories)
Evaluation	protein 30g (16% of calories)
	carbohydrate 85g (44% of calories)
	cholesterol 60 mg
	sodium 1214 mg

*For these model meals, exact nutrition information from the specified restaurant was used, and most of the items are listed in the charts following.

Little Changes Add Up to a Big Nutrition Difference*
CHANGE THIS ORDER FROM McDONALD'S

FROM:	Calories	Fat (g)	% Cals. as fat	Protein (g)	Carbo-hydrates (g)	Cho-lesterol (mg)	Sodium (mg)
Big Mac	510	26	46	25	46	75	930
French fries (large)	450	22	44	6	57	0	290
Regular Coke (large-32 oz)	300	0	0	0	82	0	30
Totals+	1260	48	34	31	185	75	1250
TO:							
McLean Deluxe	340	12	32	24	37	60	810
French fries (small)	210	10	43	3	26	0	135
Garden salad	80	4	45	6	7	140	60
Light Vinaigrette (2 tbsp)	25	1	36	0	5	0	120
Diet Coke (large-32 oz)	3	0	0	0	1	0	35
Totals+	658	27	37	33	76	200	1160

177

CHANGES THIS ORDER FROM BURGER KING

FROM:	Calories	Fat (g)	% Cals. as fat	Protein (g)	Carbohydrates (g)	Cholesterol (mg)	Sodium (mg)
Chicken sandwich (fried)	700	43	55	26	54	60	1400
French fries (medium)	400	20	45	5	43	0	240
Chocolate shake (medium)	310	7	20	9	54	20	230
Totals+	1410	70	45	40	151	80	1870
TO:							
BK Broiler chicken sandwich+	540	29	48	30	41	80	480
French fries (small)	240	10	38	4	33	0	100
Garden salad	90	5	50	6	7	15	110
Light Italian dressing (2 tbsp)	15	1	60	0	3	0	50
Diet soft drink (medium)	1	0	0	0	1	0	25
Totals+	886	45	46	40	85	95	815

*For these examples, exact nutrition information from the specified restaurant was used, and most of the items are listed in the charts following.

+Note similar percentage of calories as fat, but grams of fat are reduced by about half.

†Can request no special sauce to further reduce fat.

178

Fast Food Chains (Burgers and More) Sampler–Healthy and Not So Healthy*

Restaurant	Food Item	Calories	Fat (g)	% Cals. as fat	Protein (g)	Carbo-hydrate (g)	Cho-lesterol (mg)	Sodium (mg)
	HAMBURGERS							
Burger King	**Hamburger**	**260**	**10**	**35**	**14**	**28**	**30**	**500**
	Whopper® jr.	**410**	**24**	**53**	**21**	**29**	**60**	**550**
	Double Whopper® sandwich	860	56	59	46	45	170	920
Carl's Jr.	**Hamburger**	**200**	**8**	**36**	**11**	**23**	**25**	**500**
	Big burger	**470**	**20**	**38**	**25**	**46**	**55**	**810**
Hardee's	**Hamburger**	**260**	**9**	**31**	**11**	**33**	**20**	**460**
	Big Deluxe™ burger	530	30	51	28	36	40	790
Jack in the Box	**Hamburger**	**280**	**11**	**35**	**13**	**31**	**25**	**430**

*Based on nutrition information provided by each restaurant company.
This is a sample of representative items from each restaurant. Foods with less than 40% calories from fat and/or entrees with less than 25g of fat and side items with less than 11g of fat are in **bold.**
For beverages see Chapter 4.

Restaurant	Food Item	Calories	Fat (g)	% Cals. as fat	Protein (g)	Carbo-hydrate (g)	Cho-lesterol (mg)	Sodium (mg)
	Grilled sourdough burger	670	43	58	32	39	110	1140
McDonald's	**Hamburger**	**270**	**9**	**30**	**12**	**35**	**30**	**530**
	McLean Deluxe™	**340**	**12**	**32**	**24**	**37**	**60**	**810**
	Big Mac	510	26	46	25	46	75	930
	Jr. hamburger	**270**	**9**	**30**	**15**	**34**	**35**	**600**
Wendy's	**Plain single**	**350**	**15**	**39**	**24**	**31**	**70**	**510**
	CHEESEBURGERS							
Burger King	**Cheeseburger**	**300**	**14**	**42**	**17**	**28**	**45**	**710**
	Whopper® with cheese	720	46	58	33	45	115	1270
Carl's Jr.	Double western	970	57	53	56	58	145	1810
Hardee's	**Cheeseburger**	**300**	**13**	**39**	**13**	**34**	**25**	**690**
	Mushroom 'N' Swiss™	520	27	47	30	37	45	990

Restaurant	Food Item	Calories	Fat (g)	% Cals. as fat	Protein (g)	Carbo-hydrate (g)	Cho-lesterol (mg)	Sodium (mg)
Jack in the Box	**Cheeseburger**	**330**	**15**	**41**	**16**	**32**	**35**	**510**
	Double cheeseburger	450	24	48	24	35	75	900
McDonald's	**Cheeseburger**	**320**	**13**	**37**	**15**	**36**	**40**	**770**
	McLean Deluxe™ with cheese	**400**	**16**	**36**	**26**	**38**	**70**	**1040**
Wendy's	**Jr. cheeseburger**	**320**	**13**	**37**	**18**	**34**	**45**	**770**
	Big bacon classic	640	36	51	37	44	110	1500
	ROAST BEEF SANDWICHES							
Arby's	**Junior roast beef**	**233**	**11**	**42**	**12**	**23**	**22**	**519**
	Giant roast beef	544	26	43	33	46	72	1433
Hardee's	**Big roast beef**	**370**	**16**	**39**	**21**	**34**	**40**	**1050**

Restaurant	Food Item	Calories	Fat (g)	% Cals. as fat	Protein (g)	Carbo-hydrate (g)	Cho-lesterol (mg)	Sodium (mg)
	OTHER SANDWICHES (for chicken sandwiches, see Chapter 13)							
Arby's	French dip	368	15	37	22	35	43	1018
	Light roast beef deluxe	294	10	31	18	33	42	826
	Arby Q	389	15	35	18	48	29	1268
	Ham 'n cheese	355	14	35	25	35	55	1400
Hardee's	Hotdog	450	20	40	17	52	35	1090
Jack in the Box	Beef gyros	620	32	46	27	55	65	1310
	Country fried steak	450	25	50	14	42	35	890
	FISH SANDWICHES							
Arby's	Fish fillet	526	27	46	23	50	44	872
Burger King	BK big fish	720	43	54	25	59	60	1090

Restaurant	Food Item	Calories	Fat (g)	% Cals. as fat	Protein (g)	Carbo-hydrate (g)	Cho-lesterol (mg)	Sodium (mg)
Carl's Jr.	Carl's catch	560	30	48	17	54	60	1220
Hardee's	Fisherman's fillet™	500	22	40	24	51	60	1170
Jack in the Box	Fish supreme	590	32	49	22	51	60	1170
McDonald's	Filet-o-fish®	360	16	40	14	41	35	710
BAKED POTATOES								
Carl's Jr.	Lite potato	290	0	0	6	68	0	40
	Broccoli and cheese	530	22	37	11	76	15	930
Wendy's	Plain	310	0	0	7	71	0	25
	Chili and cheese	610	24	35	21	82	45	700
SALADS+++ (dressing not included)								
Arby's	Garden	117	5	38	7	11	12	134

+Find chicken salads in Chapter 13.
**Find nutrition information on salad dressings and suggestions for healthier use in Chapter 21.

Restaurant	Food Item	Calories	Fat (g)	% Cals. as fat	Protein (g)	Carbohydrate (g)	Cholesterol (mg)	Sodium (mg)
Burger King	Chef	205	10	44	19	13	126	796
	Garden	90	5	50	6	7	15	110
	Side	50	3	54	3	4	5	55
Carl's Jr.	Garden	50	3	54	3	4	5	75
Hardee's	Garden	190	14	66	12	3	40	280
	Chef	200	13	59	20	5	45	910
Jack in the Box	Chef	320	19	53	30	9	130	930
	Taco	470	23	44	34	30	85	1470
	Beef teriyaki bowl	580	3	5	28	124	25	930
McDonald's	Chef	210	11	47	19	9	180	730
	Garden	80	4	45	6	7	140	60
Wendy's	Caesar side	110	5	41	9	7	15	580
	Taco	580	30	47	33	51	75	1060

Restaurant	Food Item	Calories	Fat (g)	% Cals. as fat	Protein (g)	Carbo-hydrate (g)	Cho-lesterol (mg)	Sodium (mg)
	FRENCH FRIES							
Arby's	French fries (no size specified)	246	13	48	2	30	0	114
	Curly fries	337	18	48	4	43	0	167
Burger King	French fries (medium)	400	20	45	5	43	0	240
	Onion rings	310	14	41	4	41	0	810
Carls' Jr.	French fries (regular)	370	20	49	4	44	0	240
	Onion rings	520	26	45	8	63	0	840
Hardee's	**French fries (small)**	**240**	**10**	**38**	**4**	**33**	**0**	**100**
	French fries (large)	430	18	38	6	59	0	190
Jack in the Box	Seasoned curly fries	360	20	50	5	39	0	1070
	French fries (small)	**220**	**11**	**45**	**3**	**28**	**0**	**120**

Restaurant	Food Item	Calories	Fat (g)	% Cals. as fat	Protein (g)	Carbo-hydrate (g)	Cho-lesterol (mg)	Sodium (mg)
McDonald's	**French fries (small)**	**210**	**10**	**43**	**3**	**26**	**0**	**135**
	French fries (super size)	540	26	43	8	68	0	350
Wendy's	French fries (small)	240	12	45	3	33	0	150
	French fries (biggie)	420	20	43	6	58	0	260
	SHAKES							
Arby's	**Jamocha**	**368**	**11**	**27**	**9**	**59**	**35**	**262**
Burger King	**Chocolate (medium)**	**310**	**7**	**20**	**9**	**54**	**20**	**230**
Carl's Jr.	Strawberry (small)	400	7	16	9	77	30	240
Hardee's	Vanilla	370	9	22	14	59	25	210
Jack in the Box	**Strawberry (regular)**	**330**	**7**	**19**	**9**	**60**	**30**	**180**
McDonald's	**Chocolate (small–16 oz)**	**350**	**6**	**15**	**13**	**62**	**25**	**240**
Wendy's	**Frosty (small)**	**340**	**10**	**26**	**9**	**57**	**40**	**200**
	Frosty (large)	570	17	27	15	95	70	330

Restaurant	Food Item	Calories	Fat (g)	% Cals. as fat	Protein (g)	Carbo-hydrate (g)	Cho-lesterol (mg)	Sodium (mg)
	DESSERTS							
Arby's	Apple turnover	303	18	53	4	28	0	178
	Chocolate chip cookie	**130**	**4**	**28**	**2**	**17**	**0**	**95**
Burger King	Dutch apple pie	310	15	44	3	39	0	230
Carl's Jr.	Chocolate chip cookie	370	19	46	3	49	25	350
	Cheesecake	300	17	51	6	31	55	220
Hardee's	**Cool twist™ cone (vanilla)**	**180**	**4**	**20**	**5**	**29**	**15**	**80**
	Cool twist™ sundae (hot fudge)	**320**	**10**	**28**	**8**	**50**	**25**	**260**
Jack in the Box	Hot apple turnover	350	19	49	3	48	0	460
McDonald's	**Vanilla lowfat frozen yogurt cone**	**120**	**1**	**8**	**5**	**24**	**4**	**85**

Restaurant	Food Item	Calories	Fat (g)	% Cals. as fat	Protein (g)	Carbo-hydrate (g)	Cho-lesterol (mg)	Sodium (mg)
	McDonaldland cookies	**260**	**9**	**31**	**4**	**41**	**0**	**270**
Wendy's	**Chocolate chip cookie**	**270**	**11**	**37**	**4**	**38**	**15**	**150**

13

Healthier eating out
Fast Chicken

Are you ready to cluck? If the answer is yes, it's no wonder. Over the last few years, eat in/take out chicken restaurants have burgeoned to meet the convenience and nutrition demands of the '90s lifestyle. Boston Chicken and Kenny Rogers are two chains spreading their wings across the country, serving rotisserie chicken and hot and cold sides. They tout healthiness as well. Rumor has it that McDonald's is testing a home-style chicken restaurant called Hearth Express. Today, fast-food burger joints serve up chicken along with their standby burgers and fries. No matter where chicken is served, the message is: read the nutrition fine print. Though chicken gets raves for being "heart healthy," sometimes by the time it gets to the table it no longer is.

Getting to know the cuisine

With today's attention to health, some restaurants try to distance themselves from the "F" word—fried. KFC tried to make you forget that "F" stood for fried. Yet, that's still their main business. Others appear concerned with healthiness; with Kenny Rogers, for example, uses the slogan "Your Heart's in the Right Place" on their nutrition information.

Fried chicken chains have lined highways for many years. The Colonel was first on the block and for many years stuck close to its roots with good old high-fat fried chicken. As nutrition and health became salable, the fried chicken chains wanted in on the action. First they jumped out of their skin but kept frying. That was called skin-free or skinless. Today, KFC offers Rotisserie Gold Chicken in white or dark quarters. Several fried chicken chains have followed the flock while others choose to keep on frying.

Chicken infiltrated fast-food burger chain menus due to its air of healthiness. Now, most large fast-food restaurants offer several chicken items—fried chicken sandwich, grilled chicken sandwich, grilled chicken on a salad, and fried chicken pieces served with a variety of dipping sauces. Several fast-food chains make chicken their only business—Chick-fil-a is one. A mixed bag of healthy and not-so is served, with a fried chicken sandwich as their mainstay.

The newest entries in the chicken business leave their hands off the deep-fryers. Rotisserie is their scene. Meals are built around one-quarter or one-half, white or dark. Hot or cold sides are heaped on the plate, items like corn, baked beans, and cucumber salad. They top the plate with cornbread or a roll. Needless to say, there's plenty to eat even if you're not counting the calories or grams of fat. They're just as glad to see you buy a whole chicken with sides to take home for a quick and easy family meal. It's perfect for today's meal-in-a-minute mentality.

Before you order

Even though chicken chains cluck about being heart healthy, the meal can quickly change to unhealthy. Yes, even a meal of rotisserie chicken and healthy-sounding side offerings like butternut squash, Mediterranean pasta salad, or garlic parsley potatoes. So get your preplanning skills ready. You'll be quite familiar with the menu by the time you stop in for the second or third time.

One way to deal with the overabundant portions is to grab a take-out container and split the portion in two. If you are escorting the meal home, do the same. A more economical way to proceed is to buy a half-chicken and a few healthy sides and divide it into three or four meals. Consider splitting a meal (preferably just a one-quarter white meat order) with your dining partner. If you need to fill out the meal a bit, try one or two more healthy sides—an extra salad, roll, or vegetable.

A benefit of both fast-food and the eat in/take out rotisserie chains is that there's no food to greet you at the table. No bread and butter or cheese and crackers to up your fat grams before you even order. Another plus is order à la carte. You can even steer clear of the chicken and make a meal of healthier sides. That's more in sync with the Food Guide Pyramid.

Menu management

Thank goodness there are no high-fat appetizers to skirt. Chicken soup, of course, is a warm and low-fat starter. Try a cup or bowl, or small or large in restaurant parlance. Soup might be just the right added extra with a few hot or cold side items, especially if you're trying to keep the protein low and the carbos high.

On to the main course. If it's chicken in the bun for you, here are a few pointers. Make sure you know it isn't fried. The words chargrilled, grilled, or broiled tell the right tale; however, most of the chains offer both fried and grilled sandwiches. If there's a question, ask. You'll note in the table "Fast-Food and Take-Out Chicken Chains Sampler" at the end of the chapter, that the fat content varies greatly. The difference depends on whether it's a fried item and if "special sauce" is added. Most often, special sauce is mayonnaise-based, but leaving it off is possible—just ask.

At restaurants like Kenny Rogers, where the sandwich is created in front of your eyes, watch carefully and request that high-fat dressings and ingredients such as cheese be left off or used scantily. Request a heavy hand with lettuce, tomato, and onion. Try barbecue sauce, ketchup, or mustard to add zip rather than a high-fat, mayonnaise-based special sauce or salad dressing.

The broiled, grilled, or roasted chicken salad is another healthy offering that keeps the fat quotient down. However, salad dressing can lead you down the high-fat trail. A packet of regular salad dressing (the serving in most restaurants) is 4 tablespoons, or one-quarter cup. It packs on about 250–300 calories. That's sometimes double what's in the salad. Take care with the dressing: always put your own on; choose a low-, reduced-, or fat-free variety; and use less than the whole package. See Chapter 21 for more details.

Stay away from chicken salad in a sandwich or topped on a salad. It's one of those healthy-sounding foods that when made in most restaurants is just loaded with mayonnaise. Consider Boston Chicken's chunky chicken salad sandwich—763 calories, with 43 grams of fat. That means 51 percent of the calories are from fat.

Chicken pieces were the first diversification from hamburgers in fast-food chains. McDonald's led the pack and like a pack, they all followed. They're all fried and even in small quantities range from just barely healthy to disasterland. Note that we've only put two in bold in the chart following. Several sauces are quite low in fat, though the sodium content might be high. A small order of chicken pieces can make a nice complement to a garden salad, but hold the French fries.

Rotisserie chicken—the newest addition to poultry paradise—is healthy if a few steps are taken. There's no doubt when you look at the nutrition numbers that white meat, no skin or wing, is the way to fly. Next best is dark meat, no skin, and if you can purchase individual portions, the breast and leg are healthier than the wing and thigh. The skin adds fat, cholesterol, and sodium. Portions of chicken quarters are about four ounces cooked, a bit more than you need, so balance it out with a lower protein meal other times of the day.

The side items run hot and cold. They also run high and low, fat that is. Unfortunately, they all end up with more fat than is needed, even the healthy-sounding ones. Why does a serving of tomato cucumber salad or butternut squash have 10 or more grams of fat? Because fat is an easy flavoring agent. Be careful with both hot and cold sides: some unhealthy-sounding ones actually meet our standard of less than 40 percent fat and/or less than 10 grams of fat per serving: mashed potatoes with gravy, baked beans, and macaroni and cheese. Healthy-sounding sides are sometimes just too fat dense: pasta salad, potato salad, and coleslaw. Luckily, there's plenty of healthy-sounding sides that are truly healthy: rice pilaf, corn, baked beans, and fruit salad. Tank up on the carbohydrates with healthier bread offerings such as cornbread, breadsticks, or rolls.

Green Flag Words

INGREDIENTS:
chicken
starches—corn, potatoes, rice, baked beans
breads—rolls, tortillas, cornbread, breadsticks
cooked vegetables—green beans, vegetable medley

COOKING METHODS/MENU DESCRIPTIONS:
rotisserie chicken (skin removed)
roasted chicken (skin removed)
marinated
grilled
broiled

Red Flag Words

INGREDIENTS:
chicken wings
cholesterol-free or vegetable oil (still 50 calories/tsp)
potato salad
coleslaw
biscuits

COOKING METHODS/MENU DESCRIPTIONS:
fried, deep-fried
golden brown
battered and fried

crispy, extra crispy
skin-free, skinless (still fried)
chicken salad (chicken mixed with
mayonnaise)

**Special
Requests
Fast
Chicken
Style**

May I have a take-home container
so I can split this portion in
half?

May we have an extra plate?

Can you split the dinner into two
portions?

Please take the wing off the
chicken breast (if it's in front
of me, I'll eat it).

Please hold the special sauce, but
I'll take barbecue sauce (salsa,
sweet-and-sour sauce, or
ketchup) on the side.

Please put the salad dressing on
the side.

Can I get some vinegar or lemon
wedges for my salad?

Please leave the shredded cheese
off my sandwich and salad.

If you can, please load the
sandwich with lettuce and
tomato.

Please put the gravy for the
mashed potatoes on the side.

The Menu: Fast Chicken Style

Soups	✓**Chicken noodle soup** **Cream of chicken soup** ✓**Hearty breast of chicken** **vegetables**
Breads	✓**Cornbread** ✓**Yeast rolls** ✓**Tortillas** ✓**Breadsticks**
Chicken **Sandwiches**	✓**Grilled chicken fillet** **Fried chicken fillet** ✓**Barbecued chicken fillet** ✓**Roasted chicken pita** (hold special sauce)
Chicken **Salads**	✓**Chargrilled chicken** with garden greens **Garden salad** topped with chicken salad **Chicken salad**
Salad **Dressings** **(1 packet** **= 4 tbsp)**	**Thousand Island** **French** ✓**Reduced-calorie Italian** ✓**Fat-free French** **Blue cheese** **Vinaigrette**
Chicken *Remove skin* *prior to eating*	**Fried chicken white meat** **Fried chicken dark meat** ✓**Roasted chicken white meat** ✓**Roasted chicken dark meat**
Hot Sides	✓**Buttered corn** **Creamed spinach** ✓**Baked beans**

✓*Preferred Choice*
Some depending on special requests

✓**Rice pilaf**
✓**Steamed vegetables**
✓**Roasted potatoes**

Cold Sides   **Pasta salad**
Potato salad
✓**Tomato cucumber salad**
✓**Garden salad**
Coleslaw
✓**Fruit salad**

Now that you've seen what might be available on the Menu, find the Model Meal that best fits your nutrition goals. For an explanation of the Model Meals and their targeted nutritional values, see Chapter 3.

*Your Order, Please**

Healthy	30%	Calories as fat
Daily	20%	Calories as protein
Eating	50%	Calories as carbohydrate
Goals	300	mg/day Cholesterol
	3000	mg/day Sodium

❶

Low Calorie/	**McGrilled chicken sandwich**
Low Fat	**Garden salad** with Lite
Model Meal:	Vinaigrette (½ package)
McDonald's	**Vanilla frozen yogurt cone**

Estimated	calories 475
Nutrient	fat 9g (16% of calories)
Evaluation	protein 34g (28% of calories)
	carbohydrate 68g (54% of calories)
	cholesterol 190 mg
	sodium 775 mg

❷

Low Calorie/	**Chicken soup**
Low	**Cornbread muffin**
Cholesterol	**Buttered corn**
Model Meal:	**Cucumber salad**
Boston	
Chicken	

Estimated	calories 624
Nutrient	fat 24g (34% of calories)
Evaluation	protein 22g (14% of calories)
	carbohydrate 82g (52% of calories)
	cholesterol 61mg
	sodium 1374 mg

*For these model meals, exact nutrition information from the specified restaurant was used.

❸

**Higher
Calorie/Low
Fat Model
Meal: Kenny
Rogers**

White meat-¼ (remove skin & wing)
Honey-baked beans
Macaroni and cheese
Corn muffin

Estimated
Nutrient
Evaluation

calories 609
fat 16g (24% of calories)
protein 46g (31% of calories)
carbohydrate 69g (45% of calories)
cholesterol 126 mg
sodium 1676 mg

❹

**Higher
Calorie/Low
Cholesterol
Model Meal:
Boston
Chicken**

Dark meat-¼ (skin removed)
New potatoes
Zucchini marinara
Cornbread
Fruit salad

Estimated
Nutrient
Evaluation

calories 757
fat 29g (35% of calories)
protein 37g (19% of calories)
carbohydrate 87g (46% of calories)
cholesterol 153 mg
sodium 1517 mg

❺

**Low Sodium
Model Meal:
Kenny
Rogers**

Chicken noodle soup (small)
Roasted chicken sandwich
    (request small amount of
    dressing)
Cinnamon apples

Estimated
Nutrient
Evaluation

calories 665
fat 20g (27% of calories)
protein 43g (26% of calories)
carbohydrate 80g (47% of calories)
cholesterol 226 mg
sodium 1359 mg

Fast-Food and Take-Out Chicken Chains Sampler*

Restaurant	Food Item	Calories	Fat (g)	% Cals. as fat	Protein (g)	Carbo-hydrate (g)	Cho-lesterol (mg)	Sodium (mg)
	GRILLED CHICKEN SANDWICHES							
Arby's	**Chicken breast fillet**	**445**	**23**	**47**	**22**	**52**	**45**	**958**
	Grilled chicken barbecue	**386**	**13**	**30**	**23**	**47**	**43**	**1002**
Boston Chicken	**Chicken breast sandwich**	**422**	**4**	**9**	**42**	**50**	**99**	**885**
Burger King	BK broiler	540	29	48	30	41	80	480
Carl's Jr.	**BBQ chicken**	**310**	**6**	**17**	**31**	**34**	**55**	**830**

*Based on nutrition information provided by each restaurant company.
This is a sample of representative items from each restaurant. Foods with less than 40% calories from fat and/or entrees with less than 25g of fat and side items with less than 11g of fat are in **bold**.
+Does not include salad dressing. See Chapter 21 for nutrition information on salad dressings and suggestions for healthier use.
**Request none or light dressing to reduce fat content.

199

Restaurant	Food Item	Calories	Fat (g)	% Cals. as fat	Protein (g)	Carbo-hydrate (g)	Cho-lesterol (mg)	Sodium (mg)
Chick-fil-A	**Chick-fil-A chicken**	**360**	**9**	**23**	**40**	**28**	**66**	**1174**
	Chick-fil-A chargrilled	**258**	**5**	**17**	**30**	**24**	**40**	**1121**
	Chick-n-Q (barbecued)	**409**	**15**	**33**	**28**	**41**	**10**	**1197**
Hardee's	**Chicken fillet**	**400**	**14**	**32**	**19**	**48**	**55**	**1100**
	Frisco™ grilled chicken	620	34	49	35	44	95	1730
Jack in the Box	**Chicken fajita pita**	**290**	**8**	**25**	**24**	**29**	**35**	**700**
	Grilled chicken fillet	**430**	**19**	**40**	**29**	**36**	**65**	**1070**
Kenny Rogers	**BBQ chicken pita**	**356**	**7**	**18**	**34**	**39**	**118**	**905**
	Roasted chicken pita**	593	33	50	41	33	129	1527
	Chicken Caesar pita	566	32	51	37	33	99	1604
McDonald's	**McGrilled chicken classic**	**250**	**3**	**11**	**24**	**33**	**45**	**510**
Wendy's	**Grilled chicken**	**290**	**7**	**22**	**24**	**35**	**55**	**720**

Restaurant	Food Item	Calories	Fat (g)	% Cals. as fat	Protein (g)	Carbo-hydrate (g)	Cho-lesterol (mg)	Sodium (mg)
	CHICKEN SALAD[+]							
Arby's	Roast chicken	204	7	31	24	12	43	508
Burger King	Broiled chicken	200	10	45	21	7	60	110
Carl's Jr.	Chicken	260	9	31	28	11	70	530
Chick-fil-A	Chargrilled garden	126	2	14	20	8	28	567
Hardee's	Grilled chicken	120	4	30	18	2	60	520
Jack in the Box	Teriyaki bowl	580	2	3	28	115	30	1220
Kenny Rogers	Roasted chicken	355	13	33	36	24	190	641
	Chicken Caesar	587	38	58	37	24	99	1220
McDonald's	Chunky chicken	160	5	28	23	8	75	320
Wendy's	Grilled chicken	200	8	36	25	10	50	690
	CHICKEN PIECES							
Burger King	Chicken Tenders™ (6)	250	12	43	16	14	35	530

Restaurant	Food Item	Calories	Fat (g)	% Cals. as fat	Protein (g)	Carbo-hydrate (g)	Cho-lesterol (mg)	Sodium (mg)
Chick-fil-A	**Chick-fil-A Nuggets®(8)**	**287**	**15**	**47**	**28**	**13**	**61**	**1326**
McDonald's	Chicken McNuggets (6)	300	18	54	19	16	65	530
	DIPPING SAUCES (1 oz/2 tbsp)							
Burger King	**Honey**	**90**	**0**	**0**	**0**	**23**	**0**	**10**
	Barbecue	**35**	**0**	**0**	**0**	**9**	**0**	**400**
	Sweet & sour	**45**	**0**	**0**	**0**	**11**	**0**	**50**
McDonald's	**Barbeque**	**50**	**0**	**0**	**0**	**12**	**0**	**280**
	Honey mustard	**50**	**5**	**90**	**0**	**3**	**10**	**85**
	ROTISSERIE OR ROASTED CHICKEN							
Boston Chicken	**White-¼ (without skin, no wing)**	**164**	**4**	**22**	**32**	**<1**	**89**	**356**

Restaurant	Food Item	Calories	Fat (g)	% Cals. as fat	Protein (g)	Carbo-hydrate (g)	Cho-lesterol (mg)	Sodium (mg)
	White-1/4 (with skin and wing)	332	18	49	42	2	150	524
	Dark-1/4 (without skin)	218	12	50	28	<1	121	342
	Dark-1/4 (with skin)	330	22	60	34	2	151	443
El Pollo Loco	Breast	160	6	34	26	0	110	390
	Thigh	180	12	60	16	0	130	230
	Leg	90	5	50	11	0	75	150
Kenny Rogers	White-1/4 (without skin)	147	2	12	32	0	92	332
	White-1/4 (with skin)	250	10	36	39	0	152	631
	Dark-1/4 (without skin)	182	8	40	28	0	142	380
	Dark-1/4 (with skin)	239	13	49	32	0	171	565
KFC	White-1/4 (without skin, no wing)	199	6	27	37	1	97	667

Restaurant	Food Item	Calories	Fat (g)	% Cals. as fat	Protein (g)	Carbo-hydrate (g)	Cho-lesterol (mg)	Sodium (mg)
	White-¼ (with skin and wing)	**335**	**19**	**51**	**40**	**0**	157	1104
	Dark-¼ (without skin)	**217**	**12**	**50**	**27**	**0**	128	772
	Dark-¼ (with skin)	333	24	65	30	1	163	980
	HOT SIDE DISHES							
Boston Chicken	Butternut squash	247	11	40	2	37	28	978
	Steamed vegetables	**32**	**trace**	**trace**	**2**	**6**	**<1**	**13**
	New potatoes	**129**	**4**	**28**	**2**	**22**	**<1**	**156**
	Buttered corn	**181**	**6**	**30**	**5**	**31**	**<1**	**187**
	BBQ beans	**290**	**7**	**22**	**11**	**47**	**7**	**653**
	Rice pilaf	**188**	**5**	**24**	**4**	**32**	**trace**	**684**
	Zucchini marinara	**80**	**4**	**45**	**2**	**10**	**<1**	**503**

Restaurant	Food Item	Calories	Fat (g)	% Cals. as fat	Protein (g)	Carbo-hydrate (g)	Cho-lesterol (mg)	Sodium (mg)
	Mashed potatoes & gravy	205	10	44	3	27	25	514
	Macaroni and cheese	290	11	34	12	35	19	896
El Pollo Loco	Rice	110	2	16	1	19	0	220
	Corn	110	2	18	3	20	0	110
	Beans	100	3	27	5	16	0	460
Kenny Rogers	Cinnamon apples	199	5	23	0	39	13	3
	Corn on the cob	68	1	13	2	13	0	11
	Garlic parsley potatoes	259	12	42	3	35	6	867
	Honey baked beans	152	2	12	7	27	8	524
	Macaroni and cheese	197	6	27	6	30	26	661
	Mashed potatoes and gravy	149	2	12	3	30	46	444

205

Restaurant	Food Item	Calories	Fat (g)	% Cals. as fat	Protein (g)	Carbo-hydrate (g)	Cho-lesterol (mg)	Sodium (mg)
	Rice pilaf	173	5	26	3	29	0	146
	Steamed vegetables	48	<1	trace	3	9	0	59
KFC	Green beans	36	1	25	1	5	3	563
	BBQ baked beans	132	2	14	5	24	3	535
	Vegetable medley salad	126	4	29	1	21	0	240
	Mean greens	52	2	35	3	8	6	477
	Red beans and rice	114	3	24	4	18	4	315
	Mashed potatoes and gravy	70	1	13	3	15	5	370
	Macaroni and cheese	162	8	44	7	14	16	531
	Potato wedges	192	9	42	3	25	3	428
	Garden rice	75	1	12	2	15	0	576

Restaurant	Food Item	Calories	Fat (g)	% Cals. as fat	Protein (g)	Carbo-hydrate (g)	Cho-lesterol (mg)	Sodium (mg)
	COLD SIDE DISHES							
Boston Chicken	**Fruit salad**	**49**	**<1**	**0**	**<1**	**11**	**<1**	**7**
	Cranberry relish	**371**	**6**	**14**	**2**	**83**	**<1**	**<1**
	Cucumber salad	**79**	**7**	**80**	**<1**	**4**	**<1**	**182**
	Mediterranean pasta salad	**160**	**9**	**51**	**4**	**16**	**12**	**617**
	Tortellini salad	430	25	52	14	38	55	660
Chick-fil-A	**Carrot and raisin salad**	**116**	**5**	**39**	**1**	**18**	**6**	**8**
El Pollo Loco	Potato salad	180	10	50	2	21	10	340
Kenny Rogers	Pasta salad	272	17	56	6	95	46	421
	Potato salad	390	27	62	3	34	0	628
	Tomato cucumber salad	133	10	68	1	10	0	519

Restaurant	Food Item	Calories	Fat (g)	% Cals. as fat	Protein (g)	Carbo-hydrate (g)	Cho-lesterol (mg)	Sodium (mg)
KFC	Garden salad (no dressing)	16	0	0	1	3	0	10
	BREADS							
Boston Chicken	Cornbread	253	8	28	4	43	30	505
El Pollo Loco	Flour tortilla	90	3	30	3	15	0	150
	Corn tortilla	60	1	15	1	13	0	25
Kenny Rogers	Corn muffin	113	6	48	1	14	0	159
KFC	Cornbread	175	6	31	2	27	0	285
	Breadstick	110	3	25	3	17	0	15
	Sourdough roll	126	2	14	4	24	0	236
	SOUPS							
Boston Chicken	Chicken	87	3	31	12	4	31	500

Restaurant	Food Item	Calories	Fat (g)	% Cals. as fat	Protein (g)	Carbo-hydrate (g)	Cho-lesterol (mg)	Sodium (mg)
Chick-fil-A	**Hearty breast of chicken**	**152**	**3**	**18**	**16**	**11**	**46**	**530**
Kenny Rogers	**Chicken noodle–cup**	**111**	**2**	**16**	**7**	**16**	**23**	**715**
	Chicken noodle–bowl	**171**	**4**	**21**	**12**	**22**	**37**	**1148**

14

Healthier eating out
Pizza

Today, pizza is as ubiquitous as burgers and fries. It's an easily found "fast-food" and fits in perfectly with the quick and easy mindset of the '90s. You can get it by driving through, faxing in, or as a five-minute express meal. Pizza is an inexpensive meal out or an easy take-out meal for the home front. Pizza fits in for lunch or dinner and (as I recall from college days) for quite a few late-night snacks. Pizza, left from the night before (cold or microwaved) is even a good nutritional choice for breakfast. It beats the sausage biscuit or chips and soda when hunger pangs hit. Best yet, if you practice the p's and q's of eating out, pizza is a healthier choice than burgers and fries. It's a matter of what's on top, how deep, and how much.

A city or town without at least one local pizza parlor? Not a chance in America these days. Beyond the cheese, pepperoni, and onions-and-peppers pizza, the local pizza joint will fill those long sub rolls. (See Chapter 20 for more information on subs, hoagies, or whatever name you have for them in your neck of the woods.) Pizza is the mainstay of several fast-food chains. Domino's and Papa John's don't even let you sit down or order by the piece. It's a whole pie and outta here. Before just about every food could be phoned for, pizza headed the list of deliverable meals. In two other large pizza chains, Little Caesar and Pizza Hut, you have a choice: sit down or take-out. But wherever you eat it, pizza is the name of their game, although a few other offerings might sprinkle the menu—garlic bread, spaghetti, and salads.

More upscale pizza restaurants are appearing in different parts of the country. Some tout pizza that's made in wood-fired or brick ovens. From the West, it's California Pizza Kitchen, quickly marking their territory with wood-fired ovens. In the East, it's Bertucci's, growing slowly. Pizzeria Uno, from the middle of the country, Chicago, is the mature sibling when it comes to upscale pizza spots. "Original deep-dish pizza" is their pie.

Pizza is served at most "American" restaurants as well. Because it's a hit with the young, elders, and in-betweens, pizza's a regular on many menus. For instance, Houlihan's lists a five-cheese pizza (no, thanks) and a spicy grilled chicken pizza (looks good; go light on the cheese), and Chili's, another restaurant chain with an ethnic identity crisis, has multiplied their offerings of pizza.

Beyond the trend to cook pizza with new-fangled ovens, we've witnessed a move to more creativity with toppings. I call it "yuppie pizza." Ingredients such as goat's cheese, spinach, pesto, and roasted red peppers might fly solo or appear in combos. That's a far cry from "extra cheese and plenty of pepperoni." Nutritionally, it's good news. You're seeing more culinary care and nutrition consciousness in the upscale pizza world. The great taste of pizza is improving while the fat, cholesterol, sodium, and calories get axed.

Take a look at one wild (and healthy) combo from California Pizza Kitchens—Santa Fe chicken, consisting of grilled chicken breast marinated in lime and herbs, sauteed onions, and cilantro topped with fresh tomato salsa, sour cream, and guacamole (hold the last two ingredients). California Pizza Kitchens also lists several cheeseless pizzas. That's another new trend.

Before you order

From the nutritional point of view, pizza is thought of as off limits—loaded with fat, cholesterol, and calories. People who try to shed a few pounds think pizza must be erased from their future. That's simply not true. Think about it. Pizza dough is basically flour, yeast, salt, and water—no fat, no cholesterol, and only a few calories. Then tomato sauce is added, another low-calorie and low-fat item. Next in line, of course, the cheese is spread. Yes, cheese is high in calories and fat and has 20–30 milligrams of cholesterol per ounce.

How much cheese is really on one slice of medium pizza? about one ounce. A few larger chains are sprinkling part-skim cheese. Let's hope they continue. The final step is to load the toppings. The big question is will they be the low-calorie mushrooms, onions, spinach, or tomato slices? Or will you add extra cheese, pepperoni, and sausage? Just a few of the toppers Pizza Hut puts on their Meat Lover's® could break your heart, not to mention your diet: pepperoni, beef topping, pork topping, Italian sausage, ham, and bacon!

The sodium quotient in pizza is very reasonable—200–400 per slice; but if you sit down to four pieces, it adds up. Toppers such as pepperoni, sausage, and extra cheese can add sodium. Not only are they high in fat but they are higher in sodium than onions, artichokes, and eggplant.

When you know about the nutritional content of pizza, it is saddening to observe how some "weight watchers" eat it. They eat everything *but* the crust. It's analogous to eating a burger or sandwich without the bread. By now we should know enough to eat more of the bread and starch rather than the higher-fat items. Remember Skill Number 6: Order according to the Food Guide Pyramid.

Overeating is the biggest problem with pizza. One or two slices are always left on the tray begging to be eaten. Try Skill Number 7: Practice portion control from the word go. Order less. If you typically order three slices, get two. If your usual is a large pizza to share, order a medium. On the other end, practice Skill

10: Know when enough is enough. Pack it up and take it home. Remember, eat it cold or warm it up for breakfast.

Menu management

Pizza can easily be a healthy meal. Think about what's topped on and how much you order. It's best to set a limit of two to four toppers. Refer to the Green and Red Flag Toppings (following) to separate the healthy from the unhealthy. It used to be that pizza crust was thin—no options. Now, crust comes in all depths: thin, medium, and deep-dish. Pizza Hut names their types euphemistically: Thin 'N Crispy®, Hand Tossed (medium), and Pan Pizza (deep-dish). The rule of thumb is thinner is slimmer. Look at the stats in the "Pizza Sampler: The Nutrition Numbers" chart at the end of this chapter and you'll see.

Before you order, think about how many pieces fit your needs. If you are working at trimming up, one or two slices are plenty. If cholesterol is your concern, not calories, and you go vegetarian, then maybe three slices are right. Order the pizza size with the number of slices that meets the group's appetite needs.

Another bit of advice is to have a salad along with the pizza. Not only does that allow you to check off one vegetable serving but salad is filling and won't leave as much room for pizza. Most restaurants serving pizza also list salads. Even the corner pizza parlor offers a garden or Greek salad. Don't forget your salad watchwords—"dressing on the side." Crunch on the salad first, prior to delivery of the pizza. Pizzeria Uno offers Ike's house salad—a nice light salad with mushrooms, tomatoes, and rings of onion and pepper. It's served with Ike's dressing, a light oil-and-vinegar mix, always served on the side.

One benefit of pizza joints: no greasy breadsticks or garlic bread greet you at the table. At the other end of the meal, dessert is no big deal. Bertucci's doesn't list a single one.

Green Flag Toppings

part-skim cheese
green peppers
red peppers
roasted peppers
onions
herbs and spices
sliced tomatoes
mushrooms
black olives
salsa
broccoli
eggplant
artichoke hearts
pineapple
tuna
garlic
feta cheese
spinach
chicken—grilled or spicy
shrimp, crabmeat

Red Flag Toppings

extra cheese (all types)
pepperoni
sausage
anchovies
bacon
meatballs
prosciutto

**Special
Requests
Pizza
Style**

Please bring the salad dressing on the side.

Can I have some vinegar on the side also?

Please go light on the cheese.

Can I substitute spicy chicken for the sausage (or pepperoni) on this pizza?

Instead of the extra cheese, can you put on more onions and sliced tomatoes?

Can I get this pizza cheeseless?

Please wrap this up so I can take it home.

Please bring a take-home box when you bring the pizza.

The Menu: Pizza Style

Salads ✓**Garden salad** (with lettuce, green peppers, mushrooms, tomatoes)
✓**Greek salad** (lettuce or spinach topped with mushrooms, bell peppers, onions, and Greek olives)
Caesar salad (romaine leaves with egg, onions, buttery croutons, and cheese) served with thick Caesar dressing
Antipasto (cold eggplant parmesan, tomato and mozzarella salad, roasted peppers, marinated artichoke hearts, and prosciutto) served with breadsticks

Salad Dressings: **Italian**
✓**Light Italian**
✓**Olive oil and vinegar**
French
Thousand Island
Ranch

Pizza ✓**Cheese and tomato sauce**
Pepperoni
Sausage
✓**Vegetarian** (with tomatoes, onions, mushrooms, and broccoli florets)
✓**Grilled vegetarian** (grilled red and green onions, eggplant, and tomatoes)
Eggplant Parmesan and onion
✓**Grilled eggplant cheeseless**
✓**Grilled teriyaki chicken**
Cheese plus (mozzarella, ricotta, and sharp Cheddar)

✓*Preferred Choice*
Some depending on special requests

✓**Hawaiian** (with pineapple,
Canadian bacon, onion, and
tomato slices)
✓**Artichoke, olive, and capers**
(artichoke hearts, Greek olives,
and capers)
✓**Goat's cheese and roasted garlic**
(bits of cheese melted with
roasted garlic and sliced tomatoes)
Meat plus (with pepperoni,
sausage, and meatballs)

Breads   ✓**Breadsticks** (thick breadsticks
sprinkled with herbs)
Garlic rolls
Garlic bread
✓**Focaccia** (flat Italian bread topped
with herbs, sliced tomatoes, or
cheese)

Now that you've seen what might be on the Menu,
find the Model Meal that best fits your nutrition goals.
For an explanation of the Model Meals and their targeted nutritional values, see Chapter 3.

*Your Order, Please**

Healthy	30% Calories as fat
Daily	20% Calories as protein
Eating	50% Calories as carbohydrate
Goals	300 mg/day Cholesterol
	3000 mg/day Sodium

❶

Low Calorie/	**Garden salad** with Italian
Low Fat	dressing, reduced calorie, 2 tbsp
Model Meal:	**Original cheese pizza,** 2 slices
Godfather's	
Estimated	calories 582
Nutrient	fat 18g (28% of calories)
Evaluation	protein 22g (15% of calories)
	carbohydrate 83g (57% of calories)
	cholesterol 44 mg
	sodium 1037 mg

❷

Low Calorie/	**Greek salad** with Italian dressing,
Low	low calorie, with extra vinegar
Cholesterol	**Pan! Pan! vegetable pizza,** 2
Model Meal:	slices
Little Caesar's	
Pizza	
Estimated	calories 540
Nutrient	fat 24g (40% of calories)
Evaluation	protein 25g (18% of calories)
	carbohydrate 56g (42% of calories)
	cholesterol 43 mg
	sodium 1387 mg

*For these Model Meals, exact nutrition information
from the specified restaurant was used.

Higher Calorie/Low Fat Model Meal: Domino's

Veggie pizza, hand tossed, 4 slices

Estimated Nutrient Evaluation

calories 836
fat 20g (22% of calories)
protein 60g (28% of calories)
carbohydrate 104g (50% of calories)
cholesterol 76 mg
sodium 2050 mg

Higher Calorie/Low Cholesterol Model Meal: Pizza Hut

Tossed Salad, 2 cups from salad bar (all vegetables) with Ranch dressing, 2 tbsp, with vinegar
Veggie Lovers® pizza, 2 slices

Estimated Nutrient Evaluation

calories 621
fat 25g (36% of calories)
protein 28g (18% of calories)
carbohydrate 71g (46% of calories)
cholesterol 44 mg
sodium 1003 mg

Low Sodium Model Meal: California Pizza Kitchens

Field greens salad, ½ order with Balsamic Dijon vinaigrette, 1 tbsp, with extra balsamic vinegar
Grilled eggplant cheeseless pizza, 3 slices

Estimated Nutrient Evaluation

calories 593
fat 17g (25% of calories)
protein 26g (18% of calories)
carbohydrate 84g (57% of calories)
cholesterol 0 mg
sodium 1850 mg

Pizza Sampler: The Nutrition Numbers*

Restaurant	Pizza Item	Calories	Fat (g)	% Cals. as fat	Protein (g)	Carbo-hydrate (g)	Cho-lesterol (mg)	Sodium (mg)
Domino's Pizza	12″ HAND TOSSED (1 slice)							
	Cheese	**172**	**5**	**26**	**7**	**25**	**10**	**490**
	X-tra cheese & pepperoni	**228**	**9**	**37**	**10**	**25**	**21**	**652**
	Veggie	**180**	**5**	**25**	**15**	**26**	**19**	**514**
	1 slice from 12″ deep-dish							
	Cheese	280	12	39	24	63	32	1184
	X-tra cheese & pepperoni	335	17	46	15	32	27	754
	Veggie	288	12	38	12	33	16	617

*Based on nutrition information provided by each restaurant company for 1 slice of pizza. Items with less than 40% calories from fat and/or less than 11g of fat are in **bold**.

Restaurant	Food Item	Calories	Fat (g)	% Cals. as fat	Protein (g)	Carbo-hydrate (g)	Cho-lesterol (mg)	Sodium (mg)
Godfather's Pizza	MEDIUM ORIGINAL CRUST (1 slice)							
	Cheese	**242**	**7**	**26**	**10**	**35**	**22**	**285**
	Combo	318	12	34	16	37	38	569
	1 slice from medium Golden Crust							
	Cheese	**229**	**9**	**31**	**8**	**28**	**19**	**272**
	Combo	283	13	41	13	30	29	526
Little Caesar's Pizza	ROUND PIZZA (1 slice)							
	Cheese	**164**	**6**	**33**	**10**	**19**	**15**	**201**
	Pepperoni	**179**	**7**	**35**	**10**	**20**	**18**	**251**
	Vegetable	**169**	**6**	**32**	**9**	**20**	**15**	**219**

Restaurant	Pizza Item	Calories	Fat (g)	% Cals. as fat	Protein (g)	Carbo-hydrate (g)	Cho-lesterol (mg)	Sodium (mg)
Little Caesar's Pizza	PAN! PAN! (1 slice)							
	Cheese	181	6	30	10	23	16	355
	Pepperoni	198	7	32	10	23	20	413
	Vegetable	186	6	29	10	24	16	374
Pizza Hut	MEDIUM THIN 'N CRISPY (1 slice)							
	Cheese	223	10	40	13	19	25	503
	Pepperoni	230	11	43	12	20	27	678
	Meat Lovers®	297	16	48	14	20	44	1068
	Veggie Lovers®	192	8	38	11	20	17	551
	Supreme	262	14	48	15	20	31	819
	Chunky veggie	193	8	37	11	28	17	546

Restaurant	Pizza Item	Calories	Fat (g)	% Cals. as fat	Protein (g)	Carbo-hydrate (g)	Cho-lesterol (mg)	Sodium (mg)
Pizza Hut	MEDIUM HAND TOSSED (1 slice)							
	Cheese	**253**	**9**	**32**	**15**	**27**	**25**	**593**
	Pepperoni	**253**	**10**	**36**	**20**	**28**	**25**	**738**
	Meat Lovers®	321	15	42	16	28	42	1105
	Veggie Lovers®	**222**	**7**	**28**	**13**	**28**	**17**	**641**
	Supreme	289	12	37	17	28	29	894
	Chunky veggie	**224**	**6**	**24**	**13**	**29**	**17**	**633**
Pizza Hut	MEDIUM PAN® (1 slice)							
	Cheese	279	13	42	14	26	25	473
	Pepperoni	280	18	58	8	26	25	618
	Meat Lovers®	347	23	60	15	27	42	986

Restaurant	Pizza Item	Calories	Fat (g)	% Cals. as fat	Protein (g)	Carbo-hydrate (g)	Cho-lesterol (mg)	Sodium (mg)
	Veggie Lovers®	249	15	54	7	27	17	521
	Supreme	315	16	46	16	27	29	774
	Chunky veggie	**251**	**10**	**36**	**12**	**21**	**17**	**513**
Pizza Hut	MEDIUM BIGFOOT™ (1 slice)							
	Cheese	**179**	**5**	**25**	**9**	**24**	**14**	**959**
	Pepperoni	**195**	**7**	**32**	**10**	**24**	**17**	**1022**
	Personal Pan–pepperoni	675	30	40	29	76	53	1335
	Personal Pan–supreme	647	35	49	37	76	53	1313
Round Table Pizza	LARGE THIN PIZZA (1 slice)							
	Cheese	**166**	**7**	**38**	**8**	**18**	**21**	**332**

Restaurant	Pizza Item	Calories	Fat (g)	% Cals. as fat	Protein (g)	Carbo-hydrate (g)	Cho-lesterol (mg)	Sodium (mg)
	Pepperoni	**180**	**8**	**40**	**8**	**18**	**21**	**441**
	Combo	**192**	**9**	**42**	**10**	**19**	**26**	**449**
Round Table Pizza	LARGE PAN PIZZA (1 slice)							
	Cheese	310	11	32	13	40	30	631
	Pepperoni	332	13	35	14	40	32	174
	Combo	340	13	34	15	41	36	759

15

Healthier eating out

American Style

family & dinner restaurants

Mushroom burgers topped with melted mozzarella and fries on the side; Mexican salad loaded in a fried tortilla shell; or teriyaki chicken breast with a baked potato dressed with butter and sour cream and accompanied by a crisp garden salad with blue cheese dressing. And maybe it's apple pie à la mode for a finisher. That's a mere scattering of the regulars in "American" restaurants, those restaurants that are a few steps up from fast-food chains and a few steps down from the cloth napkins, fresh flowers, and ambiance of upscale restaurants.

American eating places are crowded by people in search of "R and R," rest and relaxation. You frequent these for lunch or dinner to meet family or friends, for some relief from the hectic work pace, after a weekend matinee, for weekend brunch after a fitness workout, or for a late night snack. Quick and pleasant service, a bit of taste bud pleasure, and a full gut fills the bill.

Two categories of American restaurants line America's highways, city streets, and the halls of malls. Dinner houses, or "fern bars" in the vernacular, are a bit more upscale and expensive than the family restaurants that specialize in getting the job of feeding done inexpensively. The menus overlap considerably. You'll find hamburgers, French fries, chef and taco salads, and pasta entrees on both. Many dinner and family restaurants belong to large chains. Familiar chain dinner houses are TGI Friday's, Houlihan's, and Applebee's. Growing bigger and wider is Ruby Tuesday's and Houston's. Denny's, Shoney's, and Bob Evans fit the family restaurant category. Many independently owned restaurants also feature "American" fare.

Get to know the cuisine

We use the term "American" fare, but what is it? The menus reflect a melting pot of cuisines. Bottom line: American food is a blending and "Americanization" of foods from around the world. You'll find menu offerings from America's ethnic favorites—Mexican nachos and fajitas, Chinese stir-fries and pot stickers, and Italian lasagna and pizza. As new ethnic cuisines become popular, those items fall into the melting pot of American restaurant offerings. It's already happened— TGI Friday's lists Thai chicken as an appetizer; it's a variation on satay.

This cuisine leaves much to be desired for the health-oriented diner. It's loaded with fat—think about fried mozzarella sticks, quiche, or super nachos; and it's heavy on protein—eight-ounce hamburgers and whole chicken breasts. Vegetables and fruits are hard to find, and the portions are easily enough for two. Last, but not least, the waitperson expects an entree order per person. Family style is not the serving style in family restaurants.

Burgers, grilled and topped with cheese and bacon, are the trademark of American cuisine. Contemplate the calorie count of a four-ounce cooked hamburger (and that's a small one) served on a roll with French fries and a dinner salad with Thousand Island dressing. Over 800 calories, with almost 40 grams (45 percent) of the calories from fat. That's a chunk of calories and fat in one fell swoop.

Though you'll need to skip around the menu and apply a big dose of Skill Number 8—Menu creativity, these restaurants don't need to be crossed out. Seek and you shall find a few healthy choices: peel-and-eat shrimp; blackened or Cajun chicken topped on a salad and served with potato and vegetable or on a sandwich roll; stir-fry chicken or shrimp. As healthier eating catches on, demand for lower-fat offerings grows. In just six years since the first edition of *The Restaurant Companion,* several large American restaurants have introduced healthier and lighter options. TGI Friday's features a few "lite" items—fresh vegetable baguette or Pacific Coast tuna, which ring in at 300 to 400 calories. Chili's makes their plug for health with a grilled chicken salad topped with fat-free honey-mustard dressing. How are the calories reduced a notch? It's no secret: the fat's been whisked away and the portions are shrunk. But don't have any visions of American restaurants becoming havens for the health conscious. They'll be serving up the super nachos, ten-ounce strip steaks, and fettucine Alfredo for many years to come.

Before you order

American restaurants call for you to employ all 10 Skills and Strategies (see Chapter 2). In particular, be an avid fat detective and practice menu creativity; have an action plan prior to your arrival. Chances are you've left some greenbacks at the restaurant before and you know the healthy bets only too well. Do not tempt your taste buds by even viewing the extensive bill of fare.

If you choose to peruse the menu, remember that fat is enemy number one. Steer clear of the Red Flag Words that ring out "FAT"—"stuffed with cheese," "served with blue cheese dressing," or "topped with cheese." Seek out the Green Flag Words that ring out "LEAN"—"grilled," "blackened," and "stir-fried." Keep a lid on extra fats such as mayonnaise spread on sandwiches or tossed in with tuna or chicken and butter on a grilled hamburger bun. Opt for zero-fat sandwich spreads such as mustard, honey-mustard, horseradish, or a fat-free dressing. Let the waitperson know, by asking questions, that you count your fat grams. Be specific and assertive about special requests. You'll note there are many in this chapter.

A big challenge in American restaurants is to avoid overeating. Don't start thinking about this at the end of the meal. Take a preventive approach. Employ creative strategies when ordering. Take advantage of soup or salad and half-sandwich combinations. Entertain splitting from appetizer through dessert with a dining partner. Or take the sharing route and complement two entrees to shave down the amount of protein. Share a hamburger, French fries, and spinach salad topped with light salad dressing.

If you can't convince anyone to split or share, go it alone. Order an appetizer with salad and/or soup. Split a large dinner salad or entree with yourself by requesting a doggie bag when you place your order. These tactics help you reduce the amount of food in front of you from the start so you don't overeat at the end. Don't feel compelled to order an entree just because that's the expectation. Be a rebel.

Menu management

Silverware and napkins are all that greet you at the table. Luckily no rolls and butter or chips and salsa say hello. Then it's on to appetizers. The crunchy fried variety are easy to find and lethal in fat. Even the healthy onions and mushrooms are battered, dipped, and fried in American restaurants. Frequent offerings are nachos or super nachos; that's fried tortilla chips with more high-fat goodies topped on—cheese, sour cream, and guacamole. Other tasty appetizers that add insult to injury are fried mozzarella sticks and buffalo chicken wings (fried and traditionally served with blue cheese dressing). As usual the low calorie spud skin is drowned in fat by frying, then topped with cheese, bacon bits, and sour cream. The healthiest part are the chives on top.

A few redeeming choices are shrimp cocktail, peel-and-eat shrimp with cocktail sauce, raw oysters on the half shell, and Mexican pizza. You might find a platter featuring raw vegetables with creamy dip platter. Unfortunately, the dip is 100 percent fat, but put menu creativity to work: ask for a side of low-calorie salad dressing and dip away. If your dining partners order high-fat appetizers, order a house salad or broth-based soup as your appetizer. That's easier than facing temptation when the greasy little tidbits arrive.

Soups divide down the middle—healthy and fat-dense. Here's a rule of thumb. If you can see through it or it's loaded with beans and vegetables, it's healthy. If it's white and creamy, it's loaded with fat. Common soups are the high-fat French onion (healthy before the cheese is loaded on top), New England clam chowder, potato or cheese soups. Healthier choices are chicken vegetable, black bean, chili (hold the cheese), or Manhattan clam chowder. If sodium is a concern, soup is best avoided.

Entrees are varied, from hot to cold, from Tex-Mex to Thai. You see the whole melting pot in American restaurants. You'll spot salads, sandwiches, burgers with various toppings, and hot entrees partnered with a starch and a hot vegetable. Healthy items abound— seek and you shall find. Practice Skill Number 4: Have an action plan in mind, and at least look for the type of item you want before perusing the whole menu. This limits menu ''shopping.''

The salad choices on American fare menus have grown. That is great for the health conscious, but observe what's topped on the healthy bed of greens. House salad, Cobb, taco, chicken or tuna salad, Greek, and spinach are the usuals. Some restaurants serve salads in fried tortilla shells. Request that yours arrives *sans* shell. The shell is just too crunchy and tempting to have within arm's reach.

If you choose a salad, observe the Red and Green Flag Words. Let's consider the Cobb salad: on top of greens you find chicken or turkey breast, crisp bacon, avocado, blue cheese, hard-boiled egg, black olives, and tomatoes. A few Red and a few Green words. If you like the basic ingredients, just request that a few items be left in the kitchen. Replace those with more of the health variety—tomatoes, onions, peppers. Read the salad ingredients carefully. Request what you want in and out of your salad.

Last, but not least, is the dressing. Dressing can take a salad from healthy to nutritional disaster in spoonfuls. America's favorites—Thousand Island and blue cheese—ring in at 70 calories per level tablespoon. Here are a few suggestions: take advantage of reduced-calorie or fat-free dressings; order any dressing on the side so you control the quantity; request a side of vinegar or lemon wedges to dilute the dressing. (For more details about salad dressings and suggestions for a healthy approach, see Chapter 21.)

Sandwiches are regular listings: tuna salad on a croissant and turkey club are just two regulars. Unfortunately, they are usually stacked with excess amounts of protein and/or fat. Watch out for the healthy-sounding tuna or chicken salad. These are packed with mayonnaise and thus tip the fat scale. Stick with unadulterated meats—turkey, roast beef, ham, or chicken. Ask to have the mayonnaise held, and request a side of mustard, low-calorie salad dressing, honey-mustard, barbecue sauce, or ketchup. Mexican hot sauce or horseradish work just as well. Half a sandwich with soup, salad, or baked potato might be plenty.

When zeroing in on a sandwich choice, observe the toppers. You might find an appealing grilled chicken breast sandwich, but they top it with bacon and cheese. Keep to the healthy preparations—charbroiled, teriyaki, or Cajun—and stick to the healthy toppers—sauteed onions, mushrooms, peppers, and jalapeños. Sandwiches to avoid are Reuben, Philadelphia cheese steak, clubs, and melts.

Another problem with sandwiches is their partners: potato chips, pasta salad, French fries, or creamy coleslaw. These are all loaded with fat and calories. Request that these be left off your plate, or exchange them for a healthier choice such as baked potato, rice pilaf, house salad, or steamed or sauteed vegetables.

On to one of American's favorite foods—burgers. An American menu without hamburgers and various toppings would be sacrilegious. Portions of protein are large. Take advantage of ordering the smaller size if a regular and jumbo are offered. If the quantity of meat is noted, for instance, ''six ounces (or a half-pound) of first-quality ground meat,'' remember that the amount is based on the raw weight. It cooks down by one or two ounces. A six-ounce hamburger will be a four to five-ounce hamburger when served. Hamburger toppings among the Red Flag Words are melted cheese (any type), bacon, and guacamole. Green Flag toppings include sauteed onions, peppers, and/or mushrooms, lettuce, tomato, raw onions, jalapeños, and barbecue sauce.

You might steer clear of hot entrees because you think salads and sandwiches are lighter and lower in calories. Interestingly, you'd do better with chicken or beef fajitas, chicken or vegetable stir-fry, or Cajun chicken breast. No doubt, some nutritional disasters lurk in the hot entree section—fettucine Alfredo, barbecued ribs, rib-eye steak.

American restaurants love to pile on the fats: baked potato with butter and sour cream, potatoes au gratin, creamed spinach, etc. You'll have to open your mouth and make special requests to delete the fat and add the healthier side dishes, such as rice pilaf, baked potato (toppings on the side), dinner salad, or steamed vegetables.

Desserts are best passed by. Cheesecake, some decadent chocolate cake, apple pie à la mode, or ice cream sundae are the usuals. Decent choices are fruit pie (hold the ice cream or whipped cream), sorbet, sherbet, or frozen yogurt. The portions are huge, so order dessert with at least two forks or spoons.

Green Flag Words

INGREDIENTS:
sauteed onions, peppers, and/or
    mushrooms
jalapeños
BBQ sauce
cocktail sauce
mustard, honey-mustard
lettuce, sliced tomatoes, raw
    onions
spicy Mexican beef or chicken
low-calorie or fat-free salad
    dressing

COOKING METHODS/MENU
DESCRIPTIONS:
marinated in teriyaki sauce
Cajun or blackened
mesquite-grilled
charbroiled or grilled
with oriental sauce
stir-fried
marinated
barbecued
fajitas

**Red Flag
Words**

INGREDIENTS:
cheese (grated, melted, topped
  with, smothered in, sauce)
blue cheese (crumbled, topped
  with, salad dressing)
guacamole
bacon (strips, crumbled, crisp)
sausage
sour cream
butter or cream
mayonnaise, garlic mayonnaise,
  "special" sauce

COOKING METHODS/MENU
DESCRIPTIONS:
golden fried, crispy fried
deep-fried
lightly fried
battered and fried
rolled in breadcrumbs and fried or
  sauteed
topped with cheese, bacon, and/or
  sour cream
served in or on crisp tortilla shell
large, jumbo, piled high, stacked
Alfredo

AT THE TABLE:
butter or margarine
mayonnaise
sour cream
salad dressing
cream (half-and-half) for hot
  beverages

**Special
Requests
American
Style**

Please bring me a little bowl of low-calorie dressing that I can use for the vegetable dip.

Please bring my House Salad when you bring the others their appetizers.

I'd like to order an appetizer as my main course. But will you bring it when you bring the others their entrees?

Please put the salad dressing on the side and bring some vinegar or lemon wedges.

On the blackened chicken sandwich, please leave off the cheese, but add lettuce and tomato.

On the roast beef sandwich, can you make sure they don't put any butter or mayonnaise on the bread? However, I'd like a side of mustard or horseradish.

Do you have Mexican hot sauce? Could I get a bit to use on my salad or sandwich?

Please hold the sour cream, but you can load on the onions and jalapeños.

Could I substitute a baked potato or steamed vegetables for the French fries?

I know the sandwich or hamburger comes with French fries, but could you leave them off the plate?

Could I get that sandwich served on whole-wheat bread rather than on a croissant?

We are going to split the salad and the hamburger, so could you bring an extra plate?

May I have the rest of this wrapped up to take home?

The Menu: American Style

Appetizers **Nachos** (nacho chips covered with melted Monterey Jack cheese and jalapeño peppers, served with Mexican hot sauce)
Super nachos (nacho chips covered with melted Monterey Jack cheese, refried beans, spicy beef or chicken, shredded lettuce, and tomatoes, served with Mexican hot sauce)
Buffalo chicken wings (marinated chicken wings in hot and spicy sauce, lightly fried, and served with blue cheese dressing and celery sticks)
✓**Peel-and-eat shrimp** (one-quarter pound boiled shrimp in a spicy sauce, served with cocktail sauce)
Potato skins (fried and crispy potato skins, filled with cheese and your choice of bacon bits, sour cream, and/or onions)
Mozzarella sticks (sticks of mozzarella cheese, rolled in breadcrumbs and fried; served with marinara sauce)
✓**Raw bar platter** (combination of oysters on the halfshell, steamed littleneck clams, and jumbo shrimp, served with cocktail sauce)
Chicken fingers (small pieces of tender chicken breast breaded and fried, served with choice of honey mustard or barbecue sauce)

✓*Preferred Choice*
Some depending on special requests

Soups

New England clam chowder
(creamy New England style
chowder with chunks of clams
and potato, served with oyster
crackers)
French onion soup (crock of rich
onion soup, smothered with Swiss
cheese)
✓**Chili** (spicy mixture of pinto
beans, ground beef, and sauteed
onions and peppers, topped with
onions and Monterey Jack cheese)
✓**Vegetable gumbo** (blend of
garden vegetables, onions,
tomatoes, broccoli, and green
beans simmered in Cajun spices)

Salads

✓**House salad** (blend of greens
with sliced cucumbers and
tomatoes, topped with alfalfa
sprouts; choice of dressings)
✓**Spinach salad** (fresh spinach
topped with sliced mushrooms,
eggs, bacon bits, and croutons,
served with hot bacon dressing)
Caesar salad topped with your
choice of blackened chicken, fresh
tuna, or shrimp
✓**Seafood pasta salad** (rotini
blended with baby shrimp and red
pepper, tossed with Italian
dressing, and served on bed of
mixed greens)
✓**Blackened chicken salad** (slices
of marinated and blackened
chicken breast, served with mixed
salad greens, avocado slices,
cherry tomatoes, and broccoli
florets, topped with shredded
Swiss cheese and croutons)
✓**Mexican salad** (choice of spicy
chicken or beef, served on bed of
mixed greens, with spicy Mexican
beans, red and green peppers,

tomato, and Monterey Jack
cheese, all in crispy flour tortilla
shell) Request shell be held

✓**Chef salad** (julienne sliced turkey,
ham, and Swiss cheese, served
on bed of lettuce greens, diced
tomatoes, red and green pepper
rounds, all in crispy flour tortilla
shell) Request shell be held

Choice of Salad Dressings:

House (creamy garlic)	Thousand Island
	Hot bacon
	✓Lemon vinaigrette
✓Italian	✓Oil and vinegar
French	✓Low-calorie Italian
Blue cheese	Ranch
	✓Fat-free French

Sandwiches* **Philadelphia cheese steak** (thinly
sliced beef, grilled with onions
and mushrooms, and topped with
melted cheese; served in
submarine roll)

✓**French dip** (thinly sliced beef,
topped with melted provolone
cheese, and served in submarine
roll with natural gravy)

✓**Blackened chicken sandwich**
(breast of chicken marinated and
blackened on the grill, topped
with lettuce, tomato, sprouts, crisp
bacon slices, and Cheddar cheese)

Tuna melt (creamy tuna salad,
topped with melted Swiss cheese
and served with lettuce and
tomato)

Seafood salad croissant (flaky
croissant filled with mixture of
creamy seafood salad, celery and
onions, served with lettuce and
tomato)

*All sandwiches are served with
French fries and creamy coleslaw

Burgers*	Regular hamburgers are 6 ozs. of ground beef and jumbo size are 9 ozs.

✓**American hamburger**
Cheeseburger (add slice of Swiss or Cheddar cheese)
Bacon cheeseburger (add several slices of bacon and slice of Monterey Jack cheese)
✓**Veggie burger** (add sauteed onions, peppers, and mushrooms)
Chili burger (add spicy Mexican chili)

*All burgers are served with sliced tomato on bed of lettuce, with French fries and side dish of creamy coleslaw.

Hot Entrees	✓**Fajitas** (choice of chicken or beef, grilled with sliced onions and green peppers, served with warm flour tortillas and sides of sour cream, guacamole, Mexican hot sauce)

Baby back ribs (robust portion of pork ribs, marinated and barbecued with zesty barbecue sauce, and served with fried onion rings and baked beans)
✓**Teriyaki chicken breast** (boneless breast marinated in teriyaki sauce and grilled; served with rice pilaf and sauteed vegetables)
✓**Steak** (6 oz. top sirloin served with sauteed onions and peppers)
Chicken fried steak (sirloin steak, dipped in batter, and fried; served with country gravy, baked potato, and steamed vegetables)

✓**Oriental stir-fry** (choice of chicken, shrimp, or just vegetables, stir-fried with oriental sauces, and served over a bed of Chinese egg noodles)

✓**Fettucini primavera** (sauteed broccoli, mushrooms, and red peppers, tossed with light tomato sauce, and served on bed of fettucini)

Combina- ✓**Soup and salad** (bowl of any
tions soup and house salad)

Quiche and salad (slice of ham, broccoli, and mushroom quiche, served with house salad)

✓**Soup and half sandwich** (bowl of any soup, served with half of French dip or smoked turkey sandwich)

✓**Salad and half sandwich** (house salad, served with half of French dip or smoked turkey sandwich)

Side **French fries**
orders **Creamy coleslaw**
✓**Rice pilaf**
✓**Baked potato** with choice of butter and/or sour cream
✓**Sauteed vegetables**

Desserts **Mud pie** (chocolate graham cracker crust filled with coffee ice cream and topped with fudge sauce)

✓**Deep-dish apple pie** à la mode (vanilla ice cream) or topped with whipped cream

New York style cheesecake (topped with choice of strawberry or blueberry sauce)

Ice cream (two scoops of vanilla, chocolate, or strawberry)

Hot fudge sundae (two scoops of vanilla ice cream, topped with hot fudge sauce, walnuts, and whipped cream)

✓**Sorbet** (two scoops of raspberry or lemon sherbet)

✓**Frozen strawberry yogurt** (large portion of soft-serve frozen yogurt)

Now that you've seen what might be available on the Menu, find the Model Meal that best fits your nutrition goals. For an explanation of the Model Meals and their targeted nutritional values, see Chapter 3.

Your Order, Please

Healthy	30%	Calories as fat
Daily	20%	Calories as protein
Eating	50%	Calories as carbohydrate
Goals	300	mg/day Cholesterol
	3000	mg/day Sodium

Low Calorie/ **Peel-and-eat shrimp**
Low Fat *Quantity:* 1 order (9–12 med.)
Model Meal *Exchanges:* 3 meat (lean)
Cocktail sauce for above
Quantity: 2 tbsp
Exchanges: free
Oriental stir-fry, vegetable
Quantity: 1½ cups
Exchanges: 2 fat; 3 vegetable
Chinese egg noodles with above
Quantity: 1 cup
Exchanges: 2 starch
Sorbet, raspberry (split order)
Quantity: ¾ cup
Exchanges: ½ fat; 1 starch; 1 fruit
Mineral water
Quantity: unlimited
Exchanges: free

Estimated	calories 608
Nutrient	fat 14g (21% of calories)
Evaluation	protein 32g (21% of calories)
	carbohydrate 88g (58% of calories)
	cholesterol 227 mg (high, due to shrimp)
	sodium 970 mg

**Low Calorie/
Low
Cholesterol
Model Meal**

Chili (hold the cheese)
Quantity: 1 cup
House salad (dressing on the
  side)
Quantity: 2 cups
Italian dressing (low calorie)
Quantity: 2 tbsp
Baked potato (hold butter and
  sour cream; use chili to dress)
Quantity: 1 large
Light beer
Quantity: 12 oz

Estimated
Nutrient
Evaluation

calories 595
fat 11g (17% of calories)
protein 36g (24% of calories)
carbohydrate 68g (46% of calories)
alcohol 13% of calories
cholesterol 135 mg
sodium 1146 mg

**Higher
Calorie/Low
Fat Model
Meal**

House salad (dressing on the
  side)
Quantity: 2 cups
Exchanges: 2 vegetable
Blue cheese dressing (request
  vinegar)
Quantity: 1 tbsp
Exchanges: 1 fat
Teriyaki chicken breast
Quantity: 4 oz
Exchanges: 4 meat (lean)
Rice pilaf
Quantity: 1 cup
Exchanges: 3 starch

Sauteed vegetables
Quantity: 1 cup
Exchanges: 1 fat; 2 vegetable
Wine
Quantity: 1 glass (6 oz)
Exchanges: account for calories
but don't omit exchanges

Estimated   calories 758
Nutrient   fat 26g (31% of calories)
Evaluation   protein 42g (22% of calories)
               carbohydrate 61g (32% of calories)
               alcohol 15% of calories
               cholesterol 120 mg
               sodium 1170 mg

Higher
Calorie/Low
Cholesterol
Model Meal

Blackened chicken salad (hold
cheese; request more tomatoes
and broccoli; request Mexican
hot sauce)
Quantity: 1 order
Lemon vinaigrette dressing
Quantity: 2 tbsp
Dinner roll
Quantity: 1
Deep-dish apple pie a la mode
(hold ice cream; ask for 2 forks
and extra plate)
Quantity: ½ piece

Estimated   calories 795
Nutrient   fat 31g (35% of calories)
Evaluation   protein 38g (19% of calories)
               carbohydrate 91g (46% of calories)
               cholesterol 157 mg
               sodium 1080 mg

Low Sodium Model Meal

Veggie burger (hold French fries and coleslaw)
Quantity: 1 (4½ oz cooked)
Baked potato (hold butter and sour cream; request mustard)
Quantity: 1 large
Dijon mustard for above
Quantity: 1–2 tbsp
Milk (low fat or skim)
Quantity: 8 oz

Estimated Nutrient Evaluation

calories 805
fat 30g (34% of calories)
protein 54g (27% of calories)
carbohydrate 78g (39% of calories)
cholesterol 130 mg
sodium 874 mg

16

Healthier eating out
Upscale Dining

The menus of French and Continental restaurants of yesterday have done a one hundred eighty-degree turn. That's good news for the health conscious. Goodbye to cream sauce, hollandaise, and au gratin and hello to ginger soy sauce, chipolte peppers, pineapple salsa, and sun-dried tomatoes. The new-fangled continental food is christened with several names—fusion cuisine, multiethnic fare, or new American regional cooking. Whatever the name, it's the melding of ingredients, spices, preparation techniques, and recipes from across the globe.

Fusion cuisine has evolved in part because of diners' desire to move away from heavy French foods. Also, the array of foods and restaurants available in the U.S. just continues to bloom, with Thai, Japanese, Korean, and Vietnamese foods slowly but surely muscling their way into the picture. Another contribution to this changing cuisine is the spread of Californian and Southwestern cuisine.

American-trained chefs experiment with new recipes, ingredients, and cooking techniques like smoking, grilling, and marinating. They travel, explore recipes of different cultures, trade secrets with chefs from other countries, and then integrate these into their menu mix. In turn, chefs from all sectors of the globe visit the U.S. and toss their culinary talents into the melting pot.

Here's a multiethnic sampling of menu listings you might find in a continental restaurant of the '90s: grilled tamari chicken with shiitake mushrooms and ginger soy sauce; cheese tortellini with prosciutto in a basil and cream sauce; and chicken pot pie. An eclectic and interesting menu is the goal.

No doubt, in most large cities you will still find restaurants dedicated to preparing foods in old-style French *haute cuisine.* You will also find upscale Italian, Mexican, and Chinese restaurants. For detailed information on upscale dining for each ethnic cuisine, read the chapter dedicated to that type of restaurant.

Get to know the cuisine

Since French cuisine has played such an important role in defining cooking and dining around the world, it's interesting to recap its recent history. One quality that defined French cookery, referred to as *grande* or *haute cuisine,* was its complicated and labor-intensive sauces. The sauces were started by roasting meat or poultry bones with *mirepoix*—celery, carrots, and onions. That creates the base for a stock. Stocks simmer to concentrate and intensify flavors and then are combined with butter, eggs, cream, and/or flours to thicken them. Bérnaise, béchamel, Bordelaise, and espagnole were just a few of the complex sauces. Expensive ingredients were commonly used in haute cuisine, such as truffles, pâté de foie gras, and crème fraîche. The master chefs of grand French cuisine blossomed during the nineteenth and early twentieth centuries. Haute cuisine was *the* cuisine of the upper class, clearly not standard fare in France.

Different regions of France specialized in producing or manufacturing particular ingredients or recipes. For instance, in Brittany and Normandy dairy products were a specialty. Provence was known for its sauce Provençal, made with tomatoes, garlic, and olive oil. Dijon, a city in the Burgundy region, is well known for its mustard, which contains a bit of wine. And Bordeaux, beyond being world-renowned for wine production, also claims sauce Bordelaise.

Around the middle of the twentieth century, there were changes brewing in how French chefs prepared foods. Chefs were abandoning heavy, complex sauces and high-fat ingredients for lighter, vegetable-based sauces. More chefs were traveling and returning with recipes and ingredients that they intermingled with the old ones. The result is referred to as *nouvelle cuisine*. These lighter preparation techniques spread to American restaurants.

Madeleine Kamman in *In Madeleine's Kitchen* sums up the definition of nouvelle cuisine. French cooking has been "updated for the twentieth century, simplified quite a bit, rejuvenated by foreign and ethnic ingredients, lightened in texture by both the adoption of Oriental techniques of cooking and modern man's worry about his arteries and the expanse of his waistline, and truly personalized by each cook or chef . . . exercising his/her own creativity at combining ingredients." New French cooking is no less an art form, but the bottom line is that the result is great for the health-conscious diner.

This chapter discusses restaurants where you go to "dine." Visits to upscale restaurants might be reserved for a special occasion—a birthday celebration, anniversary, or graduation, just to name a few happy events. Also, many business meals are eaten in upscale establishments.

No matter what type of food it is—French, Italian, Spanish, Chinese, or wherever it came from—you have different expectations in an "upscale" restaurant than when you buzz into a fast-food spot or fold up a slice of pizza. It's in upscale restaurants that you expect to be waited on, where you get white-glove service. Unlike the quick-order-and-bring-me-a-check restaurants, you plan to linger over your meal for two or three hours, enjoying the food and relaxing environment. It's in these restaurants that you are almost expected to eat everything from soup to nuts.

You'll perhaps be greeted with a small taste bud teaser. These restaurants often serve their own special bread, which is quickly delivered. It might be garlic rolls in a restaurant with an Italian persuasion, herb rolls or cheese bread in a place serving regional American cuisine, or jalapeño bread if you go Southwestern. The first question asked is, ''What will you have to drink?'' Maybe it's a mixed drink before dinner, wine with dinner, and a cordial to top off the meal. That can tally up to hundreds of calories. (For information on choosing alcoholic beverages, see Chapter 4.)

In upscale restaurants, you are expected to order and linger over appetizers while sipping an alcoholic drink. A salad then follows with a large main course not far behind. The fish, beef, or pasta is at least double the quantity you need. Dessert and a hot beverage are usual at the other end of the meal.

All of these factors—the length of time spent around the table, extra eats at the table, soup-to-nuts ordering, large quantities of food, elaborate preparation, alcohol and tempting desserts—can make upscale dining a challenge. Success requires persistence and just plain ''white knuckling'' it. The good old strategies of having a game plan in mind, portion control from the starting gate, and knowing when enough is enough are paramount. Remember, you don't need to keep up with your dining partners. Don't order from soup to nuts. Pick and choose which courses you want and strike the others. Avoid price-fixed menus so you don't feel hemmed in to overeat. One special strategy is to focus on the pleasure of the special occasion and/or the pleasant environment. Luxuriate in the ambiance; it helps take the importance off the food.

Before you order

You can choose to order healthy, low-fat, and calorie-conscious menu selections when eating upscale. However, you will need to ask questions and make special requests in order to get this mission accomplished. A few watchwords: don't cross the threshold starving; drink plenty of non-caloric liquids; practice out-of-sight, out-of-mouth techniques; and order the filling, low-calorie foods such as salads and broth-based soups.

Fat is, as usual, the biggest pitfall. You'll immediately be encouraged to indulge in high-fat temptations as the fresh baked bread and butter or cheese spread or whatever is plopped on the table. Limit these by politely forcing them to the other end of the table, or ask that they be whisked back to the kitchen, that is, if your dining partners agree. More fat is loaded onto appetizers such as escargot, stuffed mushrooms, or pâté. But a few healthy appetizers are usually available: shrimp cocktail, smoked salmon platter and grilled vegetable mini pizza, to name a few. Healthy-sounding salads can further add fat with high-fat ingredients such as cheese, bacon, croutons, olives, and egg yolk. Look for salads featuring mainly greens. Get dressing on the side, and lighten up on or have them hold the high-fat add-ons.

Entrees may be high in fat from the word go, such as prime rib, or have fat added to a low-fat protein food, like shrimp scampi or sole stuffed with crabmeat and served with a cream sauce. Choose a petite fillet mignon with mushrooms, shrimp with vegetables over linguini, or other preparations that feature smaller protein portions, low-fat preparations, and plenty of vegetables. Obviously, some of the decadent desserts don't exactly assist you in keeping fat controlled. But berries and a nice shot of liqueur are more than you can usually fit after the main course. That is if you plan on keeping your belt on the same notch.

When you order, pay attention to the food choice as well as the cooking method. Keep the Red and Green Flag Words in mind. The Red Flag Words point out high-fat ingredients or preparation methods. The Green Flag Words steer you toward low fat. Portion control helps limit fat and calories simply because you eat less. Practice menu creativity: order a salad when others eat appetizers and an appetizer or two for your main course; or split everything from soup to desserts with your dining partner. Don't feel pressured to order an entree. Keep the Food Guide Pyramid in mind and go heavy on the carbos and light on the protein.

For those who monitor sodium, careful ordering, special requests, and portion control from the word go help keep the milligrams reasonable. Salt and high-sodium ingredients are flavor enhancers. Salt is used liberally in sauces and gravies. Watch out for preparation methods that clearly connote high sodium—marinated, broiled in teriyaki sauce, or with lemon soy sauce. Let the waitperson know you have sodium concerns. If you have an entree, such as steak, it will be made to order. Ask that the salt be held. Also make those special requests: ask for salad dressing or sauce on the side so you can control the amount you use. The dipping technique helps you limit sodium best. Remember, you are best off with unadulterated preparations such as steamed red potatoes rather than Delmonico, a grilled petite fillet mignon instead of beef Stroganoff. These strategies also keep the fat count down.

Menu management

When the waitperson asks, "May I bring you a drink?" have a plan in mind and know what you and your dining partners will drink. That is before, during, and after dinner. It's best to avoid sweetened mixed drinks, such as piña coladas and strawberry daiquiris. Sip on wine, light beer, or wine spritzers instead. Always have a non-caloric beverage by your side. Quench your thirst with it rather than the alcoholic beverage. Don't forget that the calories in alcohol, even though it's liquid, add up quickly. A half-bottle of wine rings in at about 250 calories, a shot of distilled liquor about 100 calories. You can easily sip 500 calories.

Appetizers are often laden with fat, but there are usually some healthy ones to choose among. Look for unadulterated and unfried seafood or vegetables. Appetizers are perfect for sharing because they come in petite morsels. The small servings also make them perfect as a portion-controlled entree. The Green Flag soup words are broth, clear, beans, and vegetable. Skirt around creamy soups such as cream of, bisque, or cheese and potato which are surely fat dense. Healthy soup is a great filler. If you monitor sodium, avoid soup.

Don't pass by the salads. Order them rather than high-fat appetizers. Look for the healthy greens and low-calorie vegetables. Order salads with interesting and unique ingredients like endive, jicama, radicchio, and fruits. Be cautious about salad dressing. Get the light vinaigrette or other vinegar-and-oil-based dressing. Pour off some of the oil. Request vinegar or lemon wedges on the side to spread the dressing with fewer calories. Be on guard for the high-fat salad toppings—bacon, homemade croutons, avocado, cheese (blue, feta, Parmesan), and nuts.

On to the main course. The entree, which most frequently contains a large amount of protein, gets the most attention when you gaze at the menu. Will it be duck, lamb, or shrimp. No matter which entree you choose, you will be served a large portion. So portion control is key. Practice menu creativity: split or share complementary dishes to minimize the amount of protein, request a doggie bag, or leave a few bites on your plate.

In the decision-making process, think about choosing the lower fat, lower cholesterol fish, shellfish, and chicken. Look for preparation methods on the Green Flag list—grilled, poached, steamed, blackened, or stir-fried. Seafood items such as cioppino and bouillabaisse offer lots of food with few grams of fat.

But even though you start with healthy protein foods, such as fish or chicken, they can easily become nutritional disasters. Look at the description of chicken Kiev: breast of chicken filled with herb butter and cheese garlic, served topped with butter sauce. Compare this with chicken saute: diced chicken breast sauteed with sun-dried tomatoes, herbs, and asparagus in olive oil. Neither item is fat-free, but the latter is certainly the lower-fat choice.

Yes, seafood and chicken are often healthier choices, but unadulterated beef, lamb, or veal might be wiser bets. If you order meat, stick with a small cut—"petite," "queen," and "eight-ounce" are usual descriptions of small servings. They are still more than you need but better than the "king" and "sixteen-ounce" portions. Go for leaner cuts. A fillet mignon is leaner than a sirloin strip, rib eye, porterhouse, or prime rib. Veal is often breaded and sauteed prior to cooking. But if you spot a broiled veal chop on the menu, that's a good choice. Lamb can be high in fat, but it is most often broiled or grilled, which doesn't add much fat. If there's fat to trim once the meal arrives, do so.

Duck is thought of as quite high in fat, and with the skin on it is. However, with the arrival of nouvelle and fusion cuisines, more sliced duck breast is served. It is quite lean and the skin is gone. Often light fruit sauces or glazes are used on duck breast.

More restaurants now offer vegetarian entrees. Take a look at these to cut way back on the protein. There might be pasta dishes, Chinese stir-fries, or grilled vegetables. Be careful that vegetarian entrees don't come loaded with fat and cheese. You can go vegetarian also by ordering à la carte appetizers, soups, salads, and side items. (See Chapter 18 for more detailed information on vegetarian choices in continental restaurants.)

A starch is usually included with the entree or available à la carte. Again, search for the unadulterated (*sans* fat) starches. Baked potato, red potatoes, rice, or grains: request that no additional fat be added. If it's potatoes, ask that butter and sour cream be served on the side. Vegetables might also be included. Ask how these are prepared. Make sure that cream, cheese, and hollandaise sauces are left in the kitchen. If some vegetables are listed as sauteed, request that yours be steamed. If no vegetables come with your entree, order them à la carte. Look for grilled, steamed, or stir-fried preparations.

Dinners in upscale restaurants seem to cry out: "Have some dessert—it's a special occasion." Needless to say, they are often decadent. If you don't strictly monitor calories and fat, you might enjoy a dessert splurge situation. Often simply a taste or two of a sweet is all you want. Or share a dessert with several dining partners. Order one dessert and a round of forks. In upscale restaurants serving lighter cuisine, fruit might be found. Often it's berries with crème fraîche and liqueur. Hold the crème fraîche but drink the liqueur—it's fat free.

Green Flag Words

INGREDIENTS:
balsamic, raspberry or any vinegar
light vinaigrette
roasted peppers
sun-dried tomatoes
herbs and spices
couscous, polenta, and risotto
salsa—fruit or vegetable-based
chipolte peppers or sauces

COOKING METHODS/MENU DESCRIPTIONS:
blackened
Cajun
wine sauce—red or white (make sure not a cream sauce)
mustard sauce (make sure not a cream sauce)
tomato, garlic, and herb sauces
fruit sauce
roasted
steamed

poached
grilled
marinated
en brochette (on skewer)
available as appetizer portion
half-portions available
petite or queen-size

INGREDIENTS:

Red Flag Words

melted cheese
cheese—blue, goat's, mozzarella,
    feta, Parmesan
butter, drawn butter, cream
bacon
sausage
pistachio, orange, herb, or garlic
    butter
hollandaise, rémoulade, mornay
    sauce (other white sauces or
    mayonnaise-based sauces)
sour cream
crème fraîche
whipped cream

COOKING METHODS/MENU
DESCRIPTIONS:
creamy mushroom sauce
cheese sauce
au gratin
stuffed with seasoned breadcrumbs
Wellington
Stroganoff
garlic and herbed cream sauce
casserole (usually has butter,
    cream, and/or cheese and
    breadcrumb topping)
wrapped in bacon, phyllo dough,
    puffed pastry,
    served in pastry shell

AT THE TABLE:
butter
sour cream
salad dressing
high-fat sauces

**Special
Requests
Upscale
Dining**

Please bring me a club soda with a lemon wedge.

Please bring my salad when you serve the others their appetizers.

Please bring my appetizer when you bring the others their main course.

Could you serve the sauce on the side?

Would you serve the salad dressing on the side?

Could I get some vinegar or lemon wedges for my salad rather than the dressing?

May I have some Dijon mustard for my potato?

Please don't add butter or sour cream to my potato, but bring it on the side.

Please don't bring out the drawn butter, but I will have a good supply of lemon wedges.

Is it possible to have these vegetables steamed rather than sauteed?

Please hold the hollandaise sauce from the vegetables.

Could we get an extra plate to split this appetizer (or entree)?

Can you split the entree in the kitchen?

Can you bring several extra forks; we are going to split this dessert?

May I have this wrapped up to take home?

The Menu: Upscale Dining

Appetizers

Mussels au gratin (mussels in garlic butter sauce with cheese topping)

✓**Shrimp,** marinated and grilled (quarter pound of shrimp marinated in lemon, garlic, and spices and grilled over mesquite chips)

Stuffed mushrooms (prepared with herbs and seasoned breadcrumbs, topped with a blend of rosemary in cream sauce)

Pâté de la maison (pâté de foie gras, served with toast points)

Goat's cheese (wrapped in Bibb lettuce with sun-dried tomatoes and grilled over mesquite chips)

Escargots (snails served in traditional style, with garlic, herb, butter sauce)

✓**Vegetable melange** with mustard sauce (freshly cut raw vegetables served in a lettuce cup with curry mustard sauce)

✓**Grilled asparagus** with lemon soy sauce (fresh asparagus, grilled and basted in a light oriental sauce)

Artichoke hearts with feta cheese (artichoke hearts marinated and sauteed in olive oil, topped with crumbled feta cheese)

Soups

Soup du jour (server will describe today's special)

French onion soup (traditional style, rich onion soup, served in a crock with melted cheese)

✓*Preferred Choice*
Some depending on special requests

✓**Jellied consomme** (clear light broth, served chilled)

Cream of spinach soup (creamy soup with fresh steamed spinach)

✓**Gazpacho** (cold tomato-based soup of assorted pureed fresh vegetables)

Salads   ✓**House salad** (mixture of romaine and Bibb lettuce, with red onions, red peppers, and sprouts, served with raspberry vinaigrette dressing)

✓**Marinated tomatoes** (sliced tomatoes marinated with red onions in olive oil and balsamic vinegar, topped with crumbled feta cheese)

Melon salad with avocado dressing (slices of cantaloupe and honeydew melon, topped with creamy avocado dressing)

✓**Baby field greens** (mixture of radicchio, endive, watercress, and jicama, served with balsamic vinaigrette)

✓**Spinach salad** (fresh spinach, topped with sliced mushrooms, egg, and bacon bits, served with hot bacon dressing)

Entrees   **MEATS***

Beef Wellington (fillet of beef covered with thin layer of goose liver pâté and wrapped in flaky pastry shell, topped with Bordelaise sauce)

✓**Petite fillet mignon** with mushroom sauce (small fillet broiled to your liking, topped with light sauteed mushroom sauce)

New York sirloin strip steak, 12 ozs (center cut sirloin, broiled to your liking)

Rib-eye steak, 12 ozs (aged rib eye, broiled or blackened to your liking)

✓**Rack of lamb** (individual rack of lamb, broiled with a glaze of honey mustard sauce)

Veal Oscar (veal cutlet sauteed with lobster meat and asparagus, topped with hollandaise sauce)

POULTRY*

Chicken Kiev (boneless breast of chicken, filled with herb butter and cheese garlic, topped with butter sauce)

✓**Chicken saute** (sliced chicken breast, sauteed with sun-dried tomatoes, asparagus, and herbs in olive oil)

Duck à l'orange (one-half Long Island duckling grilled and basted with orange glaze)

✓**Duck breast with raspberry sauce** (sliced breast of duck served with light raspberry lemon sauce)

SEAFOOD*

Stuffed shrimp (four jumbo shrimp, stuffed with blend of crabmeat and seasoned breadcrumbs, baked and basted with garlic butter sauce)

✓**Poached salmon** with smoked tomato sauce and cilantro (salmon fillet, lightly poached in wine and topped with delicate tomato and cilantro sauce)

Dover sole in champagne cream sauce (dover sole, baked in a light champagne-based cream sauce)

✓**Blackened tuna** served with mango chutney sauce

✓**Seafood Cioppino** (combination of seafoods sauteed in light, seafood-based tomato sauce, served over fettucine)

*All above entrees served with choice of rice pilaf, baked potato, steamed red bliss potatoes, or fried potato puffs.

PASTA
Seafood fettucini (shrimp and scallops, topped with basil cream sauce)
Cheese-stuffed tortellini topped with sauteed broccoli and mushrooms

VEGETARIAN
✓**Oriental stir-fry** (fresh garden vegetables, stir-fried in olive oil, Tamari, garlic, and lemon, served over brown rice)
Roasted Red Peppers and Salmon Ravioli (ravioli stuffed with bell peppers and salmon, served with a spinach cream sauce)

Vegetables ✓**Squash and zucchini,** sauteed in lemon herb butter
✓**Snow peas,** sauteed with red pepper
Creamed spinach
✓**Asparagus,** steamed and topped with hollandaise sauce

Desserts ✓**Strawberries** topped with crème fraiche
Key lime pie (lightly sweetened graham cracker crust filled with tart Key lime mousse)

Peanut butter cheesecake (New York-style rich cheesecake with a hint of peanut butter flavor)
Chocolate raspberry cake (double fudge cake, iced and filled with raspberry jam)
✓**Fresh raspberries** topped with Chambord liqueur
✓**Crème Caramel** (a light egg custard with caramel topping)

Now that you've seen what might be available on the Menu, find the Model Meal that best fits your nutrition goals. For an explanation of the Model Meals and their targeted nutritional values, see Chapter 3.

Your Order, Please

Healthy	30%	Calories as fat
Daily	20%	Calories as protein
Eating	50%	Calories as carbohydrate
Goals	300	mg/day Cholesterol
	3000	mg/day Sodium

❶

Low Calorie/　**Shrimp,** marinated and grilled
Low Fat　　　(listed as appetizer but request
Model Meal　　as main course)
Quantity: 1 order
Exchanges: 3 meat (lean); 1 fat
Baby field greens (dressing on
　the side)
Quantity: 1–2 cups
Exchanges: 1–2 vegetable
Balsamic vinaigrette dressing
　(on the side)
Quantity: 1 tbsp
Exchanges: 1 fat
Red potatoes, steamed (request
　no butter)
Quantity: 2
Exchanges: 2 starch
Strawberries (hold crème fraîche)
Quantity: ½ cup
Exchanges: 1 fruit
Wine
Quantity: 6 oz
Exchanges: account for calories
　but don't omit exchanges

Estimated	calories 581
Nutrient	fat 13g (20% of calories)
Evaluation	protein 33g (23% of calories)
	carbohydrate 58g (40% of calories)
	alcohol 17% of calories
	cholesterol 166 mg
	sodium 650 mg

❷

Low Calorie/	**Gazpacho**
Low	*Quantity:* 1 cup
Cholesterol	**Blackened tuna** (chutney sauce
Model Meal	on the side)
	Quantity: 4 oz (½ order)
	Baked potato
	Quantity: 1
	Sour cream for above
	Quantity: 2 tbsp
	Snow peas with red peppers
	Quantity: 1 cup
	Mineral water
	Quantity: unlimited

Estimated	calories 589
Nutrient	fat 21g (32% of calories)
Evaluation	protein 40g (27% of calories)
	carbohydrate 60g (41% of calories)
	cholesterol 72 mg
	sodium 670 mg

❸

Higher	**House salad** (dressing on the
Calorie/Low	side)
Fat Model	*Quantity:* 1–2 cups
Meal	*Exchanges:* 1–2 vegetables

Raspberry vinaigrette dressing
(on the side)
Quantity: 2 tbsp
Exchanges: 2 fat
Petite fillet mignon
Quantity: 3 oz (½ order)
Exchanges: 3 meat (med.)
Red potatoes, steamed (request
no butter)
Quantity: 1 medium
Exchanges: 1 starch
Oriental stir-fry with brown rice
Quantity: ½ order
Exchanges: 2 fat; 2 vegetable; 2
starch
Fresh raspberries with Chambord
Quantity: ½ cup
Exchanges: 1 fruit; account for
calories but don't omit
exchanges for alcohol

Estimated
Nutrient
Evaluation

calories 858
fat 31g (32% of calories)
protein 39g (18% of calories)
carbohydrate 94 g (44% of calories)
alcohol 6% of calories
cholesterol 67 mg
sodium 790 mg

**Higher
Calorie/Low
Cholesterol
Model Meal**

Marinated tomatoes
Quantity: 1 order
Chicken saute
Quantity: 1 order
Rice pilaf
Quantity: 1 cup
Key lime pie
Quantity: ½ piece

Estimated Nutrient Evaluation	calories 888 fat 36g (36% of calories) protein 51g (23% of calories) carbohydrate 91g (41% of calories) cholesterol 188 mg sodium 1350 mg

Low Sodium Model Meal	**Spinach salad** (hold dressing) *Quantity:* 1–2 cups **Balsamic vinegar** (special request; on the side) *Quantity:* unlimited **Duck breast** with raspberry sauce *Quantity:* 4 oz (½ order) **Baked potato** *Quantity:* 1 large **Butter** for above *Quantity:* 1 pat **Asparagus** (hold hollandaise sauce and order lemon wedges) *Quantity:* 1 cup **Coffee** *Quantity:* unlimited **Amaretto** liqueur *Quantity:* 1½ oz

Estimated Nutrient Evaluation	calories 827 fat 26g (28% of calories) protein 45g (22% of calories) carbohydrate 85g (41% of calories) alcohol 9% of calories cholesterol 124 mg sodium 550 mg

17

Healthier eating out
Seafood Style

Seafood, from fin fish to shellfish, is eaten in a wide array of restaurants and served in countless ways, from healthy to loaded with fat and calories. Mesquite-grilled swordfish is on the low fat side while lobster Newburg, with its creamy rich white sauce, is not. You can eat seafood in restaurants that serve fish only hours out of the sea or in Continental restaurants, where fish is just one among many entrees. Fast-food spots, specializing in batter-drenched fried fish, French fries, and creamy coleslaw, line America's highways.

The health message is loud and clear: eat more seafood; it's good for you. Indeed, the benefits of eating fish are many but only if it's still low in fat when it enters your mouth. Many Americans know fish is good for the heart as well as the waistline. That's why we're eating more. Unfortunately, the healthiness of fish has gotten lost in the preparation. Fish when loaded with breading and deep-fried is much less healthy than a hamburger. Shrimp presented floating in a garlic butter sauce is just as unhealthy as prime rib. Fish *is* healthier but only if it is prepared healthfully. Here it is in black and white from the Center for Science in the Public Interest's report on seafood restaurants in their November, 1994, *Nutrition Action Healthletter:* broiled or grilled scallops (6 ozs).—150 calories and 17 grams of fat; broiled haddock or flounder (6 ozs.)—209 calories and 21 grams of fat; fried shrimp (6 ozs.)—441 calories and 39 grams of fat.

Due to modern transportation, restaurants purchase and serve fish just about anywhere in the country. In fact, Legal Sea Foods in Massachusetts makes the "Maine Event" available by phone. They'll deliver a complete New England Clam Bake to your doorstep within 24 hours. Frozen fin and shellfish are served nationwide in many moderate-priced restaurants and in the fast-food business. You still see more seafood served in coastal cities, however. Some seafood varieties are native to particular areas: soft shell crabs in Maryland; lobster in Maine; salmon in Washington state; and crayfish in New Orleans.

Many people never eat seafood. With some it's an allergy and others simply dislike it. Unfortunately, sometimes one's initial or childhood exposure to fish might have left a bad taste in their mouth. Frozen fish sticks or fish cakes or overcooked flounder are frequent memories. If that was your first fishing expedition, give it another whirl. One important rule to seafood enjoyment is to eat it fresh. Keep the time brief between catching and eating. Steer clear of the "fishier" fish such as bluefish or mackerel and select flounder or cod, fish that's light in taste and texture.

Some say the more you really enjoy the taste of fish, the more simply you want it prepared. If you really don't enjoy fish, you might be tempted to cover it with high-fat ingredients—butter, cream sauce, or stuffing. Because fish has gained the reputation of being healthy, many tasty and healthful low-fat preparations and sauces have been created for it such as grilling, poaching, baking with mustard sauce, and marinating in oriental seasonings are just a few baits to hook you. In any scenario, keep the fat out—that's the secret to healthier fish dishes.

Before you order

Try to eat more fish. It's low in calories, moderate in cholesterol, and low in saturated fat. The chart "Seafood's Nutrition Assets" (on pages 279–280) gives you the nutrition numbers on a variety of popular seafoods. A few cuts of red meat are noted for comparison. Just remember that health characteristics can quickly be trashed if high-fat ingredients are loaded on. All seafood, prior to preparation, range from 30–60 calories per cooked ounce. Cod, scallops, and monkfish (called the poor man's lobster) are on the low side, whereas salmon, bluefish, and mackerel are slightly higher in calories due to their higher fat content. However, much against popular belief, fin fish has as much cholesterol as most red meat. The benefit of fish in relation to lowering blood cholesterol is that it is lower in *saturated* fat. Still, hands down, any type of fish prepared in a low-fat manner will be a better choice than red meat. Even extra-lean ground beef rings in at about 75 calories per ounce cooked.

Shrimp, the well-liked crustacean, takes a beating on the subject of cholesterol. Some of the beating is deserved and some is based on misconceptions. Shrimp has about 166 mg of cholesterol for a three-ounce cooked portion, compared to red meat at 72 mg for the same portion. Squid (calamari) is even higher in cholesterol. Even though they contain a large dose of cholesterol, the saturated fat is low and the total fat content is next to nil. Plus, shrimp and squid are not foods you eat every day. Once again, eat any type of seafood prepared the low-fat way. As for other shellfish—clams, mussels, oysters, and scallops—most are moderate in cholesterol and low in saturated fat.

In addition to the nutrition assets of fish already noted, some types, particularly the fattier ones, have a lot of omega-3 fats. Salmon, bluefish, mackerel, and eel are examples. Omega-3 fats, a type of polyunsaturated fat, has some beneficial effect in lowering triglycerides. However, these studies were done with large doses of omega-3 fats from food and supplements. This research continues toward conclusions while nutritionists currently recommend the consumption of several fish meals per week. That advice is due to all the benefits from fish, not just the omega-3 fats.

As for sodium, it is low in fin and shellfish, compared with other protein foods. You'll find in the chart that a few items, such as crab, lobster, mussels, and shrimp, have a bit more sodium. Interestingly, there seems to be no correlation between the sodium content of salt and fresh water fish. The biggest problem with sodium when dining out is the added sodium in preparation, such as soy sauce in a stir-fry or butter in broiling.

When it comes to seafood, fast food generally doesn't do it nutritional justice, but progress continues. Just several years ago, choosing a fast-food fish joint meant a fat-laden meal—no options possible. Several small pieces of thickly battered and fried fish fillets were served with yet other fried food, French fries, or hush puppies or both; then healthy cabbage and carrots were coated in mayonnaise and called creamy coleslaw. Now, at least the major seafood chains—Captain D's, Long John Silvers, and Red Lobster—offer several baked or broiled options with healthier sides like rice, baked potato, or salad. You can order grilled shrimp, grilled fish sandwich, or steamed Alaskan crab legs. The chart (pp. 281–282) "Seafood Chains Healthy Sampler," gives you the nutrition numbers on a few healthier options in the large seafood chains.

Taste the new varieties of seafood, such as mahi mahi (dolphin fish, no relation to the sea mammal), monkfish, or farm-raised catfish. Don't be limited by the fish choices of your childhood. Be adventurous and try some new varieties and preparation methods such as swordfish kebabs, blackened shrimp, steamed halibut with vegetables, or salmon with pineapple salsa.

Menu management

Start with a healthy appetizer from the raw bar: oysters on the half shell, tuna sushi or sashimi, or a shrimp cocktail or ceviche while your dining partners lubricate their innards with a high-fat cup of New England clam chowder or fried calamari. At the raw bar, almost all items are very low in fat. Raw oysters, clams, and mussels are most often served with very low-calorie sauces, the most prevalent being the red tomato cocktail sauce.

A note before propping yourself up at the local raw bar. Since more raw seafood is being eaten, there has been an increase in food-borne illnesses. One infection from eating tainted raw fin fish is anisakiasis. This results from a roundworm that lives in larval form in the fish's organs. On occasion, the parasite makes its way into the flesh of the fish and eventually to the raw bar. If the fish is cooked, the parasite is killed in the process. Other food-borne illnesses can occur from eating raw shellfish. The home economists from the USDA meat and poultry hotline in Washington, DC, recommend avoiding raw seafood completely. If you choose to eat raw seafood, practice caution. Eat raw fish in restaurants that serve lots of it, and make sure the fish looks and smells fresh. Use the motto, "if in doubt throw it out."

Sushi and sashimi, also low in calories, are served with the no-fat condiments of soy sauce, wasabi (green paste-horseradish), and pickled ginger. See further discussion of sushi and sashimi in Chapter 9 on Japanese cuisine. If you go with steamed mussels or clams, pass over the drawn butter and sink them in their own next-to-no-calorie broth.

For the main course, the order of the day is "dodge the fat." You'll see "stuffed with cream sauce" and scampi on most seafood menus, but they're best avoided and you know why—fat. Luckily, on today's seafood menus you'll also spot blackened, Cajun, and steamed—three healthier preparations. Blackening is rooted in Cajun cuisine and was popularized by Paul Prudhomme, the well-known Cajun chef from New Orleans. The cooking method uses only a small amount of fat, which is placed in a very hot cast-iron skillet prior to adding the fish. A mixture of hot spices, such as garlic powder, cayenne, and white pepper, coat the outside of the fish. They form a barrier between the flesh of the fish and the hot skillet. The high heat evaporates the moisture, leaving the outer fish fibers crusty with spice and the interior juicy and flavorful.

Surimi is the crabmeat look-alike that is substituted or used in combination with crabmeat for seafood salads and casseroles in moderately priced restaurants. Surimi is most often made from pollack. On the seafood nutrition chart following, observe that surimi is low in calories, fat, and cholesterol but a bit higher in sodium than most fin fish. That's due to processing. It's also contains a bit of sugar. Surimi is much less expensive and more available than crabmeat, which is why it has gained popularity. If you spot a menu listing "seafood salad," it will likely be surimi. Even though surimi is basically healthy, it can become high fat quickly when mixed with mayonnaise or topped with a cream sauce.

As you sit with the menu in front of you, use Skill Number 5—Be an avid fat detector. Look for the Green Flag Words, which mean lower-fat preparations. Steer clear of the Red Flag Words that point out the fat-drenched offerings. Practice Skill Number 7 as well—Portion control from the word go.

Think about sharing an entree. Often times you get 8–10 ounces of fish. Split the portion with your dining partner, or put half into the doggie bag. If you split a fish entree and it's a restaurant with a salad bar, order an extra trip to the salad bar and/or more starches—baked potato, rice, or vegetables.

Try a seafood dish served over pasta such as shrimp linguini with stir-fry vegetables or fettucini with white clam sauce. Starches will be overflowing and protein will be on the wane. A grilled fish sandwich will also keep the carbos up and the protein down. Just make sure there's no dollop of tartar sauce on top. All these steps help you more closely match up with the Food Guide Pyramid—that's Skill Number 6.

Green Flag Words

INGREDIENTS:
all fin fish, and shellfish (raw and cooked)
all herbs, spices, garlic, and seasonings

COOKING METHODS/MENU DESCRIPTIONS:
broiled
blackened
Cajun style
mesquite grilled or grilled
marinated
barbecued
stir-fried (beware of increased sodium)

teriyaki (beware of increased
   sodium)
steamed
kebabs
white or red clam sauce
served with tomato or fruit salsa

INGREDIENTS:
cheese
drawn butter
breadcrumbs
stuffing

**Red Flag
Words**

COOKING METHODS/MENU
DESCRIPTIONS:
fried, deep-fried
breaded and fried, battered and
   fried
fish n' chips
hush puppies
cream or cheese sauce
casserole
lobster or seafood pie
Newburg or Thermidor
creamy chowder or bisque

AT THE TABLE:
tartar sauce
mayonnaise-based sauces
rolls and butter
oyster crackers

**Special
Requests
Seafood
Style**

Please broil dry with a few bread crumbs.

Bring me a few extra lemon wedges.

Please serve the salad dressing on the side.

Could I substitute a baked potato for French fries?

Could I substitute a dinner salad for the creamy cole slaw?

Please bring the butter and sour cream on the side.

Could I get a doggie bag at the beginning of my meal?

Please bring an extra plate; we are going to share or split in kitchen.

Please bring my appetizer as my main course, but I'll have my salad with the others.

The Menu: Seafood Style

From the   ✓**Oysters** on the halfshell served
Raw Bar   with fresh lemon and horseradish
          ✓**Cherrystone clams** on the half-
          shell served with cocktail sauce
          ✓**Assorted sashimi** served with
          wasabi, ginger root, and white rice
          ✓**Raw bar for two:** oysters, clams,
          crab claws, and shrimp

Appetizers   **Baked clams Casino**
          ✓**Steamed clams** with broth and
          drawn butter
          Cajun-fried calamari served with
          spicy tomato sauce
          Oysters Rockefeller
          ✓**Marinated calamari**
          ✓**Barbecued shrimp**
          Scallops tempura
          ✓**Shrimp cocktail** —6 large shrimp
          served with cocktail sauce

Soups   ✓**Shrimp gumbo**
          Fish chowder
          New England clam chowder
          ✓**Manhattan clam chowder**
          Lobster bisque
          Shrimp bisque

Fin Fish   The following fish are available
Entrees*   prepared in several ways: broiled,
          steamed with vegetables, mesquite-
          grilled, blackened, or basted and
          grilled with teriyaki sauce:
          ✓**Bluefish**
          ✓**Haddock**
          ✓**Halibut**

✓*Preferred Choice*
Some depending on special requests

✓**Mahi mahi** (dolphin fish)
✓**Monkfish**
✓**Redfish**
✓**Salmon**
✓**Swordfish**
The following fish are available prepared fried or Cajun-fried:
Bass
Catfish
Flounder
Haddock
✓**Broiled mackerel** with light mustard and dill sauce
Baked stuffed gray or lemon sole
Scrod, stuffed and baked, served in cheese sauce
✓**Swordfish kebabs** (choice of one or two kebabs, with marinated swordfish pieces, skewered with peppers, mushrooms, and red onions)

Shellfish Entrees*

Baked stuffed jumbo shrimp
Seafood casserole (crabmeat, shrimp, scallops, and others combined with Parmesan cheese cream sauce and topped with breadcrumbs)
✓**Broiled Maine lobster** with drawn butter and lemon, served complete with corn on the cob, creamy coleslaw, and watermelon for dessert
Lobster pie (lobster meat combined in cream sauce and served in a casserole topped with breadcrumbs)
✓**Scallops** sauteed in spicy tomato sauce
✓**Alaskan king crab** claws steamed and served with drawn butter

✓**Cioppino** (clams, shrimp, lobster, and calamari braised in tomato sauce and served over pasta)

✓**Bouillabaisse** (seafood stew with monkfish, cod, and lobster)

* **Note:** All entrees are served with a choice of two of the following items:

French fries
✓**Baked potato**
✓**Saffron rice**
✓**Rice pilaf**
✓**Tossed green salad**
Creamy coleslaw
✓**Sauteed zucchini,** yellow squash, and onion
✓**Steamed fresh broccoli** with lemon wedges

Desserts **Creamy New York cheesecake**
✓**Fresh strawberries** or raspberries served with crème de cassis and whipped cream
✓**Watermelon**
Chocolate layer cake
Apple pie à la mode with vanilla ice cream

Now that you've seen what might be available on the Menu, find the Model Meal that best fits your nutrition goals. For an explanation of the Model Meals and their targeted nutritional values, see Chapter 3.

Your Order, Please

Healthy	30% Calories as fat
Daily	20% Calories as protein
Eating	50% Calories as carbohydrate
Goals	300 mg/day Cholesterol
	3000 mg/day Sodium

Low Calorie/ Low Fat Model Meal

Tossed green salad (hold dressing; request lemon wedges)
Quantity: 2 cups
Exchanges: 2 vegetable

Swordfish kebabs
Quantity: 1 skewer
Exchanges: 4 meat (lean); 1 fat; 1 vegetable

Rice pilaf
Quantity: 1 cup
Exchanges: 3 starch; 1 fat

Coffee or tea
Quantity: 1 cup
Exchanges: free

Estimated Nutrient Evaluation

calories 530
fat 14g (23% of calories)
protein 43g (32% of calories)
carbohydrate 60g (45% of calories)
cholesterol 70 mg
sodium 670 mg

**Low Calorie/
Low
Cholesterol
Model Meal**

Tossed green salad
Quantity: 2 cups
Vinaigrette, lemon-basil (on the
    side)
Quantity: 1 tbsp
Sauteed scallops in spicy tomato
    sauce
Quantity: 1½ cups
Saffron rice
Quantity: ⅔ cup
Broccoli, steamed fresh (hold
    butter)
Quantity: ½ cup

Estimated
Nutrient
Evaluation

calories 540
fat 19g (31% of calories)
protein 42g (31% of calories)
carbohydrate 51g (38% of calories)
cholesterol 60 mg
sodium 1100 mg

**Higher
Calorie/Low
Fat Model
Meal**

Steamed mussels in white wine
Quantity: split order
Exchanges: 2 meat (lean)
Hard roll with butter
Quantity: 1 roll, 1 teaspoon butter
Exchanges: 1 starch; 1 fat
Linguine topped with shrimp and
    stir-fried vegetables
Quantity: 1½ cups (½ order)
Exchanges: 2 starch; 1 vegetable;
    2 meat; 2 fat
Fresh raspberries with crème de
    cassis (hold whipped cream)
Quantity: ¾ cup
Exchanges: 1½ fruit

Estimated	calories 687
Nutrient	fat 27g (36% of calories)
Evaluation	protein 39g (23% of calories)
	carbohydrate 72g (42% of calories)
	cholesterol 153 mg
	sodium 980 mg

Higher Calorie/Low Cholesterol Model Meal

New England Clam Bake:
Fish chowder
Quantity: ½ cup
Steamed clams and drawn butter with lemon and clam broth
Quantity: 10–15 clams; 2 tsp sauce
Broiled Maine lobster with drawn butter and lemon
Quantity: 1¼-lb. lobster; 2 tsp sauce
Corn on the cob (hold butter and salt)
Quantity: 2 ears
Creamy coleslaw
Quantity: 1 cup
Watermelon
Quantity: 2 cups

Estimated	calories 850
Nutrient	fat 29g (31% of calories)
Evaluation	protein 62g (29% of calories)
	carbohydrate 81g (41% of calories)
	cholesterol 165 mg
	sodium 1350 mg

❺

Low Sodium	**Broiled fish fillet sandwich**
Model	*Quantity:* 1
Meal*	**Rice pilaf**
	Quantity: ½ cup
	Caesar salad with dressing on the side
	Quantity: 1½ cups salad, 2 tbsp Caesar dressing
	Sherbet
	Quantity: ½ cup
	Lemon herbal tea
	Quantity: 2 cups

Estimated	calories 716
Nutrient	fat 28g (35% of calories)
Evaluation	protein 36g (21% of calories)
	carbohydrate 80g (45% of calories)
	cholesterol 110 mg
	sodium 1205 mg

*Meal and nutrient evaluation based on nutrition information from Red Lobster.

Seafood's Nutrition Assets*

Food Item	Calories	Grams of fat	% Cals. as fat	Cholesterol, mg	Sodium, mg
FIN FISH					
Bluefish	140	5	31	66	68
Catfish	132	5	32	65	72
Cod (scrod)	93	1	7	49	61
Flounder/sole	104	1	12	55	92
Haddock	98	1	7	65	77
Halibut	119	3	19	35	59
Mackerel	232	16	60	80	101
Mahi mahi (dolphin fish)	97	1	7	83	99
Monkfish	85	2	17	28	21
Salmon (sockeye)	183	9	45	74	56
Surimi (imitation crabmeat)	84	1	8	25	122
Swordfish	132	4	30	43	98

*All information is based on 4 ozs. raw/3 ozs. cooked portions, using no fat in preparation. Nutrition information is obtained from *Composition of Foods*, United States Department of Agriculture, Human Nutrition Information Services and *Agricultural Handbook Sources*, 8–15, "Finfish and Shellfish"; 8–13 "Beef Products."

Food Item	Calories	Grams of fat	% Cals. as fat	Cholesterol, mg	Sodium, mg
Trout (rainbow)	129	4	25	62	29
Tuna	123	1	8	51	41
SHELLFISH					
Clams	126	2	12	57	95
Crab (Alaskan)	82	12	15	45	911
Lobster	83	.5	5	61	323
Mussels	147	4	23	48	313
Oysters	117	4	32	93	190
Scallops	100	1	8	37	182
Shrimp	84	1	10	166	190
Squid (calamari)	104	2	14	264	49
FOR REFERENCE:					
Beef, round (low-fat example)	181	8	38	72	51
Beef, prime rib (high-fat example)	328	28	77	72	51

Seafood Chains Healthy Sampler*

Restaurant	Food Item	Calories	Fat (g)	% Cals. as fat	Protein (g)	Carbo-hydrate (g)	Cho-lesterol (mg)	Sodium (mg)
Captain D's	Orange roughy dinner (served with rice, green beans, breadstick, and salad)	537	19	32	35	56	39	2156
	Shrimp dinner (served with rice, green beans, breadstick, and salad)	457	10	20	34	56	191	2194
Long John Silver's	Baked fish with lemon crumbs, 3 pieces (served with rice, green beans, coleslaw, and roll)	610	13	19	39	86	125	1420
	Light portion fish with lemon crumbs, 2 pieces (served with rice and salad, no dressing)	330	5	14	24	46	75	640

*Based on nutrition information provided by each restaurant company. All items are low in fat and calories.

Restaurant	Food Item	Calories	Fat (g)	% Cals. as fat	Protein (g)	Carbo-hydrate (g)	Cho-lesterol (mg)	Sodium (mg)
	Ocean chef salad (nutrition information does not include salad dressing)	110	1	8	12	13	40	730
Red Lobster	Shrimp cocktail (6)	90	2	20	n/a	n/a	175	80
	Bayou seafood gumbo (12 ozs.)	350	9	23	n/a	n/a	75	1600
	Alaskan snow crab legs	200	11	50	n/a	n/a	120	1360
	Broiled flounder fillet (5 ozs.)	150	6	36	n/a	n/a	80	370
	Broiled fish fillet sandwich	230	10	39	n/a	n/a	80	450

18

Healthier eating out
Vegetarian Style

P asta primavera, red beans and rice, bean curd (tofu) with broccoli and bamboo shoots in oyster sauce, veggie burger with jicama coleslaw, or roasted spring vegetables with grilled polenta cakes—all vegetarian and low-fat offerings from a mixed bag of ethnic and American restaurants. Today, you can eat your vegetables whether you're in an exclusively vegetarian restaurant or with a meat-lover's gang in an Upscale or

Chinese restaurant. More people each year make the switch to vegetarianism. For that reason, many restaurants cater to this growing populace of diners. Today, you see one to two vegetarian entree options on most menus. You can eat vegetarian and healthy even if no vegetarian entrees are listed, simply by applying Skill Number 8—Practice menu creativity.

Vegetarianism: A mixed bag

People practice several types of vegetarianism, both in regards to foods left off the plate and their reasons for being a vegetarian. The gamut continues to stretch as more people opt for vegetarian eating habits. Several clear-cut vegetarian categories exist. *Vegans* eat the most restrictive diet. They eat no animal products, just vegetables, starches, nuts, legumes, and fruits. In addition to eliminating all animal products, they don't consume dairy products—milk, cheese, eggs. Because no complete protein sources are eaten (ones providing all essential amino acids), vegans need to be more careful about complementing proteins. By combining different categories of foods, such as grains and legumes (rice and beans) or grains and nuts (seven-grain bread and peanut butter), vegans can get a supply of essential amino acids in the course of a day. It is no longer necessary to be concerned about complementing proteins at every meal. However, nutrient deficiencies of calcium and vitamin B-12 are possible due to the elimination of dairy products and red meat.

Lacto-ovo vegetarians eat all the foods vegans do, plus they add milk and dairy products, the lacto part, and eggs, the ovo part. Some vegetarians may choose to add just dairy products but not eggs, *lacto vegetarians;* others, *ovo-vegetarians,* add eggs, but avoid dairy foods. Dairy and/or egg products provide these vegetarians with complete sources of protein. The inclusion of dairy products and eggs also makes restaurant dining a bit easier. A growing number of people who call themselves vegetarians occasionally eat seafood or poultry. The term *semi-vegetarian* has been coined to define those who eliminate only red meat.

What is the rationale for vegetarianism? Religious beliefs cause some people to restrict foods of animal origin. For instance, some Seventh Day Adventists eat vegetarian diets. In fact, several studies have demonstrated the healthiness of Seventh Day Adventists, showing their minimal risks of heart disease, diabetes, and high blood pressure, diseases Americans are famous for. Others forgo meat because of ethical or moral reasons. These people believe it is wrong to kill animals for food. Yet others are vegetarian for financial reasons. It is simply more expensive to eat foods of animal origin than vegetables, starches, and fruits.

Most people who move toward vegetarianism do so because it is healthier. Meat, whether it is beef, pork, chicken, or fish, has fat, cholesterol, and saturated fat. These are the three dietary components you want to minimize. Unadulterated vegetables, legumes, starches, and fruits have zero fat, saturated fat, and cholesterol. Sounds like vegetarianism is a smart way to eat. Even *semi-vegetarianism* is a move in the right direction. Eating less meats (red meat, chicken, and fish) is in sync with the dietary guidelines for Americans and Skill Number 6—Order according to the Food Guide Pyramid.

One caution: do not assume that vegetarians automatically eat healthier or are necessarily in tip-top nutritional shape. Some vegetarians eat large quantities of cheese, oils, creams, butter, or margarine which keeps their calorie needle pointing in the high-fat direction and weight packed on.

Get to know the cuisine

You can eat vegetarian in just about any type of restaurant from Indian to Upscale and from Italian to fast-food chicken chains. However, there is a growing cadre of exclusively vegetarian restaurants. In vegetarian restaurants you can be sure that the base of a vegetable or bean soup is a vegetable stock, not a beef or chicken base. If you are a vegan or lacto-ovo vegetarian, you want no foods of animal origin.

Today, most major cities have a few strict vegetarian restaurants, and the number is growing. It might be a small cafe near a college campus that serves pocket sandwiches stuffed with avocado, Swiss cheese, and sprouts or veggie burgers with French fries. Or you will find a more upscale restaurant serving risotto with roasted spring vegetables and tomato-basil sauce or stir-fried vegetables with a ginger and hot pepper oil sauce over brown basmati rice. Some vegetarian restaurants specialize in simply serving raw foods—there's nothing cooked on the menu.

Obviously, it is easiest to eat healthfully in a restaurant dedicated to vegetarians. But even though the number of vegetarian restaurants is growing, they are still few and far between. Also, vegetarians eat with non-vegetarian friends and associates at non-vegetarian restaurants. The fact is, you can eat vegetarian at any restaurant—even a fast-food burger spot—if you are satisfied with a double garden salad. That might change as vegetarians get more numerous and vocal. Burger King is testing a vegetarian burger in a few locations.

The challenge in going strictly vegetarian in American restaurants is that there's a focus on animal protein—the chicken-seafood-beef entree syndrome. That's certainly true for steak and seafood houses, which place a huge serving of eight to twelve ounces of protein front and center with little attention to side offerings. A different story is true in Upscale or Continental restaurants. As more people lean toward vegetarianism, Upscale restaurants cater to them by offering at least one or two vegetarian entrees. Vegetables and grains, new-fangled and old favorites are used for recipe innovations and interesting sidekicks to the plate. Roasting vegetables, grilling fruits, and tossing in grains is in vogue. That's made eating vegetarian not only easier but more fun.

Unfortunately, even ethnic restaurants in America have "Americanized" their cuisines and thereby cast more emphasis on animal protein and less on native central features such as rice, grains, noodles, and vegetables. No doubt, it's still easier to eat vegetarian in most ethnic restaurants, especially Chinese, Italian, Thai, and Indian. There are often four to five vegetarian options, along with vegetarian rice and noodle choices.

Before you order

Just because you eat vegetarian doesn't mean any non-meat menu item you glance at will be healthy. Certainly, vegetable tempura, eggplant Parmesan, and fried tofu with assorted vegetables are loaded with fat and calories. When you focus your eyes on vegetarian listings, the same 10 skills and strategies apply. In particular Skill Number 5 comes in handy—Be an avid fat detector. Vegetarian offerings quickly mound the fat with cream sauce, nuts, cheese, and frying. Gear toward the healthier preparations of steaming, stir-frying, roasting, grilling, or just plain raw. Look for dishes that feature the newly appearing interesting grains: couscous, polenta, risotto, basmati rice, soba noodles. Go for dishes that use no-fat herbs, spices, and ingredients that lend plenty of flavor—tomato-basil sauce, roasted garlic, arugula, and jicama.

Cheese loads on fat, saturated fat, cholesterol, and, of course, calories. It's a favorite in vegetarian dishes. Consider vegetarian lasagna, bean burritos topped with cheese, pizza with roasted vegetables and melted smoked gouda. To avoid cheese, it might be easier to eat vegetarian in Asian restaurants where cheese is non-existent.

If your aim is truly to eat vegetarian, you will need to decipher menus and ask questions in non-vegetarian restaurants. It's amazing what some restaurants call vegetarian—a salad with slices of grilled chicken or pizza topped with vegetables and baby shrimp. Restaurants may use the definition of "no red meat" for vegetarian. The addition of non-red meats to certain dishes might come as a surprise, which is why practicing Skill Number 9—Order foods as you want them—comes in handy. Menu items such as baked beans or black bean soup might sound vegetarian, but they might have bacon or ham added for flavor.

If you eat vegetarian in a non-vegetarian restaurant, Skill Number 8—Practice menu creativity—applies. Vegetarian menu items lurk in the appetizer and soup sections. It's often easier to eat vegetarian if you boycott the entrees and go for the appetizers, soups, salads, sides, and breads. Maybe it's grilled portabello mushrooms, mini pizza with caramelized onions, Italian minestrone, or lentil vegetable soup (make sure the base is non-meat). A salad with just vegetables can complement one or two appetizers. Look for fresh greens and go light on the cheese and nuts, and, of course, request dressing on the side. Take advantage of side items no matter what the ethnic food and enjoy a baked potato, cold couscous-vegetable salad, steamed vegetables, pico de gallo, dahl, mango chutney, and so on. Menu creativity not only keeps out the meat, seafood, and poultry but it can also help keep the portions small and calories low.

Menu management

No matter what type of restaurant, vegetarian offerings may occur in all menu categories. Check out "The Menu: Vegetarian Style," which follows. We've listed healthier vegetarian options you might find in popular cuisines and restaurant categories such as Mexican, Chinese, Italian, Thai, Upscale, and American family and dinner restaurants. For more detailed information, refer to the chapter on that specific cuisine to learn more about the ingredients, foods, and healthiest choices.

Depending on the type of restaurant, you might be tempted to break bread or a facsimile thereof. In a Mexican restaurant you know you'll get vegetarian (as long as it's fried in non-animal fat) but unhealthy taco chips. In an Italian restaurant it might be fat-drenched garlic rolls or focaccia bread. If the bread is without butter, margarine, cheese spread, or oil and adds some whole grains, have a few bites.

Carefully scrutinize the appetizer listings. Appetizers are often fried—mushroom raviolis, vegetarian egg-rolls, vegetable tempura, or vegetable samosa in an Indian restaurant. Appetizers can contain lots of fat from cheese, oils, and nuts: artichoke and cheese casserole, eggplant stuffed with spinach and pine nuts, or spanikopita (spinach and cheese pie). Look for words like "raw vegetables served with dip," but request a reduced-calorie salad dressing instead of the regular dip.

With soups it's easy to stay vegetarian whether it's cold gazpacho or fruit soup (hold the crème fraîche or sour cream), steaming pasta fagioli (bean soup), or vegetarian chili. Take care to avoid the rich and creamy. Look for soups made with vegetable stock (you might need to ask) and containing vegetables, pasta, grains, or beans.

Salad is a great filler. Search for salads that tout their assortment of vegetables and not blue, goat's, or Parmesan cheese or toasted walnuts or pine nuts. Introduce yourself to less well-known *nouveau* vegetables like arugula, baby field greens, raddichio, endive, jicama, and enoki mushrooms. Cold grain or pasta salads might be a new option, but be careful of hidden fats in the dressing. In Mexican, Middle Eastern, and Thai restaurants vegetarian salads are a possibility. As always, if there's an item of animal origin and/or high fat (cheese, nuts, and/or seeds), ask that it be left in the kitchen. Don't forget to ask for dressing on the side.

Make starch the central focus: rice topped with stir-fried vegetables, pasta loaded with ratatouille (sauteed vegetables in a tomato sauce), or biryani, the Indian rice dish partnered with saag paneer. Vegetables should also play a main role, be they roasted, grilled, sauteed, stir-fried, or steamed. Be careful of extra fats, cream sauces, cheese and cheese sauces, and nuts.

Consider making a meal out of side items. Particularly in restaurants that are designed for carnivores, not vegetarians. In a steak house, you'll have no problem eating vegetarian if you bound up to the salad bar, eat whole-grain bread, and get a baked potato on the side. In a chicken chain, go for the vegetables, starches, and breads—zucchini marinara, steamed vegetables, rice pilaf, mashed potatoes, and dinner rolls or cornbread. In fact, both Kenny Rogers and Boston Chicken offer vegetable plates.

Unfortunately, dessert presents no problems to vegetarians, unless you are a vegan and avoid eggs and dairy products. The same rules apply: share those high-fat, high-calorie choices, and when able, go for the fruit desserts.

No matter where you choose to eat, healthy vegetarian choices are available. Skirting the high-fat ingredients, zeroing in on the innovative menu preparations, controlling portions, and practicing menu creativity to assure that you *stay* vegetarian are ways to make your mission possible.

Green Flag Words

INGREDIENTS:
herbs
spices
all vegetables, raw and cooked
all salad greens
pasta
grains—couscous, risotto, polenta
rice—brown, white, basmati, long-
    or short-grain
fruit
whole-grain bread or rolls
tomato sauce
roasted garlic
beans (legumes)
tofu

COOKING METHODS/MENU
DESCRIPTIONS:
roasted
grilled
steamed
simmered
sauteed
stir-fried
primavera (make sure no cream
    sauce)
served raw
gazpacho

Red Flag Words

INGREDIENTS:
cheese—all types
cream
nuts
oils, basil or curry oil
avocados

COOKING METHODS/MENU
DESCRIPTIONS:
fried or deep-fried
Alfredo
tempura
cheese sauce
cream sauce

**Special
Requests
Vegetarian
Style**

Please bring my soup when the others are having their appetizers.

Please bring my appetizers as a main course.

I'd like these two appetizers, but I want this one as an appetizer and the other as my main course.

Does this bean and barley soup have any meat in it?

Was this vegetable soup started with a meat or chicken base?

Please bring this salad as my main course.

Please serve dressing on the side, and bring a dish of balsamic vinegar.

Please hold the cheese (or nuts) on that salad.

This salad is made with grilled chicken; could you substitute more carrots and tomatoes for the chicken? I'm a vegetarian.

Could more roasted red peppers and garlic be substituted for the baby shrimp on this pizza appetizer?

Could tofu be substituted for beef in your Chinese beef and assorted vegetables with oyster sauce?

The Menu: Vegetarian Style⁺

MEXICAN

Appetizers and Soups
Chili con queso (melted cheese with green chilies and peppers, served with fried tortilla chips)

✓**Gazpacho** (a bowl of cold tomato-based soup with diced raw vegetables, served with a dollop of sour cream) request sour cream be held.

Entrees
✓**Vegetable fajitas** (peppers, onions, and mushrooms sauteed and served with lettuce, tomato, sour cream, guacamole, and flour tortillas) hold sour cream and guacamole

✓**Cheese enchiladas** (flour tortillas filled with melted cheese and topped with enchilada sauce) served with Mexican rice and black beans

Chilies rellenos (poblano peppers stuffed with cheese, lightly fried, and served with a spicy tomato-mushroom sauce)

Tostadas (flour tortillas topped with refried beans, melted cheese, lettuce, tomatoes, onions, sour cream, and guacamole—served with salsa) ask if refried beans are vegetarian; request sour cream and guacamole be held.

Side Dishes
✓**Black beans**
✓**Pico de gallo**

⁺We have tried to demonstrate the vegetarian possibilities of various ethnic cuisines.
✓*Preferred Choice*
Some depending on special requests

Desserts	✓**Flan** with caramel sauce **Sopaipillas**

CHINESE:

Appetizers and Soups	**Vegetarian eggrolls** (Chinese vegetables rolled in eggroll skins and fried) ✓**Cold sesame noodles** (flat noodles and broccoli tossed in soy sauce with sesame seeds) ✓**Eggdrop soup**
Entrees	✓**Buddha's vegetarian delight** (assorted vegetables stir-fried with oyster sauce) ✓**Spicy string beans** (stir-fried green beans with black bean sauce) **Fried bean curd with broccoli** (stir-fried in oyster sauce) ✓**Vegetarian lo mein** (flat noodles tossed with broccoli, napa, and bean sprouts in Chinese sauces)
Rice and Noodles	✓**Vegetable-fried rice** ✓**Steamed white rice**
Desserts	✓**Pineapple chunks** **Fried bananas**

ITALIAN:

Appetizers and Soups	✓**Minestrone** (a cup or bowl of Italian vegetable soup) **Stuffed eggplant** (fried eggplant stuffed with sauteed spinach and toasted pine nuts, covered with marinara sauce)
Pizza	✓**Vegetarian pizza** (topped with roasted bell peppers, portobello mushrooms, and smoked gouda cheese)

Vegetarian pizza (topped with goat's cheese, pine nuts, and grilled eggplant)

*Entrees ✓**Pasta primavera** (sauteed spring vegetables in a light tomato sauce, topped on angel hair pasta)
Vegetarian lasagna (layers of lasagna noodles, zucchini squash, and mozzarella cheese with marinara sauce)
✓**Penne and tomato-basil sauce** (a light tomato sauce with roasted garlic and fresh basil topped on homemade penne pasta)

*Pasta dishes, available in ½ portions

Desserts ✓**Italian ice** —lemon or raspberry
Cannoli

THAI:

Appetizers and Soups **Vegetarian tofu** (deep-fried tofu served with sweet-and-sour sauce)
✓**Vegetarian basil rolls** (fresh raw vegetables and basil leaves wrapped in spring roll wrappers, served with sweet-and-sour sauce)

Entrees ✓**Vegetable boat** (assorted fresh vegetables stir-fried with tofu in Thai spices)
✓**Vegetable-ginger with braised tofu** (ginger with green bell peppers, onions, scallions, and mushrooms stir-fried with hot chili paste)
Tofu mussaman curry (mussaman curry in coconut milk with potatoes, onions, carrots, and peanuts, served with stir-fried tofu)

Rice	✓**Vegetable-fried rice** with assorted vegetables
	✓**Steamed white rice**

UPSCALE:

Appetizers and Soups	✓**Vegetable terrine** (3 layers of pureed vegetables—carrots, beets, and summer squash—topped with red bell pepper coulis)
	✓**Grilled shiitake mushrooms** with ginger soy sauce
	Goat's cheese melted and topped with roasted red bell peppers and pine nuts, served on French bread
	Artichoke and cheese casserole (artichoke hearts baked into creamy cheese sauce, topped with buttery breadcrumbs)
Salads	✓**Mixed baby greens** topped with raspberries and dates, served with a light poppyseed raspberry vinaigrette
	Arugula topped with blue cheese, fresh apples, and toasted walnuts, served with raspberry vinaigrette
Entrees	✓**Fresh roasted vegetable plate** (assorted roasted vegetables served with couscous pilaf)
	✓**Stir-fried oriental vegetables** (an assortment of snow peas, napa, carrots, and bean sprouts, served on a bed of brown basmati rice)
	Angel hair pasta topped with basil-cream sauce
Desserts	✓**Strawberries** with Framboise and crème fraîche (hold crème fraîche)
	Chocolate mousse cake

AMERICAN FAMILY & DINNER RESTAURANTS:

Salads and Soups	✓**Spinach salad** (spinach, fresh mushrooms, eggs, and alfalfa

sprouts, served with light
vinaigrette dressing)

✓**Garden vegetable salad** with
choice of blue cheese or Thousand
Island dressing (hold dressing:
request reduced-calorie dressing
on the side)

✓**Vegetarian chili** (a cup or bowl
of hot and spicy chili with onions,
peppers, tomatoes, and carrots)

Entrees   ✓**Veggie burger with French fries**
(a meatless burger made from
onions, grains, low-fat cheese,
seasonings, and fresh herbs)
request baked potato rather than
French fries)

Cheese and vegetable melt
(sauteed vegetables on an open-
faced English muffin, topped with
melted mozzarella and served with
potato chips)

Spinach and mushroom quiche
(rich and creamy Gruyère cheese
quiche with sauteed spinach and
mushrooms, served with garden
salad)

✓**Vegetable saute medley** (fresh
vegetables sauteed with basil
pesto, stuffed into a pita pocket,
and served with vinegar-based
jicama and carrot coleslaw)

Desserts   **New York cheesecake** topped
with raspberries or blueberries

Deep-dish apple pie served with
frozen vanilla yogurt

✓**Frozen yogurt**

Now that you've seen what might be available on the
Menu, find the Model Meal that best fits your nutritional goals. For an explanation of the Model Meals
and their targeted nutritional values, see Chapter 3.

Your Order, Please

Healthy	30% Calories as fat
Daily	20% Calories as protein
Eating	50% Calories as carbohydrate
Goals	300 mg/day Cholesterol
	3000 mg/day Sodium

❶

Low Calorie	**Minestrone soup**
Low Fat	*Quantity:* 1 cup
Model Meal:	*Exchanges:* 2 starch; 1 fat
Italian	**Penne and tomato-basil sauce**
	(request half-portion)
	Quantity: 2 cups
	Exchanges: 4 starch; 2 vegetables; 1 fat
	Italian ice
	Quantity: ½ cup
	Exchanges: 1½ fruit

Estimated	calories 677
Nutrient	fat 11g (15% of calories)
Evaluation	protein 16g (10% of calories)
	carbohydrate 128g (75% of calories)
	cholesterol 2 mg
	sodium 1178 mg

Low Calorie/
Low
Cholesterol
Model Meal:
Upscale

Grilled shiitake mushrooms with ginger soy sauce (order as appetizer)
Quantity: 1 order

Vegetable terrine (appetizer; request as main course)
Quantity: 1 order

Mixed baby greens topped with raspberries and dates, with poppyseed-raspberry vinaigrette dressing (request dressing on the side)
Quantity: 1½ cups

Strawberries with Framboise and crème fraîche (hold crème fraîche)
Quantity: ¾ cup strawberries and 1 oz Framboise

Estimated
Nutrient
Evaluation

calories 582
fat 16g (25% of calories)
protein 9g (6% of calories)
carbohydrate 87g (60% of calories)
alcohol 5% of calories
cholesterol 0 mg
sodium 1187 mg

Higher Calorie/Low Fat Model Meal: Thai

Vegetable basil rolls with sweet-and-sour sauce (split order)
Quantity: 3
Exchanges: 1 starch; 1 vegetable; ½ fruit
Vegetable-ginger with braised tofu
Quantity: 2 cups
Exchanges: 3 vegetable; 1 meat; 2 fat
Steamed rice
Quantity: 2 cups
Exchanges: 6 starch

Estimated Nutrient Evaluation

calories 788
fat 16g (18% of calories)
protein 23g (12% of calories)
carbohydrate 139g (70% of calories)
cholesterol 3 mg
sodium 1441 mg

Higher Calorie/Low Cholesterol Model Meal: Chinese

Cold sesame noodles with broccoli and sesame seeds (split as appetizer)
Quantity: ¾ cup
Buddha's vegetarian delight (split order)
Quantity: 1 cup
Spicy string beans (split order)
Quantity: 1 cup
Steamed white rice
Quantity: 2 cups
Pineapple
Quantity: ½ cup

Estimated Nutrient Evaluation	calories 1004 fat 22g (21% of calories) protein 25g (11% of calories) carbohydrate 170g (68% of calories) cholesterol 0 mg sodium 1904 mg

❺

Low Sodium Model Meal: American Family and Dinner	**Spinach salad** (request bacon be omitted and vinegar and olive oil be served on the side; use 1 tsp olive oil and 2 tbsp vinegar) *Quantity:* 2 cups **Vegetable saute medley** *Quantity:* 1 sandwich **Jicama and carrot coleslaw** *Quantity:* ⅔ cup **White wine** *Quantity:* 1 glass (6 ozs)

Estimated Nutrient Evaluation	calories 705 fat 26g (33% of calories) protein 25g (14% of calories) carbohydrate 75g (43% of calories) alcohol 10% of calories cholesterol 111 mg sodium 1176 mg

19

Healthier eating out

Breakfast, Coffee Shops, and Brunch

Breakfast runs the gamut of different foods, varied amounts, and myriad restaurant settings. During the hustle, bustle work week, it might be a quick fast-food breakfast sandwich or muffin and capuccino in your car or at your desk. Then again, it might be the meal you skip during the week, yet on the weekend, linger over a gastronomic brunch buffet or a deli bagel and omelet while rifling through sections of the mammoth Sunday paper.

Over the last two decades, breakfast's format has gone through dramatic changes. You've witnessed the introduction of the fast-food sandwich on a biscuit, croissant, or bagel. Muffin mania hit in the late '80s. And now coffee shops blanket the country, offering caffeinated and decaf in several flavors, capuccino, or café au lait along with muffins to help you break the fast. Bagel shops are proliferating and serve up eye-opener coffee partnered with a bagel topped with a thick layer of butter, cream cheese, and jam. Even donut shops have tried to keep pace, with offers of bagels and croissant sandwiches in addition to their well-known namesake—donuts.

According to the National Restaurant Association's last count, approximately 19 percent of consumers eat breakfast out a least once a week. That makes breakfast the meal eaten out least often. That's probably because it's the meal most frequently skipped. You've heard the familiar preachings: "Breakfast is the most important meal of the day; it gives you energy."

Unfortunately, there's a vicious cycle that many people, especially those who struggle with excess pounds, get into: the alarm clock goes off, the snooze button is smashed (once, if not several times), you're late, you make a mad dash to ready yourself for work, and—surprise, surprise—there's no time for breakfast. As the day goes on, you grab lunch. But when you finally eat, the hunger pangs shout "feed me anything, just quickly and in volume."

Fueling your once-empty tank continues until your head hits the pillow. Nighttime overeating is rationalized by the minimal calories consumed during the day. This is a pattern that deserves a change even if it means eating a cold slice of last night's pizza for breakfast. That beats the bag of chips and regular soda from the vending machine mid-morning.

Newer health and weight control information touts the benefits of breakfast. Eating in the morning gets the metabolic juices flowing. If you don't eat, your metabolism doesn't get a jump-start. So, as the morning rolls on and you don't feed your body, your brain thinks you're fasting. Your metabolic rate remains sluggish. Generally speaking, we'd all be better off if the quantities of food eaten at breakfast and dinner were reversed—make breakfast the heavy meal and dinner the lighter one. In other words, give your body energy when it burns calories and less food when it is slowing down. That's very un-American and might be unrealistic. But make a move in the right direction and swallow a few bites for breakfast.

Get to know the cuisine

Among the most popular and growing number of breakfast spots in America today are the donut, muffin, and bagel shops. Some restaurants serve all three. It's quick and easy—the *modus operandi* for life on the run. Donut shops have been around for a while, pushing the honey-glazed and chocolate-frosted. As health-conscious Americans began frowning on donuts, muffins and bagels with cream cheese were added.

Bagels used to be relegated just to delis. Today, bagels are a mainstream American food that gets an A-plus for health. That's as long as they're topped healthfully. Bagels are found coast to coast in supermarkets, donut shops, and delis. Bagel shops have multiplied. They offer the everyday plain to the obscure spinach and chocolate-chip bagel. Then the knife handlers are glad to add butter, cream cheese, whitefish salad, and more.

The newest kids on the block trying to capture the "get it quick" breakfast crowd are the coffee shops, touting an array of fresh ground beans from hazelnut to Costa Rican. Starbucks from Seattle is perking across the country setting up shop. Along with coffee, they'll sell you regular or low-fat muffins and pastries. Coffee shops are also frequented in the evening for a spot of espresso and a sweet. (See the chart "Fast Food and Coffee Shop Breakfast Sampler" on pages 315–323 farther on in this chapter for the nutritionals on coffees, muffins, donuts, etc.)

Fast-food stops are also popular for a "quick and easy" breakfast. Most of the chains have a variety of breakfast offerings from the healthy pancakes, cereal, and fat-free muffins to the not-so-healthy biscuit, sausage and egg croissant sandwich. In 1976, McDonald's was first on the fast-food breakfast block with their Egg McMuffin. As usual, they found themselves the leader of the pack. Others quickly followed suit, and now all the large fast-food chains offer breakfast.

Many cities and towns have one, two, or more pancake or waffle houses. IHOP, more formally known as

International House of Pancakes, is best known. Waffle House is another. These restaurants serve up the obvious pancakes, waffles, eggs, toast, cereal, and, of course, bacon and sausage. Home-style independent breakfast spots or diners with similar menus crop up in many cities.

Hotels and motels are other locales for breakfast. You might find yourself at one on a business trip or meeting, at a convention, or on vacation. Typically, you'll find menu listings of cereal, eggs, pancakes, French toast, Danish pastries, and fruits. Sometimes, they'll offer a breakfast buffet to speed the process of feeding many people quickly.

Delicatessens are popular breakfast stops, too, particularly for relaxing on the weekend. It's common to see people enjoying bagels with cream cheese, lox, scrambled eggs, and onions. All-you-can-eat brunches with elaborate spreads have gained success as we seek ways to relax. The foods range from chef-made omelets with your choice of ham, cheese, onions, mushrooms, and more to sliced roast beef and a wide selection of potatoes, breakfast meats, pastries, and desserts. Champagne, mimosas, or bloody Marys can be sipped. Unfortunately, most people do eat all they can. It's plenty of food for the entire day and likely enough fat for two.

No matter where or how breakfast is eaten, there are healthy choices. Maybe it's a bagel with cream cheese on the side, or fast-food pancakes, hold the butter, light on the syrup; or a fat-free muffin with fresh fruit cup from a coffee shop.

Before you order

Breakfast is thought of as the light meal of the day—just a donut, sausage biscuit, cheese croissant, or egg sandwich with bacon. It might be light in quantity, but some of breakfast's common choices are quite fat dense, meaning lots of calories wrapped in a small package of food. The challenge is to opt for quick and easy choices that are light in fat and calories: bagel with jam, fat-free muffin, English muffin, or bowl of hot or cold cereal. It's healthier to eat a larger but leaner breakfast, perhaps pancakes or waffles with fresh fruit and a glass of low-fat milk.

All things considered, take a realistic approach and set your goal at 20–30 percent of calories from fat at breakfast. Strive to keep the carbohydrates up and the protein and fat down. You'll need to save protein and fat credits for lunch and dinner. If you load up on protein in the A.M. with a two- or three-egg omelet with cheese, you'll have a rough time holding to your protein allotment for the day. That's not to mention the excess fat and cholesterol. Go for cereals, fruits, yogurt, and breads with jelly or jam—choices that forget the fat.

As for those weekend "all-you-can-eat" brunches, the best advice is to avoid them. Steer your dining companions in the direction of a restaurant with a menu. That way you can order healthfully even if your partners let loose at the buffet. If your arm is twisted or you believe in self-torture, follow a few rules of the road. First, survey the situation, peruse the buffet, check out the foods available. Plan what you will eat and in what quantity. Try a bowl of fresh fruit or salad as a first course to take the edge off your appetite. Then return to the buffet for your final trip. If there are many appealing items, take small quantities. Lastly, drink plenty of fluids and enjoy the relaxing environment and company. Schedule some extra exercise either before or after the brunch.

Menu management

Fruit: If sitting down for breakfast, before you notice, your glass is kindly filled with orange juice. You might want to reconsider. Few people realize that even a 6-ounce glass of juice provides about 80 calories. Don't get me wrong, those are healthy nutrient-loaded calories, but you'd be better off chewing fruit than slurping juice quickly. Try to order a half-grapefruit, slice of melon, or fresh fruit cup instead of the automatic glass of juice. Fruit is also commonly available served on cereals and pancakes. If you are taking the dash-in-and-out route, look for cut up fruit or a fresh fruit bowl before you resort to the commonly found juices. Best yet, think about eating or taking along a piece of fruit prior to leaving home.

Breads, Muffins, Donuts, etc.: The breakfast bread category offers some healthy choices and others that are better left on the baker's shelf. The zero-fat choices are bagels, English muffins, and toast (any type of bread). Anytime you can get whole-wheat varieties, all the better. Even though these breads have no fat to start, they become fat-dense if butter, margarine, or cream cheese is thickly spread. Keep the fat grams to zilch by spreading jam or jelly, or keep them low with a thin coat of butter or light cream cheese. Get fats on the side so you can control the quantity.

Fat begins to mount in muffins; however, there are some fat-free muffins available. Make sure, from nutrition labeling information (if available), that they are in fact fat-free and not large and loaded with calories from fat replacers. It's important to know that fat-free doesn't mean calorie-free; carbohydrate calories are often added in, and the bottom line calorie difference is miniscule. Croissants, donuts, biscuits, and pastries are high in fat and worth avoiding.

Cereals: Hot or cold cereal, especially the high-fiber types such as oat bran or oatmeal, are some of the best breakfast bargains. Cold cereals are now found at some fast-food stops and are always in hotel and sit-down restaurants. There are usually several to choose among: cornflakes, wheat cakes, popped rice, or raisin brans to name a few. Whole grain is the way to max out on fiber. Surprisingly, cold cereals have a chunk of sodium, on average about 250 milligrams. Hot cereals are always found on breakfast menus in sit-down restaurants. Try using skim or low-fat milk with cereal and top it with fresh fruit.

Pancakes, Waffles, etc.: Pancakes, French toast, and waffles are made from the same ingredients: flour, water, egg, a bit of sugar, and a leavening agent. Before the butter and syrup are melted and poured, they are reasonably healthy. Unfortunately, the portions are often double what's needed. To solve that problem, share an order or take advantage of the optional "short stack" of pancakes or half-portion of French toast. Ask that the butter be held or served on the side, and use syrup sparingly. Have some fruit tossed on top to add to the sweetness and to satisfy one of those five fruit and vegetable servings early in the day. Another way to get some sweetness on pancakes or waffles is to sprinkle a sugar substitute and request a bit of cinnamon.

Eggs and Omelets: There are two problems with eggs. The yolk is high in cholesterol, and they're often served in duplicate or triplicate. One egg yolk has about 215 milligrams of cholesterol. That means a typical three-egg omelet with cheese rings in at 700–800 milligrams of cholesterol. The American Heart Association and other health organizations advise no more than three to five egg yolks each week. Most people also pick up an egg yolk or two each week from other foods such as baked goods, custards, ice cream, and mayonnaise, so it's certainly important not to go out of your way to get three to five eggs per week. Most sit-down restaurants will serve one egg, any style. Poached is the way to go—no added fat. If it's an omelete you want, convince a dining partner to share, and have it stuffed with veggies rather than cheese, ham, or other meat.

Breakfast Accompaniments: These include the breakfast rashers of bacon, sausage, and hash browns. Most of these add fat (the meats add some cholesterol), calories, and sodium. The healthier meat choices are ham and Canadian bacon, unless you are carefully watching sodium. Breakfast potatoes, usually called hash browns or home fries, are another example of taking a healthy food, potatoes, and adding fats and sodium in preparation. Fast-food breakfast potatoes get about 55 percent of their calories from fat. It's a similar scenario to French fries. A few side items to take advantage of in a sit-down restaurant are yogurt, fresh fruit, and cottage cheese. You can do well ordering à la carte: bagel, fresh fruit, yogurt, one poached egg, and whole-wheat toast (split an order of bacon if the urge is a must).

The Menu: Breakfast and Brunch

Fruits and Juices	✓**Juices,** small or large (orange, grapefruit, apple, cranberry, tomato) ✓**Grapefruit half** ✓**Fresh fruit cup** ✓**Sliced melon**
Cereals*	✓**Cold cereal** (cornflakes, Special K, raisin bran, bran flakes) ✓**Granola** (a natural, oat-based cereal filled with nuts and grains) ✓**Hot cereal** (oatmeal, Cream of Wheat, oat bran, Wheatena) *Served with whole milk, or low-fat milk on the side. All cereals also available topped with fresh fruit.
Pancakes, French Toast, Waffles	✓**Buttermilk pancakes,** stack of 3 large* ✓**Silver dollar pancakes** (10–12 small buttermilk pancakes)* ✓**Blueberry pancakes** (3 large buttermilk pancakes filled with blueberries, topped with whipped butter, and served with blueberry syrup) **French toast** (4 halves of extra-thick bread, dipped in egg batter, and grilled)* ✓**Belgian waffle*** *Served with whipped butter on top and syrup on the side. All available with choice of bacon, sausage links, or sausage patties.

✓*Preferred Choice*
Some depending on special requests

✓**Belgian waffle with strawberries**
(thick Belgian waffle topped with
strawberry sauce and whipped
cream)

Eggs* ✓**One egg** (fried, scrambled, or
poached)
Two eggs (fried, scrambled, or
poached)
Eggs Benedict (two English
muffin halves, each topped with
Canadian bacon, poached egg, and
hollandaise sauce)
Eggs Grecian (2 eggs baked with
spinach, onions, and crumbled feta
cheese, served topped with cream
sauce)
Steak and eggs (2 eggs prepared
to order and served with 8-oz
sirloin strip)

*Egg dishes can be served with
choice of bacon, sausage links,
or ham plus home fries and 2
slices of buttered toast.

Omelets* **Western** with sauteed onions and
green peppers; covered with
Cheddar cheese and diced ham)
Florentine (filled with spinach,
onions, and feta cheese; topped
with creamy mushroom sauce)
Three-cheese omelet
(combination of Cheddar, Swiss,
and Muenster)
✓**Veggie** (filled with sauteed
onions, green and red peppers,
and mushrooms; topped with
Swiss cheese)

*All omelets made with 3 eggs
and served with choice of bacon,
sausage patties, or Canadian
bacon plus hash browns and 2
slices of buttered toast.

Breads/ Bakery	Croissant
	✓**Muffin** (choice of blueberry, raisin bran, or oat bran)
	✓**Bagel** (choice of plain, onion, or raisin; served with cream cheese)
	Danish pastry (choice of apple or cheese)
	Doughnut (honey-dipped or cinnamon)
	Biscuit
	✓**Toast** (choice of white, whole-wheat, rye, or pumpernickel)
	✓**English muffin**

Side Orders	Bacon
	Sausage, links or patties
	✓**Ham**
	✓**Canadian bacon**
	Home fries
	Hash browns
	Cream cheese
	✓**Cottage cheese**
	✓**Fruited yogurt**
	✓**Plain yogurt**
	✓**Fresh fruit cup**

Now that you've seen what might be available on the Menu, find the Model Meal that best fits your nutritional goals. For an explanation of the Model Meals and their targeted nutritional values, see Chapter 3.

*Your Order, Please**

Healthy	30%	Calories as fat
Daily	20%	Calories as protein
Eating	50%	Calories as carbohydrate
Goals	300	mg Cholesterol
	3000	mg Sodium

❶
Low Calorie/   *(From typical Coffee Shop menu)*
Low Fat
Model Meal   **Banana,** sliced
Quantity: ½
Exchanges: 1 fruit
Cold or Hot cereal (high-fiber,
   bran, oatmeal, or oat bran)
Quantity: 1 box or 1 cup
Exchanges: 1½ starch
Milk, low-fat (skim preferable)
Quantity: 1 cup
Exchanges: 1 milk

Estimated	calories 272
Nutrient	fat 4g (13% of calories)
Evaluation	protein 11g (16% of calories)
	carbohydrate 48g (71% of calories)
	cholesterol 18 mg
	sodium 342 mg

*Note: These models were developed to be slightly lower in calories and other major nutrients than model meals in other chapters because breakfast is often a lower calorie meal than dinner or lunch.

**Low Calorie/
Low
Cholesterol
Model Meal**

(From typical Donut Shop menu)

Muffin, bran, oat bran, or raisin
   bran
Quantity: 1 small
Fresh fruit (from home)
Quantity: 1 small serving

Estimated
Nutrient
Evaluation

calories 393
fat 13g (30% of calories)
protein 9g (9% of calories)
carbohydrate 60g (61% of calories)
cholesterol 0–20 mg (depending on fat
   used in muffin)
sodium 550 mg

**Higher
Calorie/Low
Fat Model
Meal**

(From typical Delicatessen menu)

Orange juice
Quantity: 6 oz
Exchanges: 1½ fruit
Egg, poached
Quantity: 1
Exchanges: 1 meat (med.)
Bagel (cream cheese on the side)
Quantity: 1 small
Exchanges: 2 starch
Veggie cream cheese for above
Quantity: 1 tbsp
Exchanges: 1 fat
Home fries
Quantity: ½ cup
Exchanges: 1 fat; 1 starch

Estimated	calories 541
Nutrient	fat 22g (37% of calories)
Evaluation	protein 16g (12% of calories)
	carbohydrate 69g (51% of calories)
	cholesterol 228 mg
	sodium 560 mg

Higher Calorie/Low Cholesterol Model Meal

(From typical Fast Food menu)

Orange juice
Quantity: 6 oz
Pancakes (hold butter)
Quantity: 1 order
Maple syrup for above
Quantity: 2 tbsp
Milk, low-fat (skim preferable)
Quantity: 1 cup

Estimated	calories 540
Nutrient	fat 7g (22% of calories)
Evaluation	protein 15g (13% of calories)
	carbohydrate 105g (65% of calories)
	cholesterol 20 mg
	sodium 737 mg

Low Sodium Model Meal

(From typical Hotel/Motel menu)

Fresh fruit cup
Quantity: 1 cup
Toast, whole-wheat (spreads on the side)
Quantity: 2 slices
Margarine for above
Quantity: 1 tsp
Jelly for above
Quantity: 1 tbsp
Yogurt, fruited
Quantity: ½ cup

Estimated Nutrient Evaluation

calories 495
fat 9g (16% of calories)
protein 12g (10% of calories)
carbohydrate 93g (74% of calories)
cholesterol 29 mg
sodium 366 mg

Fast Food and Coffee Shop Breakfast Sampler*

Restaurant	Food Item	Calories	Fat (g)	% Cals. as fat	Protein (g)	Carbo-hydrate (g)	Cho-lesterol (mg)	Sodium (mg)
	CROISSANT SANDWICHES							
Arby's	Plain croissant	260	16	55	6	28	49	300
	Mushroom/cheese croissant	493	38	70	13	34	116	935
Burger King	Croissan'wich (bacon, egg, cheese)	350	24	62	15	18	225	790
	Croissan'wich (ham, egg, cheese)	350	22	57	18	19	230	1390
Jack in the Box	Sausage crescent	580	43	67	22	28	185	1010
	BISCUITS							
Arby's	Plain biscuit	280	15	48	6	34	0	730

*Based on nutrition information provided by each restaurant company. Foods with less than 15 grams of fat and/or less than 40% calories from fat are in **bold**. For data on beverages, see Chapter 4.

Restaurant	Food Item	Calories	Fat (g)	% Cals. as fat	Protein (g)	Carbo-hydrate (g)	Cho-lesterol (mg)	Sodium (mg)
Denny's	Ham biscuit	323	17	47	13	34	21	1169
	Plain biscuit	**215**	**9**	**38**	**5**	**29**	**1**	**76**
Hardee's	Biscuit with sausage & gravy	465	30	58	11	37	15	1490
	Cinnamon 'n' raisin biscuit	370	18	44	3	48	0	450
	Canadian rise 'n' shine biscuit	570	32	51	24	46	175	1860
	Chicken fillet biscuit	510	25	44	18	52	45	1580
McDonald's	Plain	260	13	45	4	32	0	840
	Sausage biscuit	430	29	61	10	32	35	1130
ENGLISH MUFFINS								
Carl's Jr.	**English muffin with margarine**	**230**	**10**	**39**	**5**	**30**	**0**	**330**

Restaurant	Food Item	Calories	Fat (g)	% Cals. as fat	Protein (g)	Carbo-hydrate (g)	Cho-lesterol (mg)	Sodium (mg)
Denny's	**English muffin**	**150**	**1**	**6**	**5**	**30**	**0**	**410**
McDonald's	**English muffin**	**140**	**2**	**13**	**4**	**25**	**0**	**220**
	Egg McMuffin	290	13	40	17	27	235	730
	Sausage McMuffin with egg	440	29	59	19	27	255	820
OTHER BREAKFAST SANDWICHES								
Carl's Jr.	Breakfast burrito	430	26	54	22	29	460	810
	Breakfast quesadilla	**300**	**14**	**42**	**14**	**27**	**225**	**750**
Jack in the Box	Sourdough breakfast sandwich	380	20	47	21	31	235	1120
SCRAMBLED EGGS/ PLATTERS								
Arby's	Egg platter	460	24	47	15	45	346	591

Restaurant	Food Item	Calories	Fat (g)	% Cals. as fat	Protein (g)	Carbo-hydrate (g)	Cho-lesterol (mg)	Sodium (mg)
Carl's Jr.	**Scrambled eggs (no bread)**	**160**	**11**	**62**	**13**	**1**	**425**	**125**
Denny's	Steak and eggs (no bread)	800	51	57	63	22	525	740
Hardee's	Big Country Breakfast™ (bacon)	740	43	52	25	61	305	1800
Jack in the Box	Scrambled egg pocket	430	21	44	29	31	355	1060
McDonald's	**Scrambled eggs (2) (no bread)**	**170**	**12**	**64**	**13**	**1**	**425**	**140**
OMELETS								
Denny's	Ham 'n Cheddar (omelet only)	490	34	62	28	7	240	1145
	Vegetable (omelet only)	585	48	74	26	9	630	533
PANCAKES/WAFFLES								
Denny's	**Plain pancakes (3)**	**410**	**6**	**13**	**12**	**78**	**5**	**1970**

Restaurant	Food Item	Calories	Fat (g)	% Cals. as fat	Protein (g)	Carbo-hydrate (g)	Cho-lesterol (mg)	Sodium (mg)
Hardee's	Waffle	320	22	62	5	25	85	225
	Pancakes (3)	280	2	6	8	56	15	890
	Pancakes (3) with bacon strips (2)	350	9	23	13	56	25	1130
McDonald's	Hotcakes plain	280	4	13	8	54	10	600
	Hotcakes with syrup and margarine (2 pats)	560	14	23	8	100	10	750
	FRENCH TOAST							
Arby's	Toastix	420	25	54	8	43	20	440
Burger King	French toast sticks	500	27	49	4	60	0	490
Carl's Jr.	French toast	410	25	55	6	40	0	380
Denny's	French toast	325	19	53	7	30	85	310

319

Restaurant	Food Item	Calories	Fat (g)	% Cals. as fat	Protein (g)	Carbo-hydrate (g)	Cho-lesterol (mg)	Sodium (mg)
	SYRUP							
Arby's	**Maple syrup (4 tbsp)**	120	0	0	0	29	0	52
Burger King	**AM Express® dip (2 tbsp)**	80	0	0	0	21	0	20
Jack in the Box	**Pancake syrup (4 tbsp)**	120	0	0	0	30	0	5
	HOT/COLD CEREALS							
Denny's	**Grits**	160	1	trace	4	36	0	880
McDonald's	**Cheerios® (1 pkg)**	70	1	13	2	15	0	180
	Wheaties® (1 pkg)	80	1	11	2	18	0	160
	MUFFINS AND BREADS							
Arby's	**Blueberry**	240	7	26	4	40	22	200
Au Bon Pain	**Cranberry walnut**	350	13	33	7	53	15	730

Restaurant	Food Item	Calories	Fat (g)	% Cals. as fat	Protein (g)	Carbo-hydrate (g)	Cho-lesterol (mg)	Sodium (mg)
	Oat bran apple	400	10	23	7	71	0	590
	Hearth	250	2	7	10	45	0	510
	Country seed	220	4	16	9	37	0	460
Denny's	Blueberry	310	14	41	4	42	0	190
Dunkin' Donut	Bran with raisins	310	9	26	6	51	15	560
	Corn	340	12	32	7	51	40	560
Hardee's	Blueberry	400	17	38	7	56	65	310
McDonald's	Apple bran	180	1	5	4	40	0	210
DANISH AND DONUTS								
Au Bon Pain	Raspberry Danish	335	16	43	6	43	50	480
Denny's	Cinnamon roll	670	30	40	10	88	15	400
Dunkin' Donuts	Jelly-filled donut	220	9	37	4	31	0	230

Restaurant	Food Item	Calories	Fat (g)	% Cals. as fat	Protein (g)	Carbo-hydrate (g)	Cho-lesterol (mg)	Sodium (mg)
	Glazed whole-wheat ring donut	280	15	48	4	32	0	370
	Plain cake ring donut	262	18	62	3	23	0	330
McDonald's	Apple Danish	360	16	40	5	51	40	290
CROISSANTS								
Au Bon Pain	**Cinnamon raisin**	**390**	**13**	**30**	**7**	**60**	**35**	**240**
	Chocolate	400	24	54	5	46	35	220
Dunkin' Donuts	Plain croissant	310	19	55	7	27	0	240
	Almond croissant	420	26	56	8	38	0	290
POTATOES								
Burger King	Hash browns	220	12	49	2	25	0	320
Denny's	Hashed browns	210	13	56	2	20	0	425
Jack in the Box	Hash browns	160	11	62	1	14	0	310

Restaurant	Food Item	Calories	Fat (g)	% Cals. as fat	Protein (g)	Carbo-hydrate (g)	Cho-lesterol (mg)	Sodium (mg)
McDonald's	Hash browns	130	8	55	1	14	0	330
BACON/SAUSAGE								
Carl's Jr.	Bacon, 2 strips	40	4	90	3	0	10	125
	Sausage, 1 patty	200	18	81	7	0	35	530
Denny's	Bacon, 4 strips	145	12	74	8	0	20	405
	Sausage, 4 links	225	22	88	7	0	20	390
CONDIMENTS								
Denny's	Cream cheese (1 oz)	100	10	90	2	1	30	35
Jack in the Box	Country Crock Spread® margarine	25	3	100	0	0	0	40
Burger King	A.M. Express® strawberry jam	35	0	0	0	8	0	0
Jack in the Box	Grape jelly	40	0	0	0	9	0	5

323

20

Healthier eating out

Lunch Spots

(delis, food courts & more)

L unch is the meal eaten out most frequently, so says the National Restaurant Association. They estimate that over 50 percent of Americans eat lunch out at least once a week. Lunch is eaten in a wide variety of restaurants from local sandwich or sub shops to national sub chains, delicatessens, food courts, and employee cafeterias. Your restaurant choices vary based on several constraints: time allotted, work setting, surrounding restaurants, dollars and cents, and the purpose of lunch. If you have half an hour, you can't venture far. If you spend your days on the road, you'll pull into a restaurant when your hunger bell rings. If you labor at home or are retired, you might have a favorite local sandwich or sub shop. Or maybe lunch is your larger meal of the day, and you enjoy a hot meal at a family dining spot. Whatever the situation, the 10 Skills and Strategies of healthier eating out apply.

The gamut of lunch spots

In sandwich shops turkey, tuna, and seafood salad, a handful of potato chips, along with soup and salad are the order of the day. Delicatessens, or delis as it's abbreviated, are where you'll find the unhealthy choices of chopped liver and mile-high corned beef or pastrami sandwiches, along with the healthy bagels, bean and barley soup, and smoked turkey sandwich. Subs, hoagies, heroes, grinders, or whatever you call them, are found at the local pizza parlor or at sub chains like Blimpies or Subway. They stuff long rolls with salami, ham, turkey, cheese, meatballs, and more. Food courts have sprouted up in old and new malls and in renovated railroad stations. Last, but certainly not least, if you are trapped in an office park or hospital, you may count on the well-loved employee cafeteria, with choices ranging from salad bar to sandwich fixins' to burgers and hot entrees with vegetables. For each lunch spot we'll review the offerings and give you a run down of the healthy, OK, and worst choices.

Many other types of restaurants are frequented for lunch: fast-food stops, American family and dinner restaurants, pizza parlors, and quick ethnic eateries. Find detailed information on the healthier choices in these restaurants in the chapters on those cuisines.

Before you order

Lunch is the meal where filling your belly to restore your energy is more important than the quality of the food. Because lunch breeds being on automatic pilot, you might find yourself on a lunch-food jag. Everyday it's the same old tuna sandwich and chips, burger and fries, or chef salad with Thousand Island dressing. Or maybe you ride the sandwich carousel, rotating the fillers of chicken salad, seafood salad, and ham and cheese. Of course, they're all complemented with chips, French fries, or creamy coleslaw. And you slug your daily lunch pick down with a can of regular soda. Being on automatic pilot probably has you cemented into unhealthy food choices.

Let's look at the nutritionals for one typical lunch. One-half cup of tuna salad is served on whole-wheat bread spread with mayonnaise, topped with lettuce and tomato, and garnished with a good-size handful of chips. Without the can of soda, that's 600 calories and 30 grams of fat (45 percent). The calories bounce up to 750 with a can of regular soda. That's a chunk of calories for a quick, get-the-job-done lunch. And it's hardly the worst choice. Think about the lengthy sub sandwich filled with salami, mortadella, and provolone cheese. Or a deli hot pastrami sandwich served with potato salad and/or creamy coleslaw. These lunch examples show you the damage that a quick and "light" lunch can do in the calorie and fat department.

Making healthier lunch choices requires careful attention to fats. If you order a sandwich, think about choosing lean fillers. Limit the items that are pre-assembled with mayonnaise. Watch out for those high-fat sandwich accessories—potato chips, French fries, coleslaw, pasta salad, and potato salad. They are healthy starches or vegetables drenched in fat. Ask for substitutes or order alternative side dishes such as tossed salad, vinegar-based coleslaw, carrot-and-raisin salad, sliced tomatoes, and lettuce or pickles (if you can handle the sodium). If you want the crunch that you get from chips, grab a bag of popcorn or pretzels as lower-fat crunch alternatives. Because nutrition has been in the spotlight, these items are around more.

Strategy Number 4 is Have an action plan. Know what you will order before setting foot in the restaurant. More times than not, you've been at the lunch spot before and you know the offerings all too well. If you regularly eat at the employee cafeteria, you've got the listings memorized. Take advantage of eating where you work, and bring the missing healthier items from home, such as low-fat or fat-free salad dressing, raw vegetables (cucumbers, carrots, or broccoli), and fresh fruit. You can also practice this strategy in most local sandwich shops and at mall food courts.

Portion control is another critical skill. Even though it's lunch and you expect portions to be smaller, they're still large. Give sharing a chance. Maybe your dining partner orders a sliced meat sandwich and you order a Greek or large garden salad with dressing on the side.

You'd both end up with the perfect balance of vegetables, starches, and protein if you share. Or use the frequent option of soup and a half-sandwich, or salad and a half-sandwich.

Be assertive and don't be dragged by friends or coworkers to lunch spots where there's a dearth of healthy choices. And don't be talked into sharing high-fat lunch accessories such as chips, French fries, and the like. Some people simply want a partner in crime and feel better if someone else eats greasy fries or indulges in a post-lunch ice cream cone along with them.

SANDWICH SHOPS

There are local sandwich shops, sometimes called coffee shops, where tuna or chicken salad, hamburgers, soups, and salad plates are on the menu. In others the menu reads more like a blend between a sandwich shop and delicatessen. Today, some ice cream chains, Everything Yogurt and Friendly's, for example, double as sandwich shops. Newer sandwich shops have recently made waves. We'll call them health-conscious sandwich shops. Au Bon Pain on the East Coast, Schlotzsky's in the South and Central regions, and The Butcher Shoppe in Atlanta are three growing chains. You'll find sandwiches filled with grilled chicken breast, smoked turkey, lean ham, or vegetables. You can play the options with breads—baguettes, multigrain breads and rolls, croissants, and pita pockets. You even have a choice of mustards—Dijon, pommery, or good old brown. Light mayonnaise and buttermilk-based herb dressings might be available. Homemade soups and salads are regulars as well.

Healthy choices

Great healthy choices are plentiful. Don't shy away from sandwiches with the thought that bread or rolls are loaded with calories. Remember, it's what's between the bread or in the pocket that's the problem. So don't take off the top piece of bread and just eat the insides to save calories. You're practicing Skill Number 6—Order according to the Food Guide Pyramid; go heavy on the breads and light on the stuff inside.

Choose from an array of breads. The list usually includes white, whole-wheat, light and dark rye, Kaiser rolls, baguettes, multigrain rolls, croissants, and pita pockets. Try to eat whole-wheat to pick up some fiber. Whole-wheat pocket bread is a great choice, especially if you closely watch calories. Croissants are loaded with fat even before you start stuffing them.

The best sandwich meat fillers are turkey breast, sliced chicken, grilled or barbecued chicken breast, roast beef, and ham. If there are vegetarian options, go for them, as long as the vegetables aren't weighed down with too much cheese. Ask the sandwich maker to go light on the cheese. They're made to order, so you can do that. If you monitor sodium closely, ham and cheese are on the high side. And cheese just adds more sodium, protein, and saturated fat. Request that lots of lettuce, tomatoes, onions, pickles, and peppers (if available) are topped on. That expands the volume and adds a number of bites. Instruct the waitperson or sandwich cutter not to add butter, margarine, mayonnaise, or oil to the sandwich. Use mustard, vinegar, ketchup, barbecue sauce, or low-fat salad dressing to moisten the bread and spice up the sandwich.

Salads, either as an entree or a side item, are good offerings. Such entree salads as Greek, spinach, chef, and grilled chicken are regulars. Spinach and grilled chicken are best. Remember, dressing on the side and use small amounts. Spread with vinegar.

With the onslaught of frozen yogurt over the last decade, some sandwich shops have it as part of their repertory. By the same token, some frozen yogurt shops have added light sandwiches. Frozen yogurt topped with fruits or granola makes a good low-fat lunch. A kiddie or regular serving of frozen yogurt might add a sweet ending to a light lunch. Go for the low- and no-fat varieties, and be careful of the candy and chocolate toppings unless you know the nutritional lowdown.

OK choices

In sandwich shops, it's common to find the healthy-sounding choices of tuna, seafood, crabmeat, or chicken salad. That's seafood and poultry, right? Right, but it's seafood and poultry that's adulterated with lots of mayonnaise. For this reason, these items, either in a sandwich or on a salad, aren't as healthy as the un-adulterated meats. If you want one of these pre-mixed salads, ask the waitperson if they have lots of mayonnaise or are rather dry. Certainly request that no extra mayonnaise be slathered on the bread.

Other OK choices are the chef and Greek salads. On the chef salad, ask that the egg and/or cheese be left off and request that more tomatoes, carrots, cucumbers, or whatever vegetables be substituted for the cheese. A bacon, lettuce, and tomato sandwich is OK. Request crisp bacon and mayonnaise on the side. A small hamburger is also OK. Have lettuce, tomato, and onions added to max out on the volume.

A soup may please your palate. Look for broth-based soups such as chicken, beef, vegetable with noodles or rice, split pea, lentil, barley, or tomato. A cup of chili might even be available. Homemade soups are best because they'll have less sodium than canned ones. Avoid creamy soups such as New England clam chowder, creamy broccoli, cream of mushroom, or cream of anything. Perhaps a cup of soup and salad or soup and half a sandwich are on the menu.

Worst choices

Sandwich shops offer unhealthy choices worth skirting. Paradoxically, the name ''diet'' plate should be a signal to keep searching. These plates became famous back in the '50s when protein was in and carbohydrates were out. The diet plate usually is loaded with protein from a hamburger and cottage cheese and light on carbos with canned fruit and crackers. It's also best to avoid egg salad, cheeseburgers, and burgers loaded with high-fat items, grilled cheese sandwiches, ham salad, and hot dogs.

Watch out as well for the melts—tuna melt is the most infamous. You might also find cheese melted on chicken or seafood salad and cold cuts. Steer clear of combination sandwiches that pack on the meats and cheese—roast beef and turkey or ham, turkey and Swiss. These combo sandwiches end up with about six-plus ounces of meat, more protein than you need for the entire day. Club sandwiches should be left alone due to the heavy dose of bacon and mayonnaise.

DELICATESSENS

Although the word ''kosher'' is often associated with delis, very few truly kosher delicatessens exist. Kosher delis are those that purchase, prepare, and serve food according to *Kashrut*, the Jewish dietary laws. But there are many *kosher-style* delicatessens. The first foods that come to mind when you hear ''deli'' are hot pastrami or corned beef piled high on rye, knockwurst on a hot dog roll, chopped liver, and bagels spread thick with cream cheese and topped with smoked salmon (lox). Many of these foods are high in fat and sodium.

A delicatessen might not be the best restaurant choice, but if your arm is twisted, you can find some acceptable menu choices. A survival skill in delis is to practice portion control from the word go. Order appetizers, half-sandwiches with extra bread, split a sandwich, and have a cup of beet borscht or bean and barley soup. That's Strategy Number 8—Practice menu creativity.

Healthy choices

Beef brisket, turkey breast, smoked turkey, lean roast beef are all healthy if a meat sandwich is the route you take. In many delis you can order extra-lean corned beef or pastrami for an extra charge. The problem with deli sandwiches is the mountain of meat between the bread. It's usually difficult to balance the bread or roll atop the meat. Carve down the meat by splitting a sandwich and ordering an extra roll or slices of bread. Make two sandwiches out of the meat in one. Or order a half-sandwich with an extra piece of bread.

Try a healthy appetizer as a main course—for example, stuffed cabbage or gefilte fish. There are usually a few healthy soup offerings: beet borscht, matzo ball and chicken soup, and bean soup are regulars. Order a bowl of soup and a roll, crackers, salad, vinegar-based coleslaw, pickled tomatoes, sauerkraut (high in sodium), or marinated vegetables on the side. Sometimes a fresh fruit plate with cottage cheese is available.

OK choices

Other relatively nutritious choices are salad plates or bowls. Stick with the chef, turkey, or chicken salad plate. Make sure it's not chicken salad mixed with lots of mayonnaise: you want plain unadulterated chicken. Also make sure they don't scoop potato or creamy macaroni salad onto the plate. If it's included, request that it be traded for more tomatoes, carrots, cucumbers or other healthy side items. Always get salad dressing on the side. A bagel with cream cheese or veggie cream cheese is OK. Just make sure you spread the cream cheese lightly. Get low-calorie sliced tomatoes and

Bermuda (red) onions to top the bagel. Maybe a cup of chicken soup or beet borscht will round out the lunch.

The frequently found accompaniments in a deli range from nutritional disasters, such as potato salad, macaroni salad, and creamy coleslaw to good choices such as vinegar-based coleslaw, sauerkraut, large pickles, and pickled tomatoes (as long as you can handle the sodium). Limit the mayonnaise-based salads and substitute tossed salad, sliced tomatoes or onions, marinated vegetables, or beet or carrot-raisin salad.

Worst choices

Many unhealthy choices lurk in the columns of the deli menu. Avoid the high-fat meats such as regular corned beef and hot pastrami, beef bologna, salami, knock-wurst, hot dogs, liverwurst, and tongue. Also steer clear of combination sandwiches that have upward of six ounces of meat, unless you plan to share at least two ways. Delis are known for Reuben sandwiches. They add insult to injury: bread grilled with butter, corned beef, melted cheese, Thousand Island dressing, and sauerkraut. It's a fat and sodium nightmare!

Other menu listings to veer away from are large portions or platters of smoked fish such as lox, white-fish salad, and smoked sable fish. Avoid chopped liver—it packs about the most cholesterol possible per cubic inch of food.

SUBMARINE SHOPS

Depending on what part of the country you grew up in, the long sandwiches filled with anything from Italian meats to tunafish and meatballs are called subs, hoagies, heros, or grinders. By whatever name, they are a favorite lunch choice. Philadelphia put itself on the map with its well-known Philadelphia cheese steaks. They're no longer just served in the City of Brotherly Love. Chains like Mr. Steak have spread their fame and fat across the country. The famous cheese-steak, often with oil-drenched onions and peppers, are not among calorie counters' delights.

Subs (the term we'll use) are served in local pizza parlors, where pizza and salads also line the menu board. Also, several large chains, Blimpies and Sub-way, dot their sub shops across this country's highways and byways. Another chain in the New England area is D'Angelos. They serve subs, pocket sandwiches, and salads. They're unique with their "healthy d'lites" offerings.

You no longer only find Italian meats—salami, bologna, and mortadella—and cheeses such as provolone and mozzarella packed into the lengthy sub roll. Today, many items fill the bread. That means just about anything you find in a sandwich—tunafish, seafood salad, turkey, roast beef, or hot ham. Unfortunately, in most subs you also find the complimentary cheese. You can have your sandwich made on a small or large sub roll or in a pita pocket. Some places, like Subway, offer the choice of honey-wheat rolls, which offer a bit more fiber.

The broad selection of meats and breads makes a healthy choice at a sub shop easy, especially if you have a partner to share with. However, it's still important to choose carefully. Fat, saturated fat, cholesterol, and sodium are your enemies—the stuff between the bread. The bread and toppings—lettuce, tomato, onions, pickles, and peppers—are the healthiest part of the sub. Here are some surprising figures from Subway. A 12-inch roast beef sub with cheese and the regular toppers rings in at 689 calories, 23 grams of fat (30 percent), 75 milligrams of cholesterol, and 2,287 milligrams of sodium. A 12-inch tunafish salad sub with cheese tops off at 1,102 calories, 72 grams of fat (59 percent), 75 milligrams of cholesterol, and 1,500 milligrams of sodium. So even though you see some healthy-sounding words like tuna, chicken, and seafood, be careful to determine what happens to them before they reach your mouth.

Healthy choices

Let's consider the best choices. If you've got calories to spare, order the smaller size sub roll, unless you are preplanning for another meal. The load of bread will up your carbos and fill you up. If your calorie budget is tighter, fill a pita pocket instead. A pita pocket tallies around 150 calories for the bread. That's about half the calories of a small sub roll.

The healthier meats are turkey, smoked turkey, roast beef, ham, and hot ham (this is a great spicy treat). Keep the cheese to a minimum. Rejecting the cheese is best, especially if you are watching saturated fat and cholesterol. Tank up on veggies. Ask the preparer to go light on the meats but pack on the lettuce, tomatoes, onions, pickles, and peppers. The pickles and peppers will add sodium, so be clear about your personal sodium goals. State that oil and mayonnaise are strictly verboten. However, spread some extra flavor with mustard and/or vinegar—regulars on the sub fixin's line.

Splitting and sharing work well in a sub shop. Order a small or large sandwich, depending on your calorie capacity. Split it with your dining partner or save half for another meal. Complement the sandwich with some crunch and munch from a bag of pretzels or popcorn, or order a garden or Greek salad and share it.

Salads are an alternative to the sub sandwich. These are usually served with Italian bread (no butter) or a half-pita pocket. The regulars are garden salad, chef salad, antipasto, Greek salad, and tossed salad with a scoop of tunafish, chicken, or seafood salad. Some menus offer a garden or Greek salad in a pita pocket. The best choices are garden, chef (with a request to hold the cheese), or Greek. Don't forget the salad watchwords: dressing on the side with a bit of supplemental vinegar.

OK choices

If you've got a few more calories and a few more fat grams to spare, here are a few OK choices. Steak and onions, peppers, or mushrooms is OK. Steer clear of the steak and cheese. A sauteed veggie with a cheese sandwich is also OK, as is a meatball sub.

Worst choices

There are, of course, several meat fillings to put off limits. Among them are bologna, all types of salami, mortadella, cheese, sausage and peppers, and steak and cheese. A few other sandwich fillers—eggplant and chicken or veal parmigiana—are best avoided. They start off sounding healthy, but they are breaded and deep-fried and then have cheese added before they get to you.

MALL FOOD COURTS

To make sure that Americans always know there is food nearby, food courts have become a fixture in malls. New malls are built with food courts and older malls are renovated to incorporate them. The size of the food court and the diversity of its restaurants varies. The restaurants are gathered in one section, offering an array of fast food and ethnic fare. The food court in Washington, D.C.'s Union Station, about a block from the U.S. Capitol, offers members of Congress (as well as other citizens) almost any type of ethnic cuisine and good old American fare. Renovated train stations with food courts and shopping appear in other cities—St. Louis and Indianapolis to name two.

The food court restaurant stands offer American fare such as hamburgers and fries, fried chicken, hot dogs, sub sandwiches, and stuffed potatoes. There's also popular ethnic fare—Italian spaghetti and pizza, Mexican tacos and burritos, Chinese eggrolls and chop suey, and sometimes Middle Eastern gyros, souvlaki, and tabouli. Larger mall eateries might also offer a sushi bar, frozen yogurt shop, and muffin spot.

Food courts offer several advantages. Food is served quickly—you simply stand in line, order, and take it to the table or back to work. If you dine with a group, everyone has an opportunity to pick their favorite lunch fare and still eat together. The big drawback is the tremendous visual and taste stimuli and way too many choices. If you have difficulty making decisions and are easily overwhelmed by lots of food choices, the food court is not your ideal locale. If you choose a food court due to convenience or group consensus, the best advice is to practice Skill Number 4—Have an action plan.

Healthy, OK, and worst choices

When contemplating the direction to follow, keep these thoughts in mind. Look for a stand serving fresh, unadulterated foods: fruit cups, frozen yogurt with or without toppings, salads, sub sandwiches, stuffed pita pockets, Greek salad, or stuffed baked potatoes with chili or sauteed vegetables. Steer clear of the fried foods such as fried chicken or fish, French fries, deep-fried vegetables, double and triple-decker burgers, and high-fat sandwich stuffings. For more details on healthy choices at food courts, read the specific chapters on the types of restaurants you find there, from fast-food burger and chicken chains to Chinese, Italian, and Mexican restaurants.

WORK-SITE CAFETERIAS

You might find yourself in the employee cafeteria or the office building mess hall at lunch, breakfast, or dinner day after day, depending on which shift you work. Employee cafeterias run the gamut from very limited choices of soups, sandwiches, burgers, and pre-packaged salads to elaborate choices of hot entrees and vegetables, cold and grilled sandwiches, burgers and fries, a well-stocked salad bar, refrigerated and frozen yogurt, plenty of fresh fruit, and tempting desserts.

The benefit of frequenting the employee cafeteria is that it becomes a known entity—there are few surprises. You know, only too well, what the offerings are prior to your arrival. So developing a game plan is no big deal. Another benefit is that the tempting fat treats may be few and far between. An added plus is that you can develop a relationship with a server for a special favor now and then: some cooked vegetables without butter, a sandwich without mayonnaise, etc.

Yet another plus is that it's perfectly acceptable to bring part of your lunch with you. Perhaps you have a favorite low-calorie or fat-free salad dressing that the cafeteria doesn't stock. Keep the bottle in a refrigerator, and bring it with you to the cafeteria. Flip-top individual cans of tunafish are available and work well on a garden or spinach salad. Grab a piece of fruit, a handful of carrots, or cut up raw vegetables to complement a sandwich—and check off one vegetable serving. Bring a small bag of pretzels or popcorn to substitute for the high-fat potato or tortilla chips you've been buying. These ideas get you eating healthier and keep more change in your pocket.

In the long run, maybe you can create some changes in the healthiness of what's served in the employee cafeteria. Employers today are, hopefully, more concerned about their employees' health. It serves them well to feed you healthier. For starters, discuss your wants and desires with the cafeteria manager. Perhaps you should take along several coworkers, or draft a letter that others sign so the manager acknowledges the consensus. Be specific and realistic in your requests. Maybe it's lower or no-fat yogurt or a frozen yogurt machine with fruit toppings; lower-calorie or fat-free salad dressings on the salad bar, along with a bottle of red wine or balsamic vinegar; pita pockets at the sandwich and salad bars, or a bowl of fresh fruit. These are all easy requests. If talking to the cafeteria manager doesn't create change, try the employee health nurse or human resources director.

Once again, you need to pick and choose wisely at any lunch spot, be it sandwich or sub shops, delicatessens, food courts, or employee cafeterias. There will always be Healthy, OK, and Worst choices. Apply the 10 Skills and Strategies no matter where you decide to fill your tummy for lunch.

The Menu: Lunch Spots

Soups	**New England clam chowder** (creamy chowder filled with minced clams and potatoes) ✓**Chili** (thick spicy chili chock full of beef and beans) ✓**Vegetable soup** (light, brothy soup filled with fresh vegetables)
Salads*	✓**House salad** (lettuce topped with peppers, mushrooms, cucumbers, and tomatoes) ✓**Spinach salad** (spinach leaves topped with sliced mushrooms, bacon bits, sliced egg, and bean sprouts) ✓**Greek salad** (bed of lettuce topped with crumbled feta cheese, red onions, and Greek olives) ✓**Chef salad** (bed of greens topped with ham, turkey, Swiss cheese, tomatoes, and cucumbers) **Tuna, chicken, or seafood salad** (bed of greens with tomato, green peppers, and bean sprouts topped with a scoop of tuna, chicken, or seafood salad) ✓**Roasted chicken salad** (roasted chicken sliced on bed of romaine lettuce, sliced tomato, and cucumber) *Salad served with choice of dressing: blue cheese, Thousand Island, Italian, French, ranch, ✓low-calorie Italian, ✓light vinaigrette, and ✓fat-free French.

✓*Preferred Choice*
Some depending on special requests

Cold Sandwiches*	✓Smoked turkey
	✓Turkey breast
	✓Roast beef
	Egg salad
	Chicken salad
	Tuna salad
	Seafood salad
	Hot pastrami
	✓**Corned beef**, extra lean
	✓Ham
	✓Hot ham
	Club sandwich (choice of turkey or roast beef)

Hot Sandwiches*	✓**Meatball** with tomato sauce (hold cheese)
	Reuben (corned beef grilled with cheese and sauerkraut, topped with Thousand Island dressing)
	✓**Hamburgers** (plain or topped with choice or combination of cheese, bacon, or chili)
	Grilled cheese (with tomatoes and/or bacon)
	✓**Grilled chicken breast**
	✓**Bacon, lettuce, and tomato**
	Grilled hot dog
	Tuna melt (scoop of tuna salad with melted mozzarella cheese)
	Veggie cheese melt (sauteed mushrooms, peppers, and onions topped with melted Swiss cheese)

*All sandwiches can be made on a choice of: ✓submarine roll, ✓white, ✓whole-wheat, or ✓pumpernickel bread, ✓kaiser roll, croissant, or ✓pita pocket. All sandwiches can be made with lettuce, tomatoes, and/or onions and are served with pickles and hot peppers.

Combina-tions	✓**Soup and salad** (cup of any soup served with House or Spinach salad)
	✓**Soup and half-sandwich** (cup of any soup served with choice of cold sandwich)
	✓**Salad and half-sandwich** (House Salad served with choice of cold-cut sandwich)

Side Orders	**French fries**
	Onion rings
	✓**Tabouli salad**
	✓**Coleslaw** (vinegar-based)
	Potato salad
	Macaroni salad
	✓**Yogurt**
	Potato chips
	✓**Popcorn**
	Corn chips
	✓**Pretzels**

Desserts	**Chocolate-chip cookies**
	Chocolate cake
	Apple pie
	✓**Fresh fruit cup**
	✓**Assorted fresh fruits**
	✓**Frozen yogurt**

Now that you've seen what might be available on the Menu, find the Model Meal that best fits your nutritional goals. For an explanation of the Model Meals and their targeted nutritional values, see Chapter 3.

Your Order, Please

Healthy	30% Calories as fat
Daily	20% Calories as protein
Eating	50% Calories as carbohydrate
Goals	300 mg/day Cholesterol
	3000 mg/day Sodium

❶
Low Calorie/
Low Fat
Model Meal

(From typical Food Court/Mall Eatery menu)

Roasted chicken salad (dressing on the side)
Quantity: 3 oz meat; 2 cups salad
Exchanges: 3 meat (lean); 2 vegetables
Dressing: (on the side)
Quantity: 2 tbsp
Exchanges: 1 fat
Tabouli salad with lemon-herb dressing
Quantity: ½ cup
Exchanges: 1 fat; 1 starch
Apple (brought from home)
Quantity: 1 small
Exchanges: 1 fruit
Mineral water
Quantity: 10 oz
Exchanges: free

Estimated
Nutrient
Evaluation

calories 425
fat 10g (21% of calories)
protein 35g (33% of calories)
carbohydrate 49g (46% of calories)
cholesterol 73 mg
sodium 862 mg

Low Calorie/ Low Cholesterol Model Meal

(From typical Delicatessen menu)

Smoked turkey sandwich with lettuce, tomato, onion, and mustard (eat half; share half)
Quantity: 3 oz meat, 2 slices bread
Pumpernickel bread for above
Quantity: 2 slices
Pickle (avoid if monitoring sodium)
Quantity: ½
Coleslaw, vinegar-based
Quantity: ¾ cup
Low-calorie carbonated beverage
Quantity: 12 oz

Estimated Nutrient Evaluation

calories 464
fat 14g (28% of calories)
protein 30g (26% of calories)
carbohydrate 53g (46% of calories)
cholesterol 92 mg
sodium 1712 mg (998 without pickle)

Higher Calorie/Low Fat Model Meal

(From typical Submarine Shop menu*)

Roast beef sub on honey-wheat roll with plenty of lettuce, tomato, onion, pickles, and hot peppers (hold the oil)
Quantity: 1 small sub with ½ cup toppings
Exchanges: 5 meat (lean); 3 vegetable; 5 starch

*Based on nutrition information from Subway.

Cheese Popcorn
Quantity: 1 oz
Exchanges: 2 fat; 1 starch
Iced tea, unsweetened
Exchanges: free

Estimated	calories 789
Nutrient	fat 25g (29% of calories)
Evaluation	protein 38g (19% of calories)
	carbohydrate 103g (52% of calories)
	cholesterol 75 mg
	sodium 2085 (reduce by avoiding pickles and hot peppers)

❹
Higher
Calorie/Low
Cholesterol
Model Meal

(From typical Sandwich Shop menu)

Vegetable soup
Quantity: 1 cup
Grilled chicken breast sandwich with lettuce, tomato, and mustard
Quantity: 3 oz meat
Pita pocket for above
Quantity: ⅔ whole pocket
Fresh fruit cup
Quantity: ¾ cup
Milk, low fat (skim preferable)
Quantity: 1 cup

Estimated	calories 589
Nutrient	fat 10g (16% of calories)
Evaluation	protein 46g (31% of calories)
	carbohydrate 78g (53% of calories)
	cholesterol 73 mg
	sodium 1437 mg (800 accounted for by soup)

❺
Low Sodium Model Meal

(From typical Work-Site Cafeteria menu)

Salad bar: lettuce, tomato, red onion, alfalfa sprouts
Quantity: 2–3 cups
Pickled beets
Quantity: ¼ cup
Chickpeas
Quantity: ¼ cup
Tuna (individual can, 3 oz, water packed)
Quantity: ½ cup
Low-calorie Italian dressing
Quantity: 4 tbsp
Pear
Quantity: 1 small
Milk, skim
Quantity: 1 cup

Estimated
Nutrient
Evaluation

calories 593
fat 14g (21% of calories)
protein 44g (30% of calories)
carbohydrate 71g (49% of calories)
cholesterol 39 mg
sodium 857 mg (using vinegar instead of salad dressing would reduce to 600 mg)

21

Healthier eating out
Salad Bars

"**G**o have your burgers and fries, it's the salad bar for me." This is the familiar virtuous statement of the stalwart calorie watcher. You might hear it in the employee cafeteria, pizza store, steak house, or fast-food joint. That's where salad bars reside. The well-intentioned "healthy" trip to an all-you-can-eat salad bar can result in a shockingly high-fat and high-calorie meal.

Get to know the cuisine

The word "salad" brings to mind visions of lettuce, spinach, tomatoes, and peppers in a rainbow of colors. These salad fixins' offer bulk, vitamins, minerals, and, best of all, very few calories. But in and amongst the healthy vegetables lurks pasta salad, potato salad, coleslaw, pepperoni, and cheese that bounce the calories way up. The final salad blow is the topping of dressing, often packing 60–70 calories per tablespoon. So under the guise of a "healthy" food choice, the salad bar can rack up excess fat grams and calories.

However, when you bring Strategy Number 4—Have an action plan—into play and have loads of "won't power," the salad bar is a healthy choice with lots of crunch. Beyond healthy, salad bars are convenient, relatively inexpensive, quick and easy. Salad bars are especially handy and refreshing in the warm weather, when preparing a meal is particularly unappetizing and you'd be just as happy with a block of cheese and roll of butter crackers or a pint of ice cream.

Today, you find salad bars in many eateries, from fast-food stops to family restaurants and American steakhouses. Salad bars are here to stay in supermarkets as well. Supermarket salad bars capture the on-the-run lunch and dinner traffic as well as the no-time-to-cut-everything-up crowd. Salad bars are also in employee, office building, hospital, school, and even museum cafeterias. It's common to pay by the ounce at these salad bars. At family restaurants and steak houses, a trip to the salad bar can be the whole meal or simply an adjunct.

Fast-food restaurants started the salad bar trend in the early eighties, when the health craze began. Now most large chains offer some salad options. Several outlets, such as Wendy's, still offer the make-your-own salad bar. Wendy's version is now called a salad/super bar. A few chains, McDonald's, Jack-in-the-Box, and Burger King, sell pre-packaged salads—garden, chef, grilled chicken, and more. (See Chapters 12 and 13 for more information on prepackaged salads.)

Salad bars, or more appropriately "food bars," have become especially popular at steak houses. They stock everything from soup to chocolate pudding, including everything you might imagine putting on a salad. Food bars often stretch the length of the restaurant.

Americans can claim the all-you-can-eat salad bar as our invention. The biggest salad bar dilemma is that one tends to eat one's "money's worth." Translated that means you overeat. All-you-can-eat salad bars are a set up for pigging out. And since it is under the guise of health—lots of vegetables—you can fool yourself.

Salad bar "won't" power

Because a slew of foods are before your very eyes at a salad bar, a dose of won't power is needed. If you are extremely hungry, unleashing yourself at the salad bar can be disastrous. If your won't power just doesn't hold up around a tempting salad bar, order from the menu. In a steak house, where salad bars are more appropriately called food bars, ordering a small steak, baked potato, and vegetables might be a better bet than risking a trip to the salad bar.

Here are a few strategies to cure wavering self-discipline. If you are with sympathetic friends, you can coerce someone to make the salad bar trip for you. Specify your pickings after surveying the salad bar yourself, without a plate in hand. Your willing dining companion will exercise portion control for you. Another suggestion: go to the salad bar yourself, but use a smaller plate. Often small and large plates are available. If you use a smaller plate, you've automatically limited the space. This is portion control at its simplest level. Lastly, limit yourself to just one trip.

In a fast-food restaurant offering both a salad bar and pre-packaged salads, the latter might be your best bet. The pre-packaged salads in fast-food restaurants are quite small and low in calories, that is, before the large package of dressing is emptied.

Salad bar management

Have a game plan—take a minute or two to preplan, even if it's just on your walk from the parking lot or to the employee cafeteria. Think about your hunger level. If hunger is about to get the better of you, remember, your eyes are bigger than your stomach. Rather than choosing with your eyes and taste buds, make decisions with your nutrition and health goals in mind. Think about what foods you really want, and in what quantity. If you are unfamiliar with a particular salad bar, peruse it before you grab a plate.

Nutritionally speaking, salad bars can be great as part of or as the entire meal. Offerings fit into a variety of health goals. You can get plenty of carbohydrates with lots of fiber. Greens and vegetables help you keep the protein down. If you practice fat-detective skills, you can keep fat, saturated fat, and cholesterol to a minimum.

From a sodium standpoint, salad bars can range from great to disasterland. Vegetables are extremely low in sodium, but salad mixtures such as macaroni salad, coleslaw, or the ham, olives, pickles, and croutons concoction can max out the sodium count.

The best advice at the salad bar, no matter what your nutritional priorities, is to load up on the veggies—greens, cucumbers, mushrooms, raw broccoli, and carrots. So start filling your plate by stacking the raw vegetables. Vegetables give you plenty of crunch and bites with few calories. A load of raw vegetables also gives the visual image of lots of food. If you are at a salad bar that charges by the ounce, you'll end up with change in your hand by choosing the high-volume, low-density (fat) foods. "Salad Bar Choices—Good, Bad, and Ugly" at the end of this chapter offers calorie information about specific salad bar regulars.

The next set of ingredients is the slightly higher calorie, but still healthy, category of beets, carrots, and tomatoes. Certain salad bar ingredients help you add more carbohydrate without adding much fat, for example, green peas, chickpeas (garbanzo beans), and kidney beans. Chickpeas and kidney beans might also be found in three-bean salads. That's one mixed salad that is quite low in fat and calories.

Croutons, crackers, pita pockets, and hard-to-resist freshly baked breads are frequent salad bar attendees. A few croutons are fine, although they might be high in sodium. Steer clear of those fat-drenched homemade croutons that might be seen in better restaurants. If you wish to add some lower-calorie protein foods, here are several choices: plain tuna (not tuna salad), cubed ham (not ham salad), egg, feta cheese, and cottage cheese (it will not be low fat). Two of these—ham and feta cheese—are high in sodium. Tuna, chicken, and seafood salad (mixed with mayonnaise) are loaded with fat. Chunks of cheese and pepperoni contain more calories from fat than protein.

The bigger the salad bar, the more mixed up salads you see, such as pasta salad, potato salad, coleslaw, marinated vegetables, and others. Some are smart choices and others should be left in the serving bowl. Generally speaking, marinated beets, marinated mixed vegetables or mushrooms, three-bean salad, a vinegar-based coleslaw, and mixed fruit salad are fine. Small quantities (about ¼ cup) should be taken, especially if you closely monitor calories, fat and sodium.

Another group of foods that can toss on calories is the so-called "salad bar accessories." These little temptations include nuts, seeds, Chinese noodles, olives, and bacon bits. Granted, you add these in small quantities, but a little of this and that can rack up calories. Try a *little* bit of this, and *skip* some of that as your new strategy.

Salad dressings: the lowdown

The culprit for adding lots of hidden calories is the salad dressing. Regular salad dressing, the type most frequently found at salad bars, rings in at 60–80 calories per tablespoon. That's a level tablespoon, not heaping. And those scoops used to dredge up salad dressing usually hold two tablespoons. Creamy dressings that contain mayonnaise, sour cream, and/or cheese have additional saturated fat and cholesterol, which are not in oil-based dressings made with vegetable or olive oil, such as Italian or vinaigrette.

On average, we use two to four tablespoons of dressing on a salad. The packets of dressing in fast-food restaurants contain four tablespoons of dressing, or one-quarter cup. Simple mathematics tells you this calculates to 300–400 calories for the dressing! And those are practically all fat calories. "Salad Dressings: The Numbers," following, gives you the gamut of nutrition information on salad dressings.

Salad dressings can contribute lots of sodium as well. The chart shows the sodium count. Four tablespoons of either a regular or reduced-calorie dressing can provide 500 milligrams of sodium. Sometimes, you'll find that the fat-free and reduced-calorie dressings, now more frequently available in restaurants, replace fat grams with sodium milligrams. It's a taste ploy. If you need to keep the sodium count very low, try just olive oil and vinegar or lemon wedges, or dilute a small amount of salad dressing with no-sodium vinegar or lemon juice.

By no means do you need to eat an undressed salad. There are many creative strategies to keep the calorie and fat counts of salad dressings low while enjoying the taste. Today, it is common to see both reduced-calorie and fat-free salad dressings in restaurants. In fast-food restaurants you're sure to find it, but even dinner houses are beginning to be sensitive to calories counters. Don't get carried away though; these dressings still have calories. Reduced-calorie dressings have 15–30 calories per tablespoon and fat-frees come in around 20 per tablespoon.

If you want to use a regular dressing because you like the taste or there are no lower-calorie options, here are a few strategies. Use less dressing. Get used to a lightly dressed salad as opposed to a drowned one. Thin a smaller amount of salad dressing with vinegar or lemon wedges. These techniques can cut calories substantially.

If you have your won't power in gear, a game plan in mind, and some knowledge about what to go heavy on and what to layer lightly, salad bars can be a healthy diner's paradise. A few changes at the salad bar can add up to a big calorie and fat difference. The salad bar—used wisely—is a welcome option in a variety of dining establishments—family restaurants, fast-food stops, your employee cafeteria, and even the supermarket for a quick take-out lunch or dinner.

Salad Bar Choices–Good, Bad, and Ugly

Low-Calorie Vegetables (approx. 25 calories/1 cup)	**Higher-Calorie Vegetables (approx. 25 calories/½ cup)**
broccoli	artichoke, canned
cabbage (red or green)	beets, canned
cauliflower	carrots, raw
celery	onions, raw (all types)
cucumbers	tomatoes, raw

Low-Calorie Vegetables (approx. 25 calories/1 cup)

broccoli
cabbage (red or green)
cauliflower
celery
cucumbers
endive
lettuce (all types)
peppers (all types)
radishes
sauerkraut*
spinach
sprouts (all types)
summer squash, raw
watercress
zucchini, raw

Salad Bar "Accessories" (calories/tablespoon)

pickles*	2-5
hot peppers	2-5
raisins	10
Chinese noodles	20
bacon bits (soy based)	27
sunflower seeds	47
olives, green or black*	50
peanuts	50
sesame seeds	52

Starches (60–100 calories/ ½ cup)

chickpeas
(garbanzo beans)
kidney beans
green peas
croutons
(commercial)
crackers (4-6)
bread (1 slice or 1 oz)
pita pocket (½)

Lean Protein (40–80 calories/ oz.)

plain tuna
cottage cheese
egg
ham*
feta cheese*

Higher-Fat Protein (100+ calories/ oz.)

cheeses*
pepperoni*

Salad Bar Mixtures (35-50 calories/¼ cup)

marinated/pickled beets
marinated artichoke hearts
three-bean salad
marinated assorted vegetables
marinated mushrooms
pasta salad, oil based
gelatin with fruit
fruit salad

Salad Bar Mixtures (50-80 calories/¼ cup)

tuna salad
chicken salad
seafood salad
corn relish
macaroni salad
potato salad
fruit ambrosia
pasta salad, mayonnaise-based

*Items particularly high in sodium.

Salad Dressings: The Numbers*

Salad Dressings (2 tbsp/1 oz)	Calories	Fat (g)	% Cals. as fat	Protein (g)	Carbohydrate (g)	Cholesterol (mg)	Sodium (mg)
REGULAR							
Blue cheese	120	14	100	2	2	20	340
Thousand Island	120	11	83	0	5	10	220
French	120	10	75	0	10	0	220
Ranch	140	13	84	0	5	4	428
Italian	90	7	70	0	6	0	200
Honey-mustard	110	9	74	0	5	0	200
LIGHT/LOW/REDUCED CALORIE							
Blue Cheese	130	14	97	2	2	25	520
French	80	3	34	0	6	2	450
Italian	50	4	72	0	3	2	340

*Based on nutrition information provided by several restaurant companies and N-Squared Nutrient database.

350

Salad Dressings (2 tbsp/1 oz)	Calories	Fat (g)	% Cals. as fat	Protein (g)	Carbohydrate (g)	Cholesterol (mg)	Sodium (mg)
FAT-FREE							
French	70	0	0	0	16	0	360
Italian	8	0	0	0	2	0	420
Vinaigrette	24	0	0	0	6	0	300
ALTERNATIVES/DRESSING DILUTERS							
Vinegar (any type)	3	0	0	0	1	0	0
Lemon or lime juice	11	0	0	0	3	0	0

22

Healthier eating out
Airline Fare

The average airline meal, first class or tourist, is not one to write home about. In fact, the highest expectation for airline food is something edible that will fill you up until you eat again at your destination. A *Fortune Magazine* article entitled "Why is Airline Food So Terrible?" describes an airline meal this way: "Lurking beneath that glutinous gravy is meat (origin unknown); ancient-looking peas; a few sad, spindly grains of rice. And don't forget the inevitable hockey-puck hard rolls suitable for use as a blunt instrument." Few air travelers have high hopes for a four-star meal in the clouds because they know better from past experience. As the article "Better Airline Fare" in *Health Magazine* exclaimed: "No one ventures 30,000 feet in the air in search of gastronomic experience."

Airline food has and continues to receive its knocks. However, in the airlines' defense, feeding many people quickly, at a minimal cost, in a crowded plane, without the conveniences of a restaurant or even a home kitchen is, at best, a set up for failure. Take a moment and think about it. The food you eat in the air is prepared on the ground in large food service facilities hours, if not days, before departure. The hot foods are cooked, then stored until flight time. In the air they are reheated prior to delivery to your flip-down tray. With these constraints, it's no surprise that airline meals will never be memorable ones.

Another criticism of airline food is that it's hardly healthy. From peanuts, the expected handout with a beverage, to creamy salad dressings and thick gravies, airline foods are often laden with fat, calories, and salt. A redeeming factor is that portions are quite small. So even if you eat a high percentage of calories as fat, you don't eat many calories. In fact, holding onto the vision of the size of an airline meal might help you think about more reasonable portions when you are served typical large quantities in restaurants.

Healthier airline fare

Though airline food is neither particularly tasty nor healthy, the airlines get credit for increasing responsiveness to the health concerns of air travelers. With more people flying, either for business or pleasure, there are more demands for healthier foods. An article entitled "Pie in the Sky" in *Savvy Magazine* stated that a survey sponsored by Gallup and several concerned food service groups found that "it was frequent flyers who displayed the greatest unhappiness with airline food. . . . Almost three-quarters of the passengers surveyed agreed that the airline should offer more meals with lighter, natural ingredients."

Many airlines have tried to improve the healthiness of their standard fare. Some now serve pretzels rather than peanuts, or they let you play the options. More chicken and pasta is served as well as less breakfast pastries and gooey desserts. In general, less food is served as airlines tighten their money belts. If the flight is relatively short and/or it is not during a mealtime, a beverage and pretzels or peanuts is all they'll toss your way. More light snacks are served for lunch—a cold or hot sandwich with fruit and/or chips. Bagels are often served for breakfast. The airlines still have a way to go on the road to healthy yet tempting airline cuisine.

Your wish for healthier airline meals is possible. Probably the best kept secret about airline food is that anyone can order a special meal on most major carriers. In actuality, people have ordered special-diet meals on planes for many years. Low calorie, low cholesterol, low sodium, diabetes, vegetarian, children's plates, and others are available on request. You don't need a medical or religious reason to order a special meal. And there is no additional charge. All you need is a phone and a voice. Obviously, the airlines are not advertising the fact that you can order special meals because it is one more headache for them.

Special meals—yours for the asking

There's an amazing array of special meals. Some of the special-diet offerings are oriented for diabetes and low calorie (though you can't request a certain calorie level); low cholesterol; and low sodium. If you avoid certain foods due to personal preference or religious reasons, you might want vegetarian, kosher, Hindu, or Muslim meals. For the young traveler, infants', toddlers', and children's meals are available on certain airlines when ordered in advance.

Possibly the best choice is the fruit or cold seafood plate. These are often a better choice because they're served cold. Less taste and palatability damage is done to cold food than to hot when it's held for long periods. Even if you are on a low-cholesterol, fat, or sodium meal plan, the fruit or seafood plates offer a better taste choice. It will likely fit into your nutrition guidelines as well.

The fruit plate ranges from simply an array of fresh fruit to fruit with cottage cheese and/or yogurt and crackers. The seafood plate might be shrimp and/or seafood salad. It's served with greens, salad dressing, and crackers. These are lighter alternatives to the overcooked fish or chicken and vegetables, and it's enough to tide you over to your next meal or snack at your destination. Watch out though—you'll have other passengers staring at your tray with desiring eyes. They might angrily ask how you managed to get *that*. Be nice and take a minute to give them some healthy advice about how they might do the same.

How to order special meals

It's surprisingly simple to have a special meal waiting with your name on it as your plane taxis down the runway. Most of the airlines require at least 24-hours notice. It's easiest to order the special meals when you make your reservations. For frequent flyers or anyone who uses a travel agent, just specify in your record the special meals you want at which times of day. You might want a fruit plate for A.M. flights and P.M. snacks and a low-calorie meal for dinner flights. When you make specific reservations, remind the travel agent to order your requested special meals if you are on a meal or snack flights.

Sometimes you need to make the flight attendant aware of your special meal order. They might ask you to identify yourself at the beginning of meal service. Most times, as long as you are sitting in your assigned seat, the special meal or snack will be delivered as others around you are served. Be ready, however, to have the special meal request fouled up. As with any special request, much can go wrong. If you are particularly concerned, you might want to make an extra call before departure to make sure that your special request is being tracked.

Beverages and snacks

Most flyers know they will at least be served a beverage. The free choices are consistent from airline to airline—coffee, tea, carbonated beverages, mineral water, water, and juices. If you choose a hot beverage and want to add "white stuff," ask for low-fat milk. As for cold beverages, you're best off with the low-calorie carbonated ones such as club soda, mineral water, or plain water. These are all carried in large supply. Tomato juice and bloody Mary mix (hold the vodka) are also low-calorie choices. Juices, usually apple or orange, are alternatives, but don't forget that a 12-ounce can of juice runs up to almost 200 calories.

A variety of alcoholic beverages are available in flight. Regular and light beer, small bottles of wine, and distilled alcohol to be mixed with any non-alcoholic beverage on board is standard. Don't forget about the calories in alcohol. In addition, alcohol tends to be more dehydrating than usual when consumed in the air. (Read Chapter 4 for more nutrition numbers and advice on alcoholic and non-alcoholic drinks.)

It used to be that a small bag of peanuts was the expected nibble. That's changed. Now you've often got a choice of peanuts or pretzels. Opt for the healthier, low-fat pretzels. On flights longer than one or two hours but not within particular mealtime slots, you might be served a light snack. You are better off with the light cold snack. Thank your lucky stars: it's usually more palatable than a hot meal that's been cooked, chilled, and reheated. Some airlines offer special snacks—fruit, vegetarian, and low-calorie are a few. To find out if the airline serves special snacks, ask when you reserve your seat.

Be in control of in-flight nutrition

The first rule of thumb in air travel is to "expect the unexpected." Perhaps it's a delayed or canceled flight for starters. The second rule is to have a sense of humor, "go with the flow." The third rule of thumb is synonymous with the Scout's motto: "always be prepared." To establish a sense of control when you travel through the friendly skies, don't leave what you eat up to the airlines. Before you board, maybe even as you get ready for the flight, think about your travel eating plan. Ask if you will be served a meal or snack? Do you want to eat their offerings or bring your own food? Preplanning is particularly important for people who have diabetes and are on insulin or oral diabetes medications to control blood glucose. It is important for people with diabetes not to leave the type or timing of food to the airlines.

If you need or want something specific to eat in flight, obviously you need to have it on your person prior to boarding. If you don't want to pay a pretty penny for it, shop before you arrive at the airport. If you are unable to avoid airport prices, there are several healthy items for purchase. There's absolutely no problem taking on board anything from a snack to a full course meal. You just can't eat or drink during takeoff and landing.

Here are a few portable healthier snack ideas: pretzels, soft pretzels, popcorn, fresh fruit, box of raisins, bag of dried fruits, sandwich, container of non- or low-fat refrigerator yogurt, frozen yogurt available at the airport, crackers, bagel, or muffin. Snack concessioneers line your walk to the gate. Be careful to pick and choose, avoiding the nut and candy mixtures. (For more portable snack ideas and more food suggestions in the airport, review Chapter 23.)

Standard airline fare will not likely improve dramatically in the near future. Maybe there'll be small changes due to the demand for healthier food choices. The best policy is to take control. Go the healthy route, take advantage of special meals, and order ahead. If you don't want to partake in airline fare, preplan and make purchases prior to boarding. If you are a frequent flyer, just make airplane snacks part of your regular shopping list.

23

Healthier eating out
Almost Anywhere

Food—it's practically inescapable anywhere. Baseball means hot dogs and beer; movies, popcorn and candy. Road races, a zoo visit, a trip to the shopping mall, or filling your gas tank all involve eating. Food is everywhere, and it's convenient twenty-four hours a day from vending machines and convenience stores.

This calls for drastic measures. You've got to have a plan of action and know the healthier options. In this chapter you'll get some skills for selecting healthier foods almost anywhere.

Skill No. 4—Have an action plan

First, assess where you eat extra calories and what your choices are when you are out. Do you return from your trip to the vending machine with potato chips or pretzels in hand? Do you go to the ballpark ready for a jumbo hot dog, chips, and ice cream or will popcorn and a slice of pizza do the trick?

Find out if you are eating due to external stimuli, sort of reflex action. Also see when and why you eat these less than desirable foods. Once you decipher your patterns, develop a contract with yourself to change these behaviors. You have several ways to go on the attack. You can cut out the extra food—find a different path past the vending machine, or locate a gas station where it's only your gas tank you fill.

Preplanning is a critical skill to assure that healthier foods are around when you need and want them. You've got to take a few minutes, perhaps it's before you shop, to think about the foods you will need in the house. Contemplate the next week or two. Will you travel by car, train, or plane? Will you go to a sporting event, the movies, work late, etc.? What foods will you need to make sure that you eat healthy as often as possible? Can you stock your cupboards with light snack-size microwave popcorn for late night snacks? enough fruit to take a piece or two to work each day? vanilla wafers or gingersnaps to quench your sweet tooth? In the end, preplanning saves time and keeps you eating healthier.

Meals just about anywhere

If you know you'll be out and moving about, here are three options. Take food with you—a container of yogurt or a fast-food burger or grilled chicken sandwich. Eat something healthier at home or out before you reach your destination. Lastly, select from the healthy choices at your destination. Here's a list of some healthier options:

> plain hamburger
> small hot dog
> grilled chicken sandwich
> popcorn
> pretzels
> pizza
> soft pretzel
> frozen yogurt
> bagel with or without jelly or small amount of cream cheese
> corn-on-the-cob

Snacks just about anywhere

Unfortunately, when you are out, either in a mall or convenience store, unhealthy foods surround you—hot cinnamon buns, onion rings, ice cream, chips, nuts, and on and on. Here are some healthier snacks at these spots:

> dried fruit
> fruited yogurt (refrigerated)

frozen yogurt topped with fresh fruit

pretzels, soft pretzels

popcorn, preferably light

bagel with or without jelly or small amount of cream cheese

jelly beans or gum drops

pickles

diet soda

mineral water

unsweetened ice tea

water

Your other option is to take a healthier snack along. Here are some portable snacks to stock in your pantry.

boxed raisins

dried fruit

fresh fruit

fruit juice in 6-oz. cans

V-8 or tomato juice in 6-oz. cans

fat-free crackers, bran wafers, rye crackers, saltines

rice cakes

cookies—fig newtons, vanilla wafers, gingersnaps, animal crackers, graham crackers

fat-free chips in small individual bags

popcorn, popped light, or light snack-size microwaved

granola bars, low fat

granola, low fat

fruited yogurt (refrigerated)

powdered low-calorie fruit beverage to mix with water

Food is not going away. If anything, it creeps into more activities and venues. The prediction for the future is that the three-meal-a-day style of eating is fading out. What's in is grazing.

Eating nutritiously takes effort. But much can be accomplished with a bit of time and commitment. For eating out just about anywhere, develop an internal contract: 1) preplan—think through the day and week; 2) have healthier foods accessible; and 3) commit to making healthier choices whether it's at the ballpark, movie theater, or almost anywhere.